Nell Gwyn

*For Julia
with love*

Nell Gwyn

Derek Parker

SUTTON PUBLISHING

First published in 2000 by
Sutton Publishing Limited · Phoenix Mill
Thrupp · Stroud · Gloucestershire · GL5 2BU

British Library Cataloguing in Publication Data
A catalogue record for this book is available from the British Library

ISBN 0-7509-1992-2

TM   ALAN SUTTON™ and SUTTON™ are the
trade marks of Sutton Publishing Limited

Typeset in 10.5/14 pt New Baskerville.
Typesetting and origination by
Sutton Publishing Limited.
Printed in Great Britain by
Biddles Limited, Guildford, Surrey.

Contents

List of Illustrations

A Brief Chronology

1630   **29 May**. Birth of Charles II.

c. **1640**   Hortense Mancini, Duchesse de Mazarin, born.

1641   **Autumn**. Barbara Villiers born.

1645   Charles seduced by Christabelle Wyndham.

1646   Marguerite Cartaret becomes Charles's mistress.

1648   Lucy Walter becomes Charles's mistress.

1649   **9 April**. Lucy Walter's son (later the Duke of Monmouth) born.
Louise de Kéroüalle born.

1650   **2 February**. Nell Gwyn born.

c. **1650**   Mary 'Mall' Davis born.

1658   Death of Lucy Walter.

1659   **14 April**. Barbara Villiers marries Roger Palmer.
Birth of Henry Purcell.

1660   **28 May**. Charles II restored to the throne; Barbara Villiers (aka Barbara Palmer) becomes his mistress.

1661   **25 February**. Birth of Barbara's daughter Anne, later acknowledged by the King.
The theatres reopen. The first actress appears on the English stage.
Palmer is ennobled; Barbara becomes Lady Castlemaine.

1662   **25 February**. Birth of Barbara's son Charles.
21 May. The King marries Catherine of Braganza.

1663   **7 May**. The King's playhouse opens; Nell Gwyn is an orange-seller, then an actress; she is the mistress of Charles Hart and John Lacy.
Frances Stuart captivates the King.
20 September. Birth of 'Henry Palmer', Barbara's son by the King. Charles at first declines to acknowledge him.
Nell Gwyn moves into apartments at the Cat and Fiddle, Lewkenor's Lane.

1664   **5 September**. Birth of Charlotte Fitzroy, the King's daughter by Barbara.

1665   Nell appears in Dryden's *The Indian Emperor*.
The Great Plague reaches London.

1666   The Court returns to London after the plague months.
The theatres reopen.
2–7 September. The Great Fire of London.

1667   **July**. Nell Gwyn becomes the mistress of Lord Buckhurst and Sir Charles Sedley.
The Court moves to Tunbridge Wells.
Mall Davis becomes the King's mistress.
Charles makes a secret treaty with Louis XIV.
De Ruyter sails up the Thames and attacks shipping.

1668   Nell Gwyn becomes the King's mistress.

1670   Lady Castlemaine created Duchess of Cleveland.
Charles meets Louise de Kéroüalle.
8 May. Nell Gwyn gives birth to the King's son Charles (later the Duke of St Albans).
Dryden appointed Poet Laureate.
Barbara Villiers created Baroness Nonsuch.

1671   Nell Gwyn moves to 79 Pall Mall and retires from the stage.
Louise de Kéroüalle becomes the King's mistress.
25 December. Birth of James Beauclerk, Nell's second son by Charles.

1672   **29 July**. Birth of Louise's son by the King; he is named Charles Lennox.
Barbara Villiers takes the playwright Wycherley as lover.

1673   The Test Act excludes Roman Catholics from office under the Crown.
Wycherley's *The Country Wife* is performed.
Louise is created Duchess of Portsmouth.

1674/5   Part I of John Bunyan's *The Pilgrim's Progress* published.

1675   Hortense Mancini, Duchesse de Mazarin, arrives in London and becomes the King's mistress.

1677   Production of *The Rover* by Nell's friend Aphra Behn.
Purcell appointed organist at Westminster Abbey.

1678 The Popish Plot and persecution of Roman Catholics.
1679 **28 July**. Death of Nell's mother.
1680 Nell is seriously ill; her younger son James dies in Paris.
1681 The King grants Nell Burford House, Windsor.
1682 Work starts on the Royal Hospital, Chelsea.
1684 Nell's elder son created Duke of St Albans.
1685 **6 February**. Death of Charles II.
1687 **14 November**. Death of Nell Gwyn.
1709 **9 October**. Death of Barbara Villiers.
1734 **14 November**. Death of Louise de Kéroüalle.

Preface

Of all English kings and princes, Charles II – at least from his own point of view and very possibly from the State's – handled his sex life most sensibly. His attitude was a very simple one: if he wanted a woman, he had her. Rejection has never been a great problem for princes, and was certainly not so for him. Nor did his wife provide any obstacle: unlike at least one recent consort, she knew perfectly well what was expected of her when she married Charles – she was to produce an heir, or heirs, to the throne. In such arranged marriages, love and fidelity were unusual and happiness a gamble. Charles already had at least four illegitimate children when he married Princess Catherine of Braganza, and it is unlikely that she was not at least to some extent warned about his flirtatiously amorous nature before she came to England. If at first she was shocked at the extent of his public commitment to Barbara Villiers, it was soon made clear to her that she was not to interfere in the King's extramarital affairs.

She played her hand well. While she occasionally took exception to the high-handedness of his mistresses, she rarely did more than make an occasional jibe, and even managed to tolerate their company on more or less friendly terms. The result of such toleration was that she kept her husband's affection – and indeed became perhaps the only real love of his life.

The King made no attempt to hide the fact that he kept a number of mistresses. Public gossip, the balladmongers and squib-writers publicised his exploits almost as widely as the modern media could. Portraits of his mistresses were copied and hung in private houses; broadsheets commented on the size of his genitalia and the use to which they were put. Most of his subjects regarded his philandering not merely with toleration but with pride. Some people in private, in their diaries or in conversation with trusted friends, condemned him as immoral, and a few spoke out in public, though the Church was silent on the matter. Those who were interested in the politics of the State complained that he was lazy by nature and that his mistresses were one more distraction from public affairs. But in general, he was considered a good fellow out to enjoy himself, and the fact that he did so with such obvious delight made it difficult to dislike him for it. As for his women, opinions swung between disapproval and positive relish. Both Barbara, Duchess of Cleveland, and Louise, Duchess of Portsmouth, were cordially disliked, the one for allegedly interfering in politics, the other for being foreign and a Catholic. Less hoity-toity mistresses were the subjects of coarse jokes and comment. Nell Gwyn seems never to have aroused anything but admiration and even envious compliment. There is no parallel example in English history of a royal mistress so generally admired and coveted by a monarch's subjects.

The primary evidence for events in Nell's life has been examined again and again, and unless there is some remarkable discovery one cannot expect more to turn up – since she could not write, a cache of lost letters is not going to be found. The secondary sources are, happily, plentiful and vivid. The diaries of Pepys and Evelyn and other letters and memoirs of the period are rich in references to her and her two main rivals. The best and most popular parts she played during her stage career were often written for her, and clearly reflect her character and manner of speech – even describing her physical appearance. Then there are the often scabrous lampoons and verses alluding to her and her rivals – much crueller than anything that ever appeared in *Private Eye*, though much more abusive of Barbara and Louise than of Nell.

I have been familiar with the King's mistresses, and for the most part have addressed them by their Christian names. When one of them was known, at various times, as Barbara Villiers, Barbara Palmer, the Countess of Castlemaine or the Duchess of Cleveland it seems easiest and clearest to refer to her as 'Barbara' throughout; and I have done the same with Louise Kéroüalle (or Quérouaille), and with Nell (who we can be sure would have been the last to object).

I am grateful to the librarians at the British and London libraries, the staff of the Print Room at the British Museum, Melanie Christoudia and the library of the Theatre Museum, Lady Antonia Fraser, Jaqueline Mitchell and Sarah Moore, my editors, and to my wife Julia and our friend Angela Priestman for reading the manuscript and offering advice.

CHAPTER ONE

A Queen in Imagination

Lovers, fame, pleasure and gallantry crowded on her fancy; she
soon became a queen in imagination, though she never once
dreamed of becoming in reality, if not a queen, at least the
mistress of a monarch.

Anon., from, Memoirs of the Life of Eleanor Gwinn, *1752*

In 1650 – the year after the execution of Charles I – the
Commonwealth Parliament introduced an Act for 'suppressing the
abominable sins of Incest, Adultery and Fornication'. It was proposed
that all whores should be 'cauterized and seared with a hot iron on
the cheek, forehead or some other part of their body that might be
seen, to the end [that] the honest and chaste Christians might be
discerned from the adulterous children of Satan'. So Nell Gwyn was
born during a year when a career in prostitution, at whatever level,
might not have seemed promising.

As a matter of fact, Charles I had been quite as diligent as, and even
slightly more successful than, the Commonwealth in suppressing
prostitution in London: he disliked the idea of innocent passers-by
being 'pestered with many immodest, lascivious and shameless women
generally reputed for notorious common and professed whores . . .
exposing and offering themselves . . .'.[1] So, he closed brothels in
Petticoat Lane, Wapping, Bloomsbury, Charterhouse Lane and
elsewhere, and even succeeded – after a spirited battle with the
residents which involved 'pissing-pots' being tipped over the heads of
his troops – in suppressing the most celebrated house of all, Mother
Holland's Leaguer, which traded in a splendid mansion overlooking
the Thames, and had been much frequented by King James I.

However, he did not succeed in suppressing vice at the very centre
of town in Bow Street, Drury Lane and Covent Garden, where the

1

piazza was by the 1640s a centre of prostitution and was to remain so for several generations. It may be that towards the end of his reign Charles realised, as most governments do, that it is next to impossible to subdue prostitution completely, and that a more realistic attitude is to sweep it under any convenient carpet, for the Long Parliament passed an act redesignating prostitution as a public nuisance rather than a criminal offence.

However, the Commonwealth government – prompted perhaps by the great number of prostitutes who followed the army (driven no doubt by the poverty, destitution and desperation which are among the inevitable results of civil war) – was severe on the profession, attempting to treat brothels as it treated the theatre, music and the other arts. Men who insisted that naked statues should be clothed were unlikely to permit the kind of exhibitions with which prostitutes advertised their wares from windows and doorways. A contemporary libertarian described the plight of these ladies, suddenly thrown out of work: 'If you step aside into Covent Garden, Long Acre and Drury Lane, where these *Doves of Venus*, those Birds of Youth and Beauty – the Wanton Ladies – do build their *Nests*, you shall find them in such a *Dump* of Amazement to see the Hopes of their trading frustrate. . . .'[2]

But human appetites are not easily suppressed, and some houses remained open, perhaps surviving by bribery, perhaps by discretion. For those men with a troublesome sexual itch, they were badly needed because the evidence is that premarital sex was not only frowned upon, but very little practised – at least if one consults the figures for illegitimate births, which were lower during the decade after Nell's birth than for any other period between 1541 and 1841. A certain amount of petting obviously went on, but for most people it seems to have stopped short of coitus. 'Innocent' young women were very likely indeed to become pregnant; at least prostitutes knew, one way and another, the various means by which one could try to avoid it when a man declined to use sheaths, or simply didn't know how to do so.[3]

There was little sign, during the period between Nell's birth and the restoration of the monarchy ten years later, that the bawdy houses of London were less frequented than they had ever been. Indeed, it appears that most of the notable madams whose brothels thrived under Charles II (and sometimes with his active support) were already at work during the Commonwealth. While Cromwell was still Protector, a pamphleteer, one Henry Marsh, described in *The Crafty Whore* bawdy-houses 'full of Rogues, Plumers, Fylers and Cloak-twitchers . . . warehouses for all Thefts and Fellonies' which were set up 'to save the Whores caterwauling at midnight. . . .'

Whether Nell was actually born in a brothel remains open to question, for her birthplace has never been established. At least we know her birth date with perfect accuracy, for her horoscope was calculated by Elias Ashmole, the contemporary antiquary, herald and astrologer.[4] She was born on Saturday 2 February 1650 – and – if we are to trust Ashmole – at 6 a.m. (though it seems extremely doubtful that Mrs Gwyn possessed a clock, and Ashmole, using a recognised astrological technique, probably estimated the time of birth by considering the events of her life).[5]

We cannot know where Ashmole got the details of her birth, and those details were incomplete, for against *Nata* in his chart he left a blank – he did not know her place of birth. If he got the details from her – and it is quite possible – then she did not know either. Neither are there any reliable details about her ancestry. Anthony á Wood, a historian who was some twenty years older than Nell (and who therefore may be reliable), reported in his *Oxford Worthies* that she was the granddaughter of a Canon of Christ Church, Oxford, and her friend John Wilmot, Earl of Rochester, claimed that her father died in that city. But there is certainly no hard evidence to support either that fact or the suggestion that she was born there. One Frederick van Bossen proposed in a manuscript of 1688 that Nell's father was 'Thomas Gwine, a captain of an ancient family in Wales', and as a result of the speculation Hereford claimed to be her birthplace. The suggestion is enshrined in the *Dictionary of National Biography*, and Pipe Well Lane in that city was renamed Gwyn Street in her honour. The actor David Garrick, writing a century after her birth, marked 'a building at the rear of the Royal Oak Inn' as the house in which she was born. It was pulled down three years after he saw it. But Oxford remains the most likely birthplace, if we accept Dr Edward Gwyn of Christ Church as our subject's grandfather. His son Thomas, her father, is said to have married a Miss Eleanour Smith,[6] and begot two daughters, Rose (born in 1648) and Eleanour – who we know better as Nell. The dramatist Sir George Etherege had no great opinion of Mrs Gwyn, for he wrote of Nell:

> No man alive could ever call her daughter
> For a battalion of Armed men begot her.

Her daughter, however, presumably thought well of her, or at any rate remembered her kindly, for she gave her a fine funeral at St Martin's-in-the-Fields and erected a grand tomb (demolished when the church was rebuilt in 1721).

Thomas Gwyn is described by several sources as a Captain, and if he served in the army, it would surely have been in the King's interest, since Oxford was an almost rabidly Royalist town. Like so many others, he would have effaced himself as thoroughly as possible after the Commonwealth's victory and the King's execution. But tradition has it that he was nevertheless arrested and imprisoned, and that his wife escaped to London and settled in the district in which she had been born; indeed, the very street – Coal Yard Alley, Drury Lane – and prepared to earn her living as best she might.

The address now sounds thoroughly urban, but in 1650 Drury Lane was in Middlesex, and the land to the west was open country – St Martin's literally in the fields – which stretched on beyond Clerkenwell to Islington and the woods at Hampstead. However, the Lane itself had been paved for the past half-century, and within ten years of Nell's birth there was to be enormous development around the area in which she lived. The Restoration prompted a vigorous spate of town planning with the intention of beautifying the city. Developers were encouraged to build in brick and stone – far more elegant than timber – and there were regulations aimed at reducing the higgledy-piggledy appearance of the streets by forbidding jutties and overhanging windows (though balconies were allowed).

When Nell was eight or nine years old the establishment of 'the West End' began, with the Earl of St Albans building town houses in Pall Mall Field 'for the dwellings of noblemen and gentlemen of quality'. Nell's own home, in a cellar, was noisome and cluttered, yet she lived cheek by jowl with the quality; just south of Covent Garden piazza was the mansion of the Earl of Bedford, and the Earls of Craven and Salisbury were no further distant from Coal Yard Alley. Any memories of earlier years at Oxford were swamped by the realities of life in London. It wasn't a large city by modern standards, but one in sixteen of the population of England lived there – over 300,000 people, muddled together in a relatively small area, though London had expanded considerably beyond the city walls, and stretched now from Westminster to Barking and from Shoreditch to St George's Fields, growing all the time. Covent Garden piazza had been built in 1631, and before Nell was ten Lincoln's Inn Fields had been laid out, and fine houses were going up around St James's Square and in Hatton Garden. But still, if Nell heard or knew anything of Kensington, Islington or Hackney it would have been as remote villages. Even twenty years later a country market was being held in Pall Mall fields, and a cattle market in the Haymarket.

Mrs Gwyn cannot have been especially pleased to be forced back into London with two young daughters. Country folk regarded the city, understandably, as an extremely unhealthy place. Coal Yard Alley was one of a maze of 'narrow crooked and incommodious streets (fitter for a Wheelbarrow than any noble's Carriage), dark, irregular, and ill-contrived wooden Houses, with their several stories jutting out, or hanging over each other, whereby the Circulation of the Air was obstructed, noisome Vapours harboured, and verminous pestilential Atoms nourished'.[7]

The air was bad for a number of reasons. First, there was what the diarist John Evelyn described as 'the horrid smoke which obscures our churches and makes our palaces look old, which fouls our clothes and corrupts the waters'. From the hill at Hampstead a pall could be seen hanging over London; it must have been considerably worse than that which now hangs over Los Angeles, formed as it was of smoke not only from coal fires, but also from the furnaces of the brewers and dyers. In winter, it joined with fog in the notorious smogs that were to continue to plague the city for 300 years.

To the smoke and fumes were added the smells of the streets themselves. Perhaps only after a shower of rain was there even momentary relief from the reek rising from the rivers of filth that flowed in narrow channels down the centre of the streets – copious horse droppings, the débris from street stalls, and the contributions of householders, including the contents of chamber pots emptied from upper windows, which occasionally bespattered the clothes and persons of unlucky passers-by. As the meat and vegetables sold on street stalls began to rot in summer, more stenches contributed to the general thickness of the air, flies congregating where the reek was most persistent. Butchers slaughtered their beasts in backyards. Animal skins were dried in the sun before being treated with urine, while thick stenches rose as bones were rendered for glue. Evelyn listed sugar-boilers, chandlers, hat-makers, fishmongers, bakers and brewers as well as soap-boilers and glue-makers among the worst polluters.

Londoners did their best to make matters worse not only by throwing all sorts of rubbish from their windows, but by using the streets themselves as a public lavatory. Not only the common folk did this, but the courtiers too: when Charles II took his Court to Oxford, Anthony á Wood complained that 'though they were neat and gay in their apparel, yet they were very nasty and beastly, leaving at their departure their excrements in every corner, in chimneys, studies, coalhouses, cellars'.[8] Taken short at the theatre, Mrs Pepys happily 'did her business' in the open in Lincoln's Inn Fields – though she may have contravened a by-law, for by the Restoration many parishes had ordered householders to keep the 'kennel' or channel in the middle of the road clean, to prevent their pigs from rooting about in the streets, and to sweep before their doors on pain of a fourpenny fine. But who took any notice? At night you were still likely to receive a sudden assault from above:

> When brickbats are from upper stories thrown,
> And emptied chamber-pots come pouring down
> From garret windows; you have cause to bless
> The gentle stars, if you come off with piss.
> So many fates attend, a man had need
> Ne'er walk without a surgeon by his side. . . .[9]

Going about the city by day was just as trying, for different reasons; now, there was the traffic to contend with:

> If you walk out in business ne'er so great,
> Ten thousand stops you must expect to meet:
> Thick crowds in every place you must charge through,
> And storm your passage, wheresoe'ere you go,
> While tides of followers behind you throng,
> And pressing on your heels, shove you along.
> One with a board or rafter hits your head,
> Another with his elbow bores your side,
> Some tread upon your corns, perhaps in sport,
> Meanwhile your legs are cased all o'er with dirt. . . .[10]

Travelling by coach was no less irritating. Sitting in twentieth-century traffic jams we may suppose that travel was easier three centuries ago; but far from it. Narrow passages constructed for men and horses had to deal with wheeled vehicles in ever-increasing numbers. Sir William Davenant remarked on the inconvenience of streets 'contrived before those greater engines, carts, were invented', and a contemporary complained that 'the danger I once did run of my whereabouts by crowds of carts hath caused me many times to make reflection on the covetousness of the citizens and connivancy of magistrates who hath suffered them from time to time to encroach upon the streets'.[11] The irritation must have been as great for those attempting to manoeuvre their carts or carriages about those streets, breaking their wheels on the uneven cobbles and against the posts set up in the broader thoroughfares in an attempt to protect pedestrians.

As early as 1601 attempts had been made to limit the number of coaches driving within the city to 430, and the Thames began to lose its importance as a main thoroughfare, to the despair of the watermen who rowed the boats and ferries:

> Carroaches, coaches, jades and Flanders mares
> Do rob us of our shares, our wares, our fares;
> Against the ground we stand and knock our heels
> Whilst all our profit runs away on wheels.[12]

To the coaches of the bettermost were added the Hackney Hell Carts or hired coaches, and by 1634 the streets were 'so encumbered with the necessary multitude of coaches that many of our subjects are thereby exposed to great dangers and the necessary use of carts and carriages for provisions thereby much hindered'. Just as we are today implored not to use our cars for short journeys, so it was positively ordered, in 1635, that hackney coaches should only be used to take people from London into the country, and that 'no person should make use of a coach in the city except such persons as could keep four able horses for His Majesty's service'.[13]

Cromwell made a serious effort to deal with the traffic jams that brought many streets to a standstill. In 1654 his government prohibited 'wheels shod with iron' in the parish of St Giles's-in-the-Fields, and forbade hackney coachmen from standing for hire in the streets or feeding their horses 'within three yards of any man's door'. After the Restoration efforts were made to make the streets less offensive by laying down strict regulations under which all rubbish had to be retained until it was collected by official scavengers.

The city in many ways remained a village in all but size: step from what passed for the main streets, and one found oneself in a spider's web of little alleys, one giving off the other and frequently dead-ending in a small court, usually presided over by a tippling-house, or in a garden with fruit and flowers, or a set of stables with a pond in which to water and wash the horses and a hayloft in which to store their food.

Looking today towards the city from the south bank of the Thames – say, from the reproduction of Shakespeare's Globe Theatre – it is still just possible to guess how it may have looked in the 1660s, when over 100 church spires were the highest things to be seen, for the houses of London were usually only single-storeyed, as opposed to those in other European cities, which tended to rise rather than spread. St Paul's, the greatest church in Europe (after St Peter's in Rome) was almost derelict, the spire having fallen some time previously, and the nave, battered by Cromwell's horses, still used as a market. Nell, while she may not have often ventured eastward into the centre of the city itself, knew the London of Shakespeare's time – before the Great Fire of

1666 – with its oak-framed houses, overhanging so that they made the streets almost like tunnels. Well-heeled citizens owned their own houses, one family to a building, though there were also lodging houses where rooms could be taken. And, of course, there were the mansions of wealthy merchants such as Sir Nathaniel Hobart, whose house in Chancery Lane was rented at the very considerable sum of £55 a year. Finally, the palaces of the great men of the State were set in their own gardens, sometimes large enough to be called parks, running down to the Thames. From their gates rode out their owners in fine dress, their horses' tails beribboned. Nell, her sister and mother, may have thrown them an envious glance; in Coal Yard Alley, they had a living to make, like their neighbours, and found it no easier than anyone else in their condition.

As with so much in Nell's life, we must rely on gossip and anecdote for an account of the years between her birth and the first reports of her engagement at the King's Theatre in Bridges Street, where, at the age of thirteen, she became an orange-girl. This was in 1663 (the theatre opened on 7 May), and we have only a few hints about what she had been doing until then. She would certainly have been doing something; families as hard up as Mrs Gwyn's did not allow growing girls to do nothing.

How much should we rely on the anonymous author of the first biography of Nell, the *Memoirs of the Life of Eleanor Gwinn*, published in 1752?[14] Nell died in 1687, so it is extremely unlikely that the anonymous author ever met anyone who had known her; and fables cluster so thickly around the notorious that his book must be treated with some wariness. However, in the absence of any other evidence it is at the very least worth reporting what he says, even when it is unlikely to be true. He asserts, for instance, that Mrs Gwyn decided after the Restoration to send Nell into the country (to relatives in Yorkshire) to protect her from the wave of sensuality that threatened to swamp the town, but that the child 'heard this proposal with ineffable contempt; she'd seen enough of life to make her fond of the town, and though she was then in the full possession of her virtue, she began to entertain some thoughts of yielding it, rather than to be sent to the country to live in obscurity and contract rustic habits, by which she would lose all power of pleasing for ever . . .' She had 'observed how gaily many ladies lived, who had no other means of supporting their grandeur but by making such concessions to men of fortune, and stipulating such terms as both of them could well afford to comply with; and as she was sensible that many succeeded upon the town with half her accomplishments . . .' and 'as her person was admirably calculated to inspire passion, she imagined if she was arrayed in the pomp of tragedy heroines, her figure alone, without any theatrical requisites, would make her pass upon the town . . . This thought filled her with rapture; lovers, fame, pleasure and gallantry crowded on her fancy; she soon became a queen in imagination, though she never once dreamed of becoming in reality, if not a queen, at least the mistress of a monarch, and being filled with that kind of royalty which is more substantial than a two hours glitter on the stage.'[15]

Certainly most people welcomed relief from the strict moral code that the Commonwealth had attempted to impose, and that was recalled by the large number of teenage children carrying such forenames as Temperance, Kill-sin and Steadfast-on-High. The President of Cromwell's Parliament was Praise God Barebones, and his brother was If-Christ-had-not-died-thou-hadst-been-damned Barebones. One wonders whether any Fail-nots or Redeemeds or Meeks found employment in the hundreds of brothels that opened in the first summer of Charles II's reign. It seems most probable that Nell did – in fact if Pepys is to be trusted, we have her own word for it, for in 1667 he reported a dispute between her and Beck Marshall (one of the actresses in the King's Company). Beck had called Nell 'Lord Buckhurst's whore', to which Nell replied 'I was but one man's whore, though I was brought up in a bawdy-house to fill strong water to the guest; and you are a whore to three or four . . .'[16]

Nell's sister Rose, older by two years, seems to have started work as an oyster-girl – oysters were popular and cheap, and on sale at most street corners. Nell, twelve or thirteen years old, perhaps helped her – though the often scurrilous poems written about her later have her selling vegetables or fresh herrings, and already honing her wit not only on her customers but on her sister. At the time, Mrs Gwyn was working as a barmaid at the Rose Tavern in Russell Street, on the corner of Bridges Street (now Catherine Street). This was usefully next door to the theatre in Drury Lane, and was one of over four hundred taverns within the city, some large, fashionable and respectable, some smaller, less fashionable, and less respectable. The Rose appears to have been neither one nor t'other, and Mrs Gwyn herself seems to have veered to the less exemplary end of the market. She did not have the means to set up her own brothel, but catering to the appetite of the Rose's customers, probably organised a small ring of prostitutes on offer at the bottom end of the market, working from the streets. Rose, in her mid-teens, may have been one of them, and eventually began to work full-time at Madam Ross's well-known and popular establishment in Lewkenor's Lane, on the site of the present Macklin Street off the top of Drury Lane. It was a street already associated with thieves and whores: Jonathan Wild, the notorious Bow Street runner and thief-taker, later hanged for theft, kept a bawdy house there, and Jack Sheppard, the highwayman, was taken there after his second escape from Newgate. We can suppose that Madam Ross's was the 'bawdy-house' to which Nell referred. And she may have lost, or sold, her virginity there, being

> . . . by Madam Ross exposed to town,
> I mean by those who will give half a crown

as the satire put it.[17]

Oscar Wilde's line about living in the gutter but looking at the stars can be applied to Nell. It is even suggested that from the first time she set her eyes on King Charles himself, she was ambitious to be noticed by him, for anecdote reports that it was in a fit of desperation at seeing the King ride through London with his bride, the former Princess Catherine of Braganza, that she allowed herself to be offered to one of Madam Ross's clients, a young London merchant called Duncan. The dramatist Sir George Etherege, whose flirtations with actresses certainly included some familiarity with Nell, reports that Duncan kept her for some time in lodgings at the Cock and Pie Inn, and that much later she, when the King's mistress, got a commission in the Guards for him.

However that may be, it seems almost certain that in one way or another Nell started her career as a child prostitute. How else could she – pretty, totally uneducated, living in poverty – make a substantial income? What other path could she tread that might possibly lead to anything like a reasonable income? The new King's Theatre was rising nearby, and while the theatres were not quite the dens of iniquity that modern readers have been led to suppose, Nell would certainly have noticed that fine gentlemen did not attend the theatres only for the pleasure of watching the play. The next step must have seemed an obvious one: surely there was some man of substance to whom she could sell herself? Perhaps even someone at Court, for by now it was clear that it was not only the King who was seriously addicted to sex.

CHAPTER TWO

High Desires

Nor are his high desires above his strength
His sceptre and his prick are of a length.

Earl of Rochester, from 'A Satire on Charles II'

In view of what we know of the nature of King Charles II, one should perhaps not be surprised that on 29 May 1660, his first night in London after his return to his kingdom, he shared his bed in the Palace of Whitehall with one Barbara Palmer.[1] As an anonymous poet put it:

Of a tall stature and of sable hue
Much like the son of Kish,[2] that lofty Jew.
Twelve years complete he suffered in exile
And kept his father's asses all the while.
At length by wonderful impulse of fate
The people call him home to help the State,
And what is more they send him money too,
And clothe him all from head to foot anew;
Nor did he such small favours then disdain
But in his thirtieth year began to reign.
In a slashed doublet then he came to shore,
And dubbed poor Palmer's wife his Royal Whore.[3]

The generous nature of the King's sexuality declared itself early, and sustained him and a large number of women throughout his life. Most of those women merely catered to his enthusiastic sexual appetite, but a few were really notable not only because they retained his attention for more than a night or two, but because they were individuals whose personalities have survived for three centuries, and remain as sharply defined as that of the King himself. Nell Gwyn was one of them.

13

A Mrs Christabella Wyndham was Charles's first sexual partner. She had been appointed one of the child's foster-mothers by his first governess, the Countess of Dorset, when he was one year old, and she seduced him (rather, perhaps, than the other way around) in 1645 when he was fifteen. Mrs Wyndham was said to be extremely beautiful, so it was presumably a pleasant enough experience, and pupil and mistress seem to have thrown themselves into the affair with enthusiasm. Lord Clarendon[4] viewed their romps with some misgiving, especially since there was precious little reticence: Mrs Wyndham would often smother her young lover with kisses in full view of the Court. The following year, on holiday in Jersey, the Prince chose a mistress for himself – the twenty-year-old Marguerite Carteret, daughter of Sir George Carteret, Seigneur of Trinity Manor. It is possible, though far from proven, that Charles's first illegitimate son was a result of the affair; but the sons and daughters of almost every woman with whom he slept seem at one time or another to have claimed royal blood, and all such claims should be treated with a certain amount of suspicion.

It would be tedious to list everyone Charles bedded between that summer in Jersey and his first encounter with Barbara Palmer. In exile, during the Interregnum, he and his friend Rochester[5] cut a swathe through the Continent's available women. It is difficult to blame him: what young man, with little to do, and with the knowledge that almost every woman who attracted him would be delighted to oblige, would hesitate to take advantage of his position? It is also difficult to blame the women, for apart from being the King of England – even if his office was for the time being in abeyance – he was also by now an extremely handsome young man.

It had not always been the case. His mother Queen Henrietta Maria found him at birth, 'so black that I am ashamed of him'[6] and when he was two she was still dissatisfied with his appearance: 'He is so ugly I am ashamed . . . but his size and fatness supply what he lacks in beauty.'[7] But once the baby fat had vanished and the clumsiness of adolescence was past, Charles became what he was to remain: a personable, tall, well-framed man. Perhaps the most vivid word-portrait of him was drawn by Sir Samuel Tuke, writing in 1660:

He is somewhat taller than the middle stature of Englishmen; so exactly formed that the most curious eye cannot find any error in his shape. His face is rather grave than severe, which is very much softened whensoever he speaks; his complexion is somewhat dark, but much enlightened by his eyes, which are quick and sparkling. Until he was near twenty years of age the figure of his face was very lovely, but he is since grown leaner, and now the majesty of his countenance supplies the lines of beauty. His hair, which he hath in great plenty, is of a shining black, not frizzle, but so naturally curling into great rings that they do very much recommend his person when he either walks, dances, plays at pall mall, at tennis, or rides the great horse, which are his usual exercises. To the gracefulness of his deportment may be joined his easiness of access, his patience in attention, and the gentleness both in the tune and style of his speech; so that those whom either the veneration for his dignity or majesty of his presence have put into an awful respect are reassured as soon as he enters into the conversation.[8]

Certainly that was a description meant to commend the King to his subjects, and was necessarily complimentary; but that the man was attractive enough cannot be doubted. There are many supporting descriptions. He was naturally extremely healthy and vigorous. His constitution was good, and his energy furious. He generally rose every morning at six – earlier in summer – and those forced to rise with him were often astonished at his freshness and energy after a late night and a bout with one of his mistresses. He enjoyed 'taking his usual physic at tennis' at least once a day, and would often appear at the tennis court before it was light enough to see properly; sometimes men who came to see him on important national business were summoned to tennis. He loved riding from his earliest year, and for most of his life was happy to ride a considerable distance simply to dine with a friend. There are records of his travelling sixty miles on horseback, rising at dawn and returning at midnight – and on one occasion retiring at midnight at Whitehall, rising at three the following morning and riding over thirty miles to Audley End for the Newmarket races.

When not hunting, he walked – three or four hours a day by his watch, 'which he commonly did so fast that, as it was really an exercise to himself, so it was a trouble to all about him to keep up with him'.[9] Many contemporaries remarked on the fact that only his sound constitution protected him from the usual ravages that accompanied so indefatigable a lover. It certainly seems that he had the advantage, if that is what it is, of being well endowed. Rochester, who should have known, tells us so:

> Nor are his high desires above his strength:
> His sceptre and his prick are of a length.[10]

His reputation as a lover of women was much enhanced during his exile: his enemies put it about that his Court in Bruges was a cesspit of debauchery. 'I think I may truly say,' said one Commonwealth spy, 'that greater abominations were never practised than at Charles Stuart's Court. Fornication, drunkenness and adultery are esteemed no sin amongst them.'[11] This was perhaps slightly to over-egg the pudding, though Pepys suggested that the King had had at least eighteen mistresses before he left the Continent, and certainly before he returned to London he had fathered two daughters and a son.

The King's most constant mistress during his time at Bruges was Elizabeth Killigrew, eight years his senior and the sister of the chaplain to his brother the Duke of York. Her complaisant husband (husbands tended to be complaisant when the King applied himself to their wives) was one Francis Boyle, later Viscount Shannon. Charlotte Jemima Henrietta Maria Fitzroy was born to Elizabeth in 1651. Six years later Charles Fitzcharles was born to Catherine Pegge, the daughter of a middle-class English squire; he became Earl of Plymouth in 1675.[12] Catherine bore Charles a daughter the following year, but the child died a few days after birth.

When in Paris, Charles resorted to the twice-widowed Lady Byron, née Eleanor Needham, the daughter of Viscount Kilmorey, and a number of other young women, some round about his own age but mostly somewhat older, also passed the time pleasantly with him during the boring years of his exile. In addition, he had platonic affairs with at least two women – the beautiful widowed Duchesse de Châtillon and Princess Henrietta Catherine of Orange, a Dutch Protestant. A pretty and vivacious young woman, the latter fell almost instantly in love with Charles, as he did with her; he courted her enthusiastically (under the name of Don Lauren) and told his friend Taafe[13] that she was 'the worthiest to be loved of all her sex'. The moment he heard the news of Cromwell's death (on 3 September 1658) Charles proposed to Henrietta – but nothing came of it, partly because of the objection of Mary, Dowager Princess of Orange, her mother. Charles was sanguine, and wished her well in her later marriage to another man.

His earliest really serious affair was with Lucy Walter, the daughter of a Welsh Royalist squire who had been brought to the Hague by her uncle, the Earl of Carbery. The Baronne d'Aulnoy described her: 'Her beauty was so perfect that when the King saw her . . . he was so charmed and ravished and enamoured that in the misfortunes which ran through the first years of his reign he knew no other sweetness or joy than to love her, and be loved by her.'[14] Charles's attachment to Lucy must have begun before June 1648, for their son was born on 9 April 1649, was christened James Crofts, and later in life became Duke of Monmouth. By his looks, apart from anything else, he was clearly his father's son. There is a portrait of him by Jacob Huysmans and a miniature by Samuel Cooper, in both of which his father's face is strongly recalled.

Lucy Walter seems to have been more like Nell Gwyn than any other of Charles's mistresses. Though his sexual tastes were clearly catholic, it seems that what he enjoyed above all was high spirits, individuality and enthusiastic sensuality, all of which both women possessed in no uncertain terms. Though better born than Nell, Lucy evidently had the capacity to throw off gentility and behave with the kind of unaffected, ribald sexuality that aroused the King. John Evelyn, in his diary, describes her as a 'brown, beautiful, bold but insipid creature'[15] – by insipid meaning inelegant and not especially intelligent. Most of her contemporaries thought her no better than she should be: 'a strumpet', Evelyn said; 'of no good fame', wrote Clarendon; 'a common whore', claimed Pepys. None of these descriptions need necessarily be pejorative in a mistress, however, and they certainly seem to apply, for Lucy when she was only fourteen had already attached herself to Algernon Sidney, a colonel in Cromwell's army, who passed her on to his brother Robert. Under the name of Mrs Barlow she was living as Robert's mistress at the Hague when Charles saw and appropriated her.

Charles spasmodically renewed his relationship with Lucy, taking her to Paris and then to Jersey. She was not faithful to him, bearing a daughter to another man while he was absent; and at one time she planned to marry Sir Henry de Vere, the English resident in Brussels. Or he planned to marry her. Charles approved, but the marriage did not take place. Perhaps as far as Sir Henry was concerned, her reputation was simply too damaged. The King did not trouble himself about reputation – a common whore was good enough for him, when appetite was aroused. But enough was enough, and when Lucy made herself notorious by a number of rash liaisons the King asked Taafe to attempt at least to keep her out of trouble, preferably by spiriting her away to some quiet corner of Europe: 'Advise her, both for her sake and mine, that she goes to some place other than the Hague, for her stay there is very prejudicial to us both,' Charles told his friend in 1665.[16] But Taafe was not very successful. He made her his own mistress, perhaps hoping to have additional influence over her, but the ruse did not work, and the only result of it was another bastard.

The King was concerned about Lucy's influence on their son – and that her ill reputation might reflect upon the boy. He was not a nobody, after all. Indeed, rumour had it that Charles had secretly married Lucy, and made James the legitimate heir to the throne. No definite proof of a marriage has ever been found, and given Lucy's character (perfectly clear before the King ever met her) it seems extremely unlikely.

Charles's enemies were quick to use Lucy as a weapon with which to beat the King, and she continued to provide plenty of ammunition. She took a lover, Tom Howard, who turned out to be a spy of Cromwell's. She aborted two more bastards by unknown fathers, was accused of murdering a servant (but was acquitted) and was unwise enough to take young James to England, where she was promptly arrested and imprisoned as 'the wife or mistress of Charles Stuart'. She managed somehow to argue her way out of prison, and fled again to the Continent, where Taafe guaranteed her a regular pension from the King. The latter was in fact destitute and unable to pay any of his bills, let alone a pension to a mistress, but that did not prevent him from promising her a large sum, which seems never to have been paid in total – she received, for a while, about £400 a year.

In 1658, after a great deal of difficulty, the King's agents managed to persuade Lucy to give James up. She was understandably distressed, but it had to be done: the boy could not go on living with a woman whose reputation could scarcely have been lower, and in a house in Brussels that could almost have been described as a brothel. Besides, he had received no schooling, was almost completely illiterate, and had no idea of how to behave in polite society. The King appointed a respectable guardian, and nominated a tutor. The boy's education began. Lucy never saw him again. She dragged herself to Paris after him, but died the same year, of 'a disease incident to her profession', as it was tactfully put, and lies buried in an unknown grave.

But now approaches the only other woman to establish a firm relationship with Charles before he met Nell: Barbara Palmer, a cousin of the Duke of Buckingham, whose sexual magnetism was such that she was able to exercise as much influence over the King as many of his advisers – and certainly more than any other woman.

Barbara was born in 1641, the daughter of William Villiers, Viscount Grandison, a Royalist who was killed in the service of Charles I at the siege of Bristol before his daughter was two years old. Her family was seriously impoverished as a result of the war, and her early years are obscure. She appears first as the 15-year-old mistress of the 23-year-old widowed Lord Chesterfield. From the first, she was seen as a beauty: she became the 'fairest and lewdest' of Charles II's mistresses. Dark auburn hair and bright blue eyes made her striking, and her figure was equally so – she looked fine in rich, formal clothes, but the general view was that the lighter her clothing was, the greater effect her beauty made. She was quite open in her appetites, writing Chesterfield letters demanding his 'company' (and not for taking tea), and it seems to have been the common assumption that she put herself about. Pepys is always praising her beauty – indeed, he was besotted with her – but he also repeated the claim of the malignant wit Harry Killigrew that she 'was a lecherous little girl when she was young, and used to rub her thing with her fingers or against the end of forms, and that she must be rubbed with something else'.[17]

In 1659 Barbara married Roger Palmer, a well-educated scholar, mathematician, and diplomat. His father (no doubt aware of Barbara's devotion to Chesterfield) opposed the match, declaring that 'if [his son] was resolved to marry her he foresaw he should be one of the most miserable men in the world'.[18] Indeed, she swiftly became bored with her husband and life of domesticity in the country, and slipped away to Chesterfield whenever she could. Early in 1660, perhaps in an attempt to entertain her, Palmer took her with him to Holland. He went in order to give Charles a generous cash present – like a number of other gentlemen, he was laying up preferment against the Restoration. Barbara must surely have met the King; whether she seduced or was seduced by him we cannot know, though we may safely infer the event, for Charles wrote her husband an enthusiastic letter of thanks for a gift 'which I can hardly value or ever reward enough . . . You have more title than one to my kindness, and you may believe I am very well pleased to find so much zeal and affection to run in a blood. You shall find that I have a full sense of it and that I will always be your affectionate friend.'[19] It may not merely have been the cash to which the King referred; at all events in late February 1661 Mrs Palmer bore the King a daughter – at least, that is the supposition, for though her husband was confident that the child was his, and she was known as Anne Palmer, the King later acknowledged her (thirteen years after her birth).

Barbara's languishing looks were to be copied by many of the Court ladies. Sir Peter Lely painted her a number of times. When Pepys went to the studio of the painter and engraver William Faithorne to buy some prints for his wife, he was so struck by Faithorne's rendering of the portrait of Barbara which Lely had done for Lord Sandwich that he bought three copies and had one mounted, varnished and framed.[20] A number of other gentlemen did the same. Barbara's beauty impressed Lely considerably; he thought her so ravishing that 'it was beyond the compass of art to give [her] her due, as to her sweetness and exquisite beauty'.[21] He painted her not only as herself but as the Magdalen, the Virgin, Minerva; perhaps his finest portrait of her is as St Catherine of Alexandria, holding the sword and palm leaf of her martyrdom.[22] It is difficult not to suppose that the characterisation was a joke, though it followed a convention common at the time. Her figure, in the portrait, is full – might she even have been pregnant with one of Charles's six bastards? – and she is clad in a magnificent gold dress, a swathe of light blue silk thrown over her shoulders and a pettish lock of dark hair falling over her forehead. She looks straight at the viewer with a candid gaze, a full and voluptuous lower lip and slightly lowered eyelids strongly suggesting the strength of her erotic attraction.

The contrast between Barbara and Nell could scarcely be more firmly marked than by comparing this portrait and Lely's study of Nell with her infant son, later the Duke of St Albans. Both women were less than respectable, and though both were not only the mistresses of the King but were well known for having had previous liaisons, Barbara was far too much a lady to be painted in the nude; Nell, as an actress, is unlikely to have hesitated, and Lely clearly enjoyed painting her unclothed, lying, it appears, on the white sheet of a bed, her left hand almost seeming to invite a companion to take his place at her side, while her son toys with the corner of sheet which covers her genitals, as though about to whisk it naughtily away.

The figures of the two subjects were clearly quite different, as can be seen not merely from the Lely nude but from other depictions, including his portrait of Nell in a brown satin dress, apparently feeding a pet lamb – the symbol of innocence, if you please! – with her right hand and toying with a sceptre-like wand with her left. (Innumerable copies of this exist, some better than others, scattered about the galleries of the world from London to Columbus, Ohio.) The *décolletage* of Barbara's gown suggests a full bosom and an equally lavish body; Nell's small, pert breasts and slim body speak of provocative agility. Her smart little face, slightly raised eyebrows and quizzical look add to the impression that she would be fun to be with. There is no saint in the calendar for whom she could appropriately pose.

Sadly, the other portraits of Nell on the whole fail to provide a very powerful idea of her physical appearance: the rather sober painting (by Simon Verelst) displayed by the National Portrait Gallery shows her gazing coolly at the observer as though calculating his worth. An engraving by Gerard Valck – one of the engravers who turned out versions of paintings by Lely, the admired miniaturist Cooper and others – was well thought of. It bears the legend:

> The sculptor's part is done, the 'features' hit
> Of Madam Gwyn, no art can show her wit.

However, it is unconvincing – this time the lamb at her side is garlanded, her breasts almost entirely exposed, her head a mass of artificial curls, strongly in contrast with the urchin cut of the Lely nude.

Writing to *The Times* in 1950, the tercentenary year of her birth, the then Director of the National Portrait Gallery, Henry Mendelssohn-Hake, pointed out that 'it is difficult to find any first-hand portrait of her that is reliable enough to be used as a touchstone. Her popularity has endowed hundreds of portraits of anonymous ladies with her name.'[23] For some time the gallery itself displayed a portrait bought in 1858, which was said to be of Nell. It eventually proved to be that of Katherine Sedley (though at least it was by Lely). A portrait said to be of Nell hung for years in William III's state bedroom at Hampton Court, which in fact was a likeness of James II's second wife, and indeed is not even faintly like Gwyn. Over the past three centuries almost every unattributed portrait of a woman of the period which has turned up has been firmly claimed as a likeness of Nell Gwyn, and various curators of the National Portrait Gallery have spent many hours assuring proud owners, often to their distress and usually to their disbelief, that the portrait recently discovered in their attic was not that of Charles's best-known mistress. Many of the portraits would deceive only determined romantics, and are about as convincing as Millais's painting of his daughter as Nell, mounted on a horse painted by Landseer – or indeed the various films of her story, the first, in 1921, starring the Hon. Lois Sturt (a lady chosen 'because of her likeness to the Lely portrait'), another in 1926 with Dorothy Gish in the part (released while a musical comedy by Clifford Bax was playing at the Everyman Theatre in London with Isabel Jeans in the leading rôle), and a subsequent sound film with the sublimely miscast Anna Neagle.

Lely painted Nell a number of times. It has been said that Charles liked to watch the process, whether at Lely's studio or at one of Nell's houses. In a sale of the work found in Lely's studio at the time of his death was an unfinished portrait of 'Mrs Gwyn'. But even he may have misrepresented her to an extent: the current taste was for plump women, and by all accounts Nell was never that.

Barbara, whatever the contrast with the rival who was soon to join her in the King's favour, was clearly an extremely sexy lady, whose amorous adventures were not restricted by her relationship with the King. Her lovers were many and varied, and by no means confined to members of her own class. There was to be Jacob the rope-dancer, for instance – Jacob Hall, who performed out of a booth at Bartholomew Fair, and attracted a great deal of attention with a 'variety of rare feats of activity and agility of body, as doing of somersaults and flipflaps, flying over thirty rapiers and over several men's heads, and also flying through several hoops',[24] as his advertisements announced. Watching the lithe movements and the rare feats of agility, Barbara found him attractive, wondered how he looked 'under his tumbling clothes', and sent for him in order to find out.[25] She obviously enjoyed making love, not merely as a matter of social advancement or money, but as a matter of simple straightforward carnal pleasure.

As usual with affairs at Court, Pepys follows Barbara's story from the first. Sitting up late writing letters in an office in King Street, Westminster, in July 1660, he overheard 'great doings of music at the next house' – the house in which the Palmers were living. 'The King and Dukes there with Madam Palmer, a pretty woman that they have a fancy to make her husband a cuckold.' He and a friend stood for a while at a closed-up connecting door between the two houses, listening to the music.[26]

By the end of the year, he noticed that Barbara was on fondling terms with several male members of the Court. Attending service at Whitehall Chapel in October (the day after watching the regicide

Major-General Harrison hanged, drawn and quartered – 'looking as cheerfully as any man could do in that condition') he 'observed how the Duke of York and Mrs Palmer did talk to one another very wantonly through the hangings that parts the King's closet and the closet where the ladies sit'.[27] On 20 April the following year, he watched the King ceremonially appointing the Lord Chancellor in the Banqueting Hall and creating a number of peers, and in the evening went to see the King's company perform John Fletcher's *The Humorous Lieutenant* at a royal command performance at the Cockpit in Whitehall. Though it had a good cast, with Charles Hart (soon to be Nell's lover) in a leading rôle, Pepys did not care for it. He had eyes for the audience, however: 'so many great beauties, but above all Mrs Palmer, with whom the King does discover a great deal of familiarity'.[28] Soon the King was 'following his pleasures more than with good advice he would do – at least, to be seen to all the world to do so – his dalliance with my Lady Castlemaine being public every day, to his great reproach'.[29]

Charles made Roger Palmer an Irish Earl in November 1661, not out of any respect he felt for the man, or even as a delayed response to Palmer's generous financial aid of the year before, but in order that his child by Barbara (or rather children – for she was pregnant again) should be properly recognised. Palmer became Baron of Limerick and Earl of Castlemaine, and his wife, of course, Lady Castlemaine. The title was restricted to 'children gotten on Barbara Palmer, [Palmer's] now wife'.[30] A few months later she bore a son, known at his birth as Charles Palmer, later as Charles Fitzroy, Duke of Southampton. The baby was the final cause of the separation of Barbara and her husband, who had become a Roman Catholic and insisted on the child being baptised into that faith. This was extremely embarrassing for his real father, and Barbara had Charles baptised a second time by a minister, with the King present as a witness. Roger Palmer regarded this as the last straw, and after a furious row Barbara left the house in King Street (taking with her almost everything that was movable), and Roger left the country for France.

The King now gave his mistress permission to live in rooms in the Palace of Whitehall. They were spacious enough to house her and – in due course – the five children she bore him (or at least which were acknowledged by him), and one whose paternity remains uncertain. In 1662 she became a Catholic, and the King allowed her to construct an oratory. When a minister tentatively enquired whether this was altogether wise, Charles answered that he was less concerned with women's souls than with their bodies, and opposition was dropped.

Pepys kept an appreciative eye on Barbara, and continued to admire her. One day in 1662 he and his wife were walking in the rose garden in the middle of the Palace of Whitehall, and there saw an impromptu washing line with 'the finest smocks and linen petticoats of my Lady Castlemaine, laced with rich lace at the bottoms, that ever I saw; and it did me good to look upon them'.[31] Barbara was showing off: during the 1660s a display of fine underclothes became a particular indication of class distinction. Nell, too, was proud of her underclothing, and in particular of its cleanliness, which in an age when men and women even of high rank were often dirty and verminous, was another sign of class.

By now the King had made it quite clear that his Court was to be, as far as sexual morality went, extremely permissive. The men and women surrounding the King were not much less culpable, as far as that went, than the monarch himself. The country was not greatly concerned; having suffered under the mean-spirited narrowness of the Puritans, ordinary men and women rather enjoyed the spectacle of their superiors having a good time, although here and there voices were raised against it.

Pepys once more provides an interesting insight. Though by no means averse to pleasure, he found himself agreeing with an MP (Sir Thomas Crew):

that the King doth mind nothing but pleasures and hates the very sight or thoughts of business. That my Lady Castlemaine rules him; who he says hath all the tricks of Aretin[32] that are to be practised to give him pleasure – in which he is too able, having a large [prick]; but that which is the unhappiness is that, as the Italian proverb says, *Cazzo dritto non Vuolt consiglio*.[33] . . . If any of the sober councillors give him good advice and move him in anything that is to his good and honour, the other part, which are his counsellors of pleasure, take him when he is with my Lady Castlemaine and in a humour of delight and then persuade him that he ought not to hear or listen to the advice of those old dotards or counsellors that were heretofore his enemies when God knows it is they that nowadays do most study his honour.[34]

But Charles, of course, had to marry and provide a legitimate heir. What woman, coming into a Court such as his, could contrive to cope with the innumerable social as well as emotional difficulties with which she would be presented? The answer is, a remarkable woman.

Catherine, the daughter of John, Duke of Braganza, was born in 1638, two years before her father became King of Portugal. She was eighteen when her father died in 1656. Her younger brother Alfonso became king, with their mother, the strong-minded Queen Louisa, as regent. King John had proposed, when she was only seven, that Catherine should marry the English Prince of Wales. Though Charles I was half-hearted about the proposal, the Portuguese Court continued to cling to the ambition, so when the monarchy was restored in England a formal proposal was made, with a number of sweeteners: in return for the alliance, England would be given the port of Tangiers, thus allowing it to command the Mediterranean, Bombay (with its riches), the promise of religious freedom for Englishmen living and trading in Portugal, and actual cash – 2 million Portuguese *crusados*, or some £300,000. Lord Clarendon was delighted with the terms, immediately assured the Portuguese ambassador in London of the King's admiration of the Infanta's reputation for 'piety, virtue and comeliness', and asked if it might be possible to take possession of Tangiers immediately as a gesture of goodwill.

Edward Hyde, 1st Earl of Clarendon, was one of the most important and influential men in the kingdom. He had supported Charles I, then fled abroad with young Charles, and been his principal adviser during his exile. He had been appointed Lord Chancellor while the King was still in exile, and at the Restoration was confirmed in the post, his position strengthened by the marriage of his daughter Anne to James, Duke of York, the heir-presumptive to the throne.

Unpopular with the majority of the King's friends and supporters, his advice was nevertheless usually regarded and for the most part taken. He was in favour of the proposed marriage, and in a secret council meeting persuaded Charles that recognition of and respect for Catherine's Catholic convictions, and an agreement to protect Portugal from Spain and Holland, constituted a reasonable price to pay for an advantageous marriage.

The Spanish and the Dutch were less pleased when rumours of the alliance reached them. The Spaniards sent their London ambassador around to Whitehall to spread the rumour that Catherine was infertile – and, as a matter of fact, ugly – and to volunteer to cover the Portuguese offer of £300,000 with an equal sum if the King could be matched with a Spanish princess (care would be taken that she was a beauty).

The French, however, came down on the side of the Portuguese match, and Charles's mother actually travelled to England on behalf of the French government to encourage him to agree to it. On 8 May 1661, the British Parliament heard that marriage negotiations had been completed, and both houses presented the King with an address of congratulation. Just over a month later the marriage treaty was signed.

Catherine arrived at Portsmouth in May 1662, and when offered a glass of ale demanded a cup of tea instead – not perhaps a particularly good augury, suggesting a possible lack of interest in one of the pleasures of her new countrymen and women, and hinting at luxurious tastes, for tea was very expensive. The marriage took place immediately: first came a secret, Catholic contract, followed by a relatively public marriage ceremony conducted by the Bishop of London in the house of the Governor of Portsmouth. The Queen was not well when Charles met her at Portsmouth – she was in bed with a fever or, some say, was painfully menstruating. Charles paid his respects, and kissed her, but seems to have been somewhat relieved that he did not have to go to bed to her: 'It was happy for the honour of the nation that I was not put to the consummation of the marriage last night,' he wrote to Clarendon, 'for I was so sleepy by having slept but two hours in my journey as I was afraid that matters would have gone very sleepily.'[35]

Piety, virtue and comeliness, Clarendon had said. Piety and virtue, certainly. Catherine had been brought up in seclusion – it was said that she had been outside the royal palace only ten times in her life – and had had virtually no education; she could not even speak French, which was regarded as a necessity in every European court. (She did make some effort to learn a few words of English before setting sail.) She seems to have spent most of her time as a young girl at prayer, and when she had left the palace it had been to make pilgrimage to some saint's shrine. The one popular recreation she did enjoy was dancing, though she was not actually a good dancer.

As to her comeliness, this had perhaps been somewhat over-emphasised both by Clarendon and in the portraits sent to England to advertise her beauty to the King. In betrothal portraits, as in lapidary inscriptions, an artist is not on oath. Some observers who were among the first to see her in person unkindly suggested that it was her appearance rather than Charles's rough journey from London that made him hesitate to consummate the marriage: Catherine was, they pointed out, not a specially beautiful woman (buck teeth and a long nose, according to some English observers). But the King would no doubt in due course do his duty. He promised his beloved sister Minette, who was living in France, that he would 'entertain' his bride rather better than her husband, 'Monsieur', entertained her, though since he was notoriously a homosexual, this was not perhaps saying a great deal.

Catherine was accompanied to England by a number of confessors and by six substantial and unattractive ladies-in-waiting, each armoured in an unfashionable farthingale, which the Englishmen immediately asserted were worn for the purpose of keeping men away. The women insisted that none of them could occupy a bed in which any man had *ever* slept, which threw the organisers of the occasion into some confusion. Carpers aside, most of those who were introduced to her found the Queen herself by no means unattractive. Her and her attendants' complexions were 'olivaster [olive-coloured] and sufficiently unagreeable' (thought the diarist John Evelyn) but she was 'of the handsomest countenance of all the rest, and though low of stature, prettily shaped, languishing and excellent eyes, her teeth wronging her mouth by sticking a little too far out' but 'for the rest sweet and lovely enough'.[36]

The Queen proved by no means averse to pleasure. It was soon noticed that she liked showing off her delightfully small ankles and feet (almost as petite as Nell Gwyn's, it was said), used make-up (perhaps rather too heavily) and enjoyed wearing breeches, coats and caps, in a deliberately masculine style. A few people considered her as not a great deal less loose in her behaviour than the King's mistresses – 'an ill-natured little goblin . . . designed for nothing but to dance and vex mankind'.[37] She was a good archer, and impressed professional archers sufficiently for them to invite her to become their patron. Whether she had taken up the sport because she knew that her astrological Sun-sign was Sagittarius, we cannot say, but the Honourable Fraternity of Bowmen presented her with a silver badge bearing the inscription *Reginæ Catharinæ Sagitarii.*

She not only came to appreciate English ways and English virtues but also to enjoy English sports and even to an extent English society. She became almost alarmingly fond of gambling at cards (on one famous occasion she won at the astonishing odds of 1,000 to one) and even, to Pepys's disgust, played on Sunday.[38]

She also came to appreciate Charles, and schooled herself if not to ignore, at least to tolerate mistresses he kept during the whole of their married lives. She even allowed herself to joke about them. When Charles, pleading a cold, retired to his bed one night with Nell, Catherine decided to visit him to commiserate with him on his illness. His servants unaccountably failed to warn her off, and she approached his bedroom unannounced. Mrs Chiffinch, one of a husband and wife team of panders and pimps,[39] who was lurking nearby – on this fairly early visit, she had accompanied Nelly to the Palace of Whitehall – managed to warn Charles just in time, and Nell slipped under the bed. Seeing an unmistakable, diminutive foot and ankle insufficiently concealed, the Queen simply remarked: 'Ha, I will be off, then. I see it is not you who had the cold.'

Though he is said to have remarked, on first seeing her, that he 'thought they had brought me a bat, instead of a woman',[40] the King, all in all, was satisfied with his bride. She might have had neither the lively personality nor the vigorous sensuality which he appreciated in women, but on reflection, he told Clarendon that though her appearance was:

> not so exact as to be called a beauty . . . her eyes are excellent good, and [there is] not anything in her face that in the least degree can shock one. On the contrary she has as much agreeableness in her looks altogether, as ever I saw . . . And if I have any skill in physiognomy, which I think I have, she must be as good a woman as ever was born. Her conversation, as much as I can perceive, is very good; for she has wit enough . . . I am confident never two humours were better fitted together than ours are . . . I cannot easily tell you how happy I think myself; and I must be the worst man living (which I hope I am not) if I be not a good husband.[41]

No member of a European royal family contracting a marriage with an unfamiliar member of another, knew quite what to expect on a personal level. Portraits were exchanged and opinions sought – but there was very often too much at stake politically for the prospective bridegroom to be told the whole truth about his bride, or vice versa. Catherine may well have learned before leaving Portugal that her prospective husband was no monk, but whether she knew the extent of his self-indulgence is another matter.

Most people with any position at all in society in London certainly knew what was going on; Pepys's comments on the immorality of the Court and King tell us this, and Pepys was himself not particularly chaste. The King's appetite demanded instant satisfaction: one is reminded of President John F. Kennedy and his alleged remark that if he did not have a girl a day, he got a severe migraine. If Lady Castlemaine was not available, and there was no accessible Court lady in the Palace, Charles would simply send out for a companion. His pimp was the Page of the Royal Bedchamber and Keeper of the King's Privy Closet, William Chiffinch, whose wife loyally assisted him in the procurement of young women, whether from the streets, the stage or the Court. Chiffinch had succeeded his respectable brother Thomas as Page, and accumulated considerable wealth as the result of activities which included bribery and blackmail – he is said to have amassed over £14,000 during his lifetime.[42]

He was in many ways a personable character, with a frank and friendly, open look which belied his scheming and unscrupulous nature; he was 'a good fellow', a pleasant drinking companion, who knew everyone at Court, and everyone's business; everyone knew his business, too, and even the 'respectable' winked as 'Chiffinch step'd to fetch the female prey', as a lampoon put it.[43]

The Queen could scarcely have been unaware of Mr and Mrs Chiffinch's activities, or of the procession of girls who made their way into her husband's rooms, though like Mrs Kennedy (the parallel is an irresistible one) she took care not to notice them. She was almost certainly told, before her marriage, the name of his principal mistress, and Clarendon may have played some part in ensuring that she was fully aware of the situation. In his memoirs, he remarks that 'when the Queen came to Hampton Court she brought with her a formed resolution that she would never suffer the Lady who was so much spoken of to be in her presence'.[44] Perhaps she believed that Charles would at least be discreet; but discretion was never his strong point – and even if he had wished to exclude the heavily pregnant Barbara from the Palace, she would certainly not have suffered it. Her rooms were almost next to those occupied by the Queen, and she remained firmly ensconced in them.

Clarendon's son, Lord Cornbury, provides an early signal of a coming drama. Writing to a friend, he remarks that 'there are great endeavours used to make —— ——, you know who, a Lady of the Bedchamber, but it is hoped by many they will not take effect; a little time will show us a great deal, I will say no more of this for fear of burning my fingers'.[45] Indeed, when the King submitted to the Queen the list of her Ladies of the Bedchamber, Lady Castlemaine's name was at the head of it.

The 'Bedchamber Crisis', as it was called, was a severe test of Catherine's character, and the way in which she and the King behaved during it had the potential to make or break their relationship. It was also a test of the hold Barbara had over the King. This was always considerable, and at the time of Charles's marriage was still at its most powerful. Though his marriage was important to him and to the State, and though from the first he was by no means repelled by Catherine, he was certainly not about to risk losing the extremely beautiful, sexually magnetic Barbara, whose age (she was now forty-two) had by no means diminished her appeal, and whose services to him over the previous two years had been so enthusiastic and seductive.

Among her other qualities were very high spirits, which could be focused in strong displays of temper. It was perhaps one of the things that most intrigued and attracted the King: when she was roused, he ceased to be her monarch and became just another infuriating man. He was difficult to offend, especially when the miscreant was a woman, but she occasionally managed it. She never hesitated to make her feelings and opinions known – the latter rather too strongly in political matters; John Evelyn called her 'the curse of the Nation' not so much on moral grounds as because of the political influence she was supposed to have. It was the general perception – shared, indeed, by those close to him – that Barbara occupied time and attention which the King should have been giving to affairs of state. Instead, he

> Knows not what to do
> But loll and fumble here with you.
> Amongst your ladies, and his chits,
> At cards and Councils here he sits.
> Yet minds not how they play at either,
> Nor cares not when 'tis walking weather.
> Business and power he has resigned
> And all things to your mighty mind . . .[46]

Poets and balladeers always expressed themselves forcefully, especially where Barbara was concerned:

> Then there's Castlemaine,
> That prerogative Queen:
> If I had such a bitch I would spay her.
> She swives like a stoat,
> Goes to't hand and foot,
> Level-coil with a prince and a player.[47]

No protests about her behaviour were in the least effective during the years that immediately followed Charles's marriage. Even the Queen was not immune from her malign influence: the King reluctantly agreed to dismiss Lady Gerard, one of Catherine's ladies-in-waiting, when his mistress had a disagreement with her. He gave way to Barbara in every respect. The Queen began to believe that he was literally bewitched by her – that she was using magic to keep him ensnared. There is no doubt that she held him very firmly indeed, while she was able, by simple exuberant erotic power. He scarcely ever dined with Catherine, preferring to eat in private with Barbara, where the inevitable dessert could follow without delay.

It is unnecessary to speculate about the nature of her hold over him: if Charles's sexual nature was not unlike Jack Kennedy's, there is also a parallel with King Edward VIII and Wallis Simpson. Mrs Simpson was also the subject of rumours – that she had learned her sexual techniques in the brothels of the Far East. Whatever the truth, it is clear that from the first her power over the Prince of Wales had a sexual basis, possibly sado-masochistic,[48] and that he believed that she was the only woman who could satisfy him. Charles was similarly captivated by Barbara; yes, she was amusing, yes, she was high-spirited, but above all she had taken his measure sexually, and most historians agree that she was not excelled in this respect by any of his mistresses. She herself was very much in thrall to sex, and while she was satisfying Charles, she was also engaged with a number of other lovers – and so blatantly that one wonders whether the King got some kind of sexual gratification from knowing about them – about Sir Charles Berkeley and Lord Sandwich, Sir William Wycherley and Henry Jermyn and even a Groom of the King's Bedchamber, James Hamilton.

Nell Gwyn did not see herself as a rival to Barbara – though the man in the street had some fun with the idea.[49] There is no real sign that the King's relish for Barbara ever worried Nell, and it is understandable when one remembers that really she had nothing to lose. If Barbara should take against her, there was always her popularity as an actress to fall back on; and she probably realised quite soon that Barbara's star was on the wane. Charles, after all, was always susceptible to a new face. There had been an example of this as early as 1663, a year after the King's marriage, when the Queen's ladies-in-waiting were joined by a fifteen-year-old French girl called Frances Stuart, recommended by the King's sister as 'the prettiest girl in the world, and one of the best fitted of any I know to adorn a court'. Her fame as a beauty lives, for she is still remembered as 'La Belle Stuart', and she was the original model for the engraving of Britannia prepared by Philip de Rothier for the coin of the realm.

Pepys was an admirer from the first: soon after her appearance at Court, he was walking in Pall Mall when the King and Queen rode by, prettily hand in hand; Lady Castlemaine followed, a yellow plume in her hat, but looking 'mighty out of humour'. Then, 'above all, Mrs Stuart . . . with her hat cocked and a red plume, with her sweet eye, little Roman nose, and excellent *taille*, is the greatest beauty I ever saw I think in my life; and if ever woman can, doth exceed my Lady Castlemaine; at least, in this dress.'[50] Three years later, Pepys was describing Barbara as 'a much more ordinary woman than ever I durst have thought she was, and indeed is not so pretty as Mrs Stuart . . .'[51]

Unfortunately, Frances's beauty was not spiced with intelligence. One opinion was that 'never had a woman more beauty, or less wit'. It was soon said about the Court that she was so astonishingly foolish that a man could get all her clothes off simply by admiring her ankle, calf, thigh, her shoulders, breasts, waist: she was ready to display them all, if sufficiently complimented. Alas for Charles, this was as far as she was prepared to go. Barbara, realising that the King was besotted with the little stranger, actually went so far as to persuade her to go through a fake marriage ceremony at which Barbara played the groom and Frances the bride. They were escorted to bed, and the stocking was thrown – at which point Barbara generously forfeited her position in favour of the King. But Frances was having none of it, and allowed the King no more familiarities than usual. There seem to have been plenty of these, though they were on the innocent side. The King, Pepys reported, 'gets her into corners and will be with her half an hour together, kissing her to the observation of the world . . . but yet it is thought that this new wench is so subtle that she lets him do not anything more than is safe to her'.[52]

It was the royal pimp, Chiffinch – who had his nose into most of the labyrinthine affairs at Court – who finally removed La Belle Stuart from the scene, four years after her first appearance at Court. He discovered that the 26-year-old recently widowed Duke of Richmond was as intent on pursuing Frances as the King, and as far as she was concerned with better hope of success (though he seems to have been a rather boring man). Others knew about this, too: John Evelyn told Pepys that Frances:

> was come to that pass as to resolve to have married any gentleman of £1,500 a year that would have had her in honour – for it was come to that pass that she could no longer continue at court without prostituting herself to the King, whom she had so long kept off, though he had liberty more than any other had, or he ought to have, as to dalliance . . . She had reflected upon the occasion she had given to the world to think her a bad woman, and that she had no way but to marry and leave the Court, rather in this way of discontent than otherwise, that the world might see she sought not anything but her honour.[53]

It seems that Chiffinch reported to Barbara Villiers one night that Frances had sent Charles away from her rooms because she had a headache, but that things were not quite what they seemed. Barbara went to Charles at midnight and informed him that Frances was at that moment entertaining another man. Though he demurred, she insisted on his accompanying her to Frances's rooms, where they were met by her maids, who informed them that she was in bed with a sick headache and not to be disturbed. But something about their demeanour roused his suspicions even more keenly than Barbara had contrived to do, and he insisted on their admitting him. He found Frances in bed, certainly – but with the Duke of Richmond sitting by her.

The Duke withdrew, and Frances told the King that he had proposed marriage; unless Charles could do the same – she said sardonically – perhaps he would give them his blessing? He did not. But the couple certainly had the support of the Queen, and perhaps of Clarendon – Charles certainly later suspected it. In any event, in a last bid to entice her to his own bed Charles offered to make Frances a Duchess and to provide her with a generous income. However, she met Richmond at the Bear Tavern in Southwark, he took her to his home, Cobham Court, in Kent, and they were married on 30 March.[54]

That was in 1667; four years earlier, for an hour or two Frances had served to take the King's mind off the problem of what to do about Barbara, who had made such a fool of him by cajoling him into appointing her Lady of the Bedchamber to the Queen. He must surely have realised that the action was almost criminally silly – a prime example of his capacity for, as Rochester famously put it, never saying a silly thing but equally never doing a wise one. One can only suppose the fact that his mistress was pregnant at the time made it sufficiently difficult for him to refuse her, and he also felt, as he explained rather disingenuously to his sister, that 'he had undone this lady and ruined her reputation, which had been fair and untainted till her friendship with him',[55] and must make amends by giving her an unequivocal position at Court.

Made both unavailable and perhaps (she believed) unattractive by her pregnancy, Barbara probably felt insecure – though goodness knows she must have known Charles well enough by then to have realised that he was not going to give up his way of life simply because his duty to the country had forced him to marry. At all events, she did not go out of her way to ingratiate herself with Catherine. It would have been tactful for the King's pregnant mistress to retire from Hampton Court while the royal honeymoon was being spent there; she remained in her rooms. When the other ladies in residence at Hampton Court lit fires outside their bedroom doors as a mark of respectful and celebratory welcome, she declined to do so.

The King gave Clarendon the not altogether pleasant task of assuring Catherine that he was not going to change his ways, and that she would have to reach an accommodation with him. The Queen may also have had some intimate talks with other Court ladies: Barbara was not a particular favourite at the Court – she behaved too autocratically for that – and sympathy was on Catherine's side. But all they could do was confirm what the embarrassed Clarendon told her, which was that Charles was a man to whom sex was important, who had always gratified it with a selection of women, and who was not going to change his ways.

The Queen decided to make the best of things. There was not much else she could do, but she did it well, ingratiating herself with almost everyone at Court. She became very friendly with Charles's son James, and even the Wits[56] came to like and admire her. So in his own way did Charles. Indeed, the King came to love her as much as he was capable of loving any woman – which was not, in fact, a great deal. There is little evidence that he really loved any of the women with whom he slept – he liked some of them (certainly Nell), found many of them sexually almost irresistible (Nell again, but probably more intensely, Barbara), but that was as far as it went. This is not to say he treated them ill – indeed most of the people close to the throne would have said that he was far too indulgent to them. But that is not love. However, he admired Catherine – her piety (not a characteristic of any of his mistresses) and also her wit, which was not as coruscating or as cruel as Nell's, but which could be quietly effective. When Lady Castlemaine was once tactless enough to suggest to Her Majesty that she had been rather a long time dressing, and to wonder at her patience, 'I have had so much reason to use patience that I can very well bear with it,' the Queen replied.[57] Her retort was soon applauded in and out of Court.

But though the Queen settled into her position remarkably well, and came to enjoy the King's growing love as well as his respect, she had some difficulty in conceiving an heir. It was not that Charles did not do his part – in fact the number of times he slept with his wife was remarked upon almost with surprise – but the rumour began to circulate that perhaps the Queen was infertile. The balladeers, as usual, were among the first to point the finger:

> Our good King Charles the Second
> Too flippant of treasure and moisture,
> Stooped from the Queen infecund
> To a wench of orange and oyster.
> Consulting his *cazzo*,[58] he found it expedient
> To engender Don Johns on Nell the comedian.[59]

'Nell the Comedian' may have had her first intimate meeting with the King at Tunbridge Wells, where the Queen decided to take the waters in the hope that they might help her to conceive an heir to the throne. There, she was to find herself in the company not only of her husband but of Nell and Mall Davis – two members of the first generation of English actresses.

CHAPTER THREE

From the Pit to the Stage

Fate now for her did its whole force engage
And from the pit she mounted to the stage;
There in full lustre did her glories shine,
And long eclips'd, spread forth their light divine.

Earl of Rochester, from 'A Panegyric upon Nelly'

Of all the popular pleasures restored with the monarchy, theatre-going was one of the most welcome. In 1642 a parliamentary ordinance had forbidden the public performance of plays, the playhouses had been closed down, and many of them wrecked. 'Popular stage-plays', the arch-puritan William Prynne had written, were 'the very pomp of the Devil, which we renounce in baptism, if we believe the Fathers . . . sinful, heathenism, lewd, ungodly spectacles, and most pernicious corruption; condemned in all ages as intolerable mischiefs to churches, to republics, to the manners, minds and souls of men.'[1]

The actors had done their best to argue their case:

Oppressed with many calamities and languishing to death under the burden of a long and (for aught we know) an everlasting restraint, we the comedians, tragedians and actors of all sorts and sizes belonging to the famous private and public houses within the city of London and the suburbs thereof . . . in all humility present this our humble and lamentable complaint. . . .

It is of all other our extremest grievance that plays being put down under the name of public recreations, other public recreations of far more harmful consequences [are] permitted still to stand in *statu quo prius*, namely that nurse of barbarism and beastliness, the Bear-Garden, where upon their usual days those demi-monsters are baited stave and tail; the gentlemen of handed masons and the like rioting companions resorting thither with far worst stink than the ill-formed beasts they persecute with their dogs and whips; pickpockets, which in an age are not heard of in any of our houses, repairing thither, and other disturbers of the public peace which dare not be seen in our civil and well-governed theatres, where none use to come but the best of the nobility and gentry.[2]

But the complaint was not heard; bear-baiting continued, and the theatres remained closed. There were clandestine productions of plays in a number of private houses during the Interregnum, and towards the end of Cromwell's life – in 1656 – there was some official relaxation of the prejudice against stage spectacles: the Protector allowed Sir William Davenant to give a musical entertainment at Rutland House in Aldergate Street during which the singers appeared in costume, and some scenery was mounted on a modest platform. Three months later, Davenant produced *The Siege of Rhodes*, an opera written by three composers – Henry Lawes was the best known – and with scenery painted by John Webb, an excellent scenic artist. Mrs Coleman, who sang the part of Ianthe, was the first woman singer to appear on any British stage.

It was not until 9 July 1660 that, two months after returning in triumph to London, Charles II issued an order for a warrant giving Davenant and Thomas Killigrew the right to set up two companies of actors in the city, thus making those two men the paramount movers and shakers in the theatre of the Restoration. They had both been associated with the theatre during the closing years of the reign of Charles's father. Davenant grew up in Oxford at The Taverne, an inn kept by his father, a prominent Oxford businessman with a particularly beautiful wife, Jennet. Shakespeare used to pass through Oxford on his way to and from Stratford-upon-Avon, and sometimes performed there. The rumour grew up (first repeated by that famous tittle-tattler John Aubrey) that the playwright stayed several times at The Taverne and shared a bed there with Mrs Davenant, and that little William Davenant was the result of the encounter. He, according to Aubrey, 'would sometimes when he was pleasant over a glass of wine with his most intimate friends . . . say that it seemed to him that he writ with the very spirit [of] Shakespeare, and was contented enough to be thought his son'.[3] The anecdote was much embroidered both in Davenant's time and afterwards. The boy became a page (to the Duchess of Richmond) and later a hanger-on at Court, and took to writing poetry and plays, some of which were produced with mild success. He was appointed Poet Laureate in 1638 by Charles I, succeeding Ben Jonson. He organised masques with music, which were produced at Court; he fought for the King, escaped to France during the Interregnum, and was knighted by Charles II at the Restoration.

Killigrew was a Londoner, and stage-struck at an early age: he used to go to the Red Bull 'and when the man cried to the boys "who will go and be a devil, and he shall see the play for nothing?" then would he go in, and be a devil upon the stage, and so get to see plays'.[4] He also became a page – but to Charles I himself – and in 1642 was arrested on a charge of fighting for his monarch. He managed to contrive his release, joined Charles II in Paris, and at the Restoration was appointed Groom of the Chamber and accorded the same profitable honour as Davenant.

The theatrical rights granted to the two men were very considerable. They were allowed to set up their own companies of actors and build theatres in which to perform 'tragedies, comedies, plays, operas, music scenes and all other entertainments of the stage whatever' and, for the first time in British theatrical history, they were permitted to train actresses to play female parts. Their rights were also exclusive: no other companies were to be tolerated. One of Killigrew's first acts was to suppress a rival company run by a manager called Michael Mohun, whose Red Bull Company had acted clandestinely in Cromwell's time, and showed signs of continuing to do so. Killigrew had Mohun imprisoned in October 1660 – though when Mohun was released Killigrew employed him and many members of his company at the King's Theatre.

Another renegade company was to be seen at the Cockpit in Drury Lane, managed by John Rhodes, who employed two of the best actors of the time – Edward Kynaston and Thomas Betterton. Action was taken against Rhodes, too; his actors were re-employed by Davenant for his Duke's Company. Kynaston had been a wonderful performer of Shakespeare's female rôles, and was still not too old to wear petticoats convincingly; Betterton, still in his middle thirties, was at the height of his powers, a great Hamlet and probably the finest actor of the time; after Davenant's death in 1668 he became a joint manager of the Duke's Company, and ended his life as a prominent director of opera (mounting the premières of Purcell's *Fairy Queen* and *King Arthur*).

Davenant's and Killigrew's companies divided up the traditional stock of plays between them: Davenant claimed the sole rights to produce some of Shakespeare's plays (including *The Tempest, Macbeth, King Lear* and *Hamlet* – a vehicle for Betterton) while others fell to Killigrew (including *Othello, Julius Caesar* and *A Midsummer Night's Dream*). Though the latter had the rights to fewer Shakespearean plays, he had a monopoly of Ben Jonson's work, which was almost as popular, and of the best of Beaumont and Fletcher.

In March 1660, Davenant had leased a tennis court in Lincoln's Inn Fields from a Thomas Lisle with the intention of converting it into a theatre. The idea for this was copied from the French. Tennis courts intended for the playing of 'real' or 'royal' tennis had been used as theatres in Paris as early as 1548. They were long, rectangular halls – something like 100 feet long and 30 feet across – with a gallery at one end, and lit by skylights. There was little possibility of elaborate staging, for there were no wings, and merely a flat stage; but in 1644 when the Théâtre du Marais, originally a tennis court, was burned down, the reconstruction showed just how the shell of such a building could be 'improved' for staging plays: it was redesigned with two ranges of nine boxes on each side of the hall, a gallery (known as the *paradis*) above, and four more ranges of four boxes facing the stage. An 'amphitheatre' was later constructed towards the back of the theatre, sight-lines were improved, and special boxes were reserved for an orchestra. The Lincoln's Inn Theatre must have been very like the earlier building, without wings and with doors opening onto the stage at each side.

On 5 November 1660, Killigrew established himself, with the King's Company, at the Red Bull Theatre (until his new theatre was ready). The Red Bull Theatre, which he had known as a boy, was at the upper end of St John Street in Clerkenwell, and had been built in 1605. Over half a century later it was dilapidated and in bad order; Killigrew seems to have used it only for a day or two, probably because he was eager that his company should be performing somewhere on the day that Davenant, with his Duke's Company, took possession of the Salisbury Court Theatre. This had formerly been a barn in the grounds of Salisbury House, built round about 1629 and used as a theatre until 1642. It had been gutted by the Puritans, and reopened optimistically by one William Beeson, of the second generation of a theatrical family. If Beeson had ambitions as a theatre manager, however, they were to be disappointed, for the exclusivity of the deal Charles had given Davenant and Killigrew was fatal to him. Davenant moved his company in, but only used the place briefly (the Duke's Company also played at the Apothecaries' Hall). When he left it for his new theatre, the Dowager Countess of Exeter moved in, presumably after some redesigning; finally, it perished in the Great Fire.

It was in June 1661 that Davenant and his company occupied the newly built theatre in Portugal Row, on the south side of Lincoln's Inn Fields, opening with his own opera *The Siege of Rhodes* – an enormous success.

The theatre that Killigrew rented in Rider's Yard, Bridges Street – the site of a riding school – for £50 a year had far greater possibilities for elaborate scenery and production than Davenant's. It was at the time the largest theatre in London – the first on the site of the present Theatre Royal, Drury Lane. Killigrew and his partners (the actors in his company) had planned to spend £1,500 on its construction, but then as now builders wildly overran their estimate, and the final cost was £2,500. Killigrew broke away from the long, slender auditorium based on the tennis court, and planned one 'nearly of a circular form, surrounded, in the inside, by boxes separated from each other, and divided into several rows of seats'; the benches in the pit 'rose one behind another like an amphitheatre and

[are] covered with green cloth'.[5] Pepys, who took his wife to the theatre the day after its opening, admired it, with some reservations; it was 'made with extraordinary good contrivance', but the corridors were very narrow, the boxes so far from the stage that the actors must surely be inaudible, and the orchestra pit (a new feature) so deep that the musicians' sound suffered.[6]

One of the major assets was the provision for elaborate scenery. Flats ran across the stage in grooves behind the proscenium and made flamboyant scenes possible. When John Evelyn, Pepys's fellow diarist, went to see Dryden's *The Indian Queen* there he found the stage 'so beautified with rich Scenes as the like had never been seen here as happily (except rarely any where else) in a mercenary theatre'.[7]

To make the best use of daylight (the theatre was lit through a rather leaky glass roof, though wax candles could give added light on the stage) performances began at three in the afternoon, and audiences – as at the rival theatre – were good, often completely filling the 700 or so seats. The upper gallery (seats, $1s$[8]) was crowded with the poorer sort, the middle gallery (at $18d$[9] a seat) popular with the middle classes – Pepys and his wife almost invariably sat there; and the boxes ($4s$[10] a seat) full of aristocrats ogling the masked women in the pit, who had paid $2s\,6d$[11] for the privilege of displaying themselves – but also of seeing the play, for it would be wrong to suggest that the women who thronged to the pit were all whores.

Nell was not as stage-struck as the boy Killigrew had been. She never seems to have appeared as an extra, and it is unlikely that she made for the theatre because she believed she could act. In any case, neither she nor anyone else would have supposed that women could appear on a public stage until the thing actually happened. Women's parts had always been played by boys – and very successfully so. The situation only changed with Killigrew's patent for the Duke's Theatre (issued on 20 April 1662) and Davenant's of the following year, which stated (not, one suspects, without a certain amount of irony) that:

Forasmuch as many plays formerly acted do contain several profane obscene and scurrilous passages and the women's parts therein have been acted by men in the habit of women at which some have taken offence, for the preventing of these abuses for the future we do hereby strictly command and enjoin that from henceforth no new play shall be acted by either of the said Companies containing any passage offensive to piety and good manners . . . And we do likewise permit and give leave that all the women's parts to be acted in either of the said two Companies for the time to come may be performed by women so long as these recreations which by reason of the abuses aforesaid were scandalous and offensive may by such reformation be esteemed not only harmless delights but useful and instructive representations of human life to such of our good subjects as shall resort to the same.

This was a revolutionary change, and it was vigorously welcomed not only by the actors but by their audience – a remarkable turnabout, for less than forty years previously, when a company of French actresses had performed at Blackfriars they had been hissed, booed, and so pelted with apples and other missiles that they were driven from the stage. But the influential men about the Court had mostly spent their time in exile in France, where actresses were a matter of course; they had no objection to the custom – and the general public greeted the change as a welcome aspect of the altering moral climate of the time. If a few Englishmen – in particular the Puritans – still disapproved of women appearing on the stage, they were in a considerable minority.

For some time, it was not invariable practice to cast women: Kynaston, for one, continued to play female parts for a while. On one occasion when the King went to see him act, the theatre manager had to apologise for a late curtain: 'the Queen was not shaved yet'. Kynaston, who appears to have been exclusively heterosexual, was 'so beautiful a youth that the ladies of quality prided themselves in taking him with them in their coaches to Hyde Park, in his theatrical habit, after the play',[12] and when Pepys went to see him in *The Loyal Subject* and *The Maid's Tragedy* he thought him 'the loveliest lady that ever I saw in my life' and 'the prettiest woman in the whole house'. Yet when the actor put on male clothes for the last act of the latter play, Pepys applauded him as 'the handsomest man in the whole house', and within a week he played both Arthiope, the heroine of *The Bloody Brother*, and Otto, the hero.

The new, first generation of actresses had to be trained – and Killigrew farsightedly set up a stage school at the Barbican for the purpose. Nell, however, as far as we know never attended it – nor did she need to at first, when her (legendary) job in the theatre was selling oranges. She was employed by 'Orange Mall' – one Mary Meggs, who paid Killigrew 6s 8d a day[13] for a licence to sell 'oranges, lemons, fruit, sweetmeats and all manner of fruiterers' and confectioner's wares'. ('Orange Betty' Mackerell obtained a similar licence from Killigrew at the Duke's Theatre.)

Mall was clearly a character. She knew all the inside gossip of the theatre – Pepys often went to her for the latest news. She was an obliging pimp, happy to carry messages from gentlemen to ladies in the audience, but was useful in other ways – on one occasion she saved the life of a patron who was choking to death (presumably on one of her sweetmeats) by thrusting her fingers down his throat. She stood no nonsense from anyone, and was clearly not to be crossed: in 1669 Rebecca Marshall, one of the actresses, got on the wrong side of her, and was well cuffed – Mall was arrested for assaulting her 'to the disturbance of His Majesty's actors'. Nell's sister Rose was one of Mall's girls for a while, though she was already established as a rather successful prostitute, among whose clients was Harry Killigrew, the theatre owner's son, which cannot have harmed her prospects or indeed Nell's.

The orange girls, well drilled by Mall, stood with their backs to the stage with baskets of fruit on their arms, crying 'Oranges, will you have any oranges?'[14] Their fruit was expensive – sixpence, or half the price of the cheapest seats[15] – but the generous purchaser often acquired additional services, for the girls like Mall herself acted as go-betweens, carrying notes from gallants to the racier women in the audience, whom Dryden described in a prologue:

> The play-house is their place of traffic, where
> Nightly they sit to sell their rotten ware. . . .

For while he nibbles at her amorous trap
She gets the money, but he gets the clap.
Entrenched in vizor mask they giggling sit
And throw designing looks about the pit,
Neglecting wholly what the actors say.
'Tis their least business there to see the play.[16]

Most of the orange girls also made a choicer fruit than oranges available to male theatre-goers after the performances, and Nell, having been introduced already to prostitution – even if she was not a child prostitute herself, she certainly knew about her sister's amorous activities – may have sold her wares with the rest of them.

The orange girls were a cheerful, rough-and-ready lot, but at least they were one rung up the ladder from the common street whores of Dog and Bitch Lane, Lukener's Lane, Moorfields, Ratcliffe Highway and East Smithfield. Some of these had rooms in bawdy houses, where a measure of protection was offered by such madams as the notorious Mother Cresswell and Damaris Page (signatories in 1668 of the petition to Barbara Villiers 'for protection against the company of London apprentices' who regularly attacked brothels and demolished them).[17] But the alleys and lanes were thick with amateurs – there was said to be 3,600 street prostitutes practising in London in the early 1660s, which at a conservative estimate suggests that of every fifty women in the city three were likely to be walking the streets or trading in taverns, especially those near convenient open spaces such as Lincoln's Inn Fields or St James's Park.

Nell may or may not have been, briefly, one of them; the theatre pit was safer, and there was likely to be a better class of client there. But she soon rose from the pit to the stage itself. This was not because she thought she could make a better living as an actress, or because to be an actress was much more respectable than to be an orange girl. It did not take long for actresses to gain a reputation for loose living. They were ill paid (receiving about 30*s* a week as opposed to the actors' average of 50*s*)[18] but it was very easy indeed for them to acquire 'admirers' – indeed, one would have had to be very strong-minded to resist the approaches of the gentlemen, especially those in the pit and boxes. As the satirist Tom Brown put it: ''Tis as hard a matter for a pretty woman to keep herself honest in a theatre, as 'tis for an apothecary to keep his treacle from the flies in hot weather, for every libertine in the audience will be buzzing about her honey-pot.'[19] And they were free to buzz, or so it appeared. Though the King issued a decree in February 1664, that 'no person of what quality soever do presume to enter at the door of the attiring house, but such as do belong to the company and are employed by them', his order was a great deal more honoured in the breach than the observance. The men in the audience viewed the actresses as sexually available, on or off stage, and there is plenty of evidence to show that the more determined of them were hot in pursuit: Rebecca Marshall, one of the most handsome of the women, was forced to ask the King for protection against Sir Hugh Middleton, and a certain Mark Trevor assaulted her and pursued her with a sword when she rebuffed him. A few actresses were virtuous, but like Margaret Cavendish, the poetical Duchess of Newcastle, were thought merely eccentric for preserving their virginity. Even the playwrights portrayed the female players as accessible:

> Item, you shall appear behind our scenes
> And there make love with the sweet chink of guineas
> The unresisted eloquence of ninnies.
> Some of our women will be kind to you,
> And promise free ingress and egress too.[20]

We should not forget that some of the male actors were no better than their sisters: Kynaston (notoriously) but also Charles Hart and Cardell Goodman, and no doubt other less well-known male players, were all kept at one time or another by female admirers. But it was the women on whom the satirists of the time focused: such players as the Elizabeths Boutell, Cox and Barry:

> There was chestnut-maned Boutell, whom all the town fucks,
> Lord Lumley's cast player, the famed Mrs Cox,
> And chaste Mrs Barry, i'th'midst of a flux
> To make him a present of chancre and pox.[21]

In short, the terms actress and whore were synonyms. Nell found one noun as good as the other; a 'protector', as wealthy as might be, was just the ticket for her, and as Rochester put it:

> As men commence at University
> No doctors 'till they've masters been before,
> So she no player was 'till first a whore.[22]

She continued for the time being to sell her oranges, and perhaps herself, at the King's Theatre. The 1752 biography says that '. . . no sooner had she appeared in the pit and behind the scenes with her oranges than the eyes of the players, and those sparkish gentlemen who frequent the theatres, were fixed upon her, all anxious to know the story and birth of the handsome orange wench. . . .'[23] But selling herself to those who rightly considered her as available, if that is what Nell did, she must have realised that showing off her beauty on the stage would be a wonderful advertisement, which with any luck could gain her a wealthy lover – or perhaps several.

Soon, she was in a rather happier position than her sister. Rose, for some reason, was sacked from the theatre, and went off and married a highwayman, John Cassells. Then she was arrested for burglary, and thrown into Newgate Gaol. One way and another, though convicted, she was eventually released 'from this woeful place of torment'[24] – probably as a result of special pleading by Harry Killigrew, her lover (or by now ex-lover). Killigrew may have used his influence on Nell's behalf too, for very soon afterwards she got her wish, and was seen for the first time on the stage of his father's theatre. As an anonymous versifier put it:

> Fate now for her did its whole force engage,
> And from the pit she's mounted to the stage;
> There in full lustre did her glories shine,
> And long eclips'd, spread forth their light divine:
> There Hart's and Rowley's soul she did ensnare,
> And made a king the rival to a player.[25]

Rowley – the King – was to come. First, Nell fell under the protection of Charles Hart, and of his colleague John Lacy. Both were players. Hart was a true relative of Shakespeare – the eldest son of William Hart, son of the playwright's sister Joan, to whom Shakespeare left £5 in his will. John was a boy actor before the closure of the theatres, trained by a popular older performer, Richard Robinson. He had an early success as the Duchess in James Shirley's *The Cardinal* in 1641, the first part that 'gave him any reputation'.[26] During the Civil War he served in Prince Rupert's regiment as a lieutenant of horse, then carried on acting in clandestine performances during the Interregnum – in private houses out of town 'where they had pits for the gentry and acted by candle-light'[27] (at Holland House, for instance). In 1647 he and fellow players were giving Beaumont and Fletcher's *The Bloody Brother* at such a venue (for a few silver pieces contributed by the wealthier members of the audience) when foot soldiers broke in and carried them off to prison, where they were stripped of their costumes and turned naked into the street.

After the Restoration Hart continued his career, much admired by Dryden, for one, who said of his performance as Dorante in *Mistaken Beauty* (an adaptation from Corneille) that the part was 'acted to so much advantage as I am confident it never received in its own country'. He was clearly a fine actor: it was said that he was so involved in every part he played that it was impossible to distract him once the performance was under way: he 'was a man of that exactness and grandeur on the stage, that let what would happen, he'd never discompose himself or mind anything but what he then represented, and had a scene fallen behind him, he would not at that time look back to see what was the matter . . .'[28] An anonymous courtier remarked that he 'might teach any king on earth how to comport himself'.

The 1752 biography of Nell Gwyn says that he was 'a promising genius [who] had made a rapid progress on the stage, and was held in esteem not only for his present accomplishments but for the attainments he was likely soon to be master of. He was of a constitution sanguine and amorous, he felt the passions he represented, and as love is inseparable from a heart capable of tender sensations, so it is not to be doubted but he made some advances to Nell . . .' The anonymous biographer goes on to claim that it was Hart who 'prevailed upon her to quit her profession of orange-selling, and though players then did not attain to so high a pinnacle of wealth as in modern times, yet he offered to share his salary with her, and to live with her with that constancy and freedom [in] which a husband is bound in honour to live with his wife'.[29]

John Lacy was an older man, a comedian who was one of the chief actors of Killigrew's company, and a minor playwright who also wrote for the company. He had started life as a dancing master: in his youth he was 'of a rare shape of body and good complexion'.[30] He was a great favourite of Charles II, who commissioned a portrait of him in three of his comic rôles. He had served as a soldier during the war – it is said in the same troop as Nell's father, which may be one reason why he took her up. Apart from teaching her to dance, he assisted Hart in teaching her something about acting, for he had also played 'straight' rôles, including Tartuffe and Falstaff; one critic said that he 'performed all parts that he introduced to a miracle, insomuch that I am apt to believe that as this age never had, so the next never will have his equal – at least not his superior'.[31]

Nell became mistress of both men – the young Hart and the decidedly middle-aged Lacy. Colley Cibber claimed that 'Hart introduced Mrs Gwyn upon the dramatic boards. And has acquired the distinction of being ranked among that lady's first felicitous lovers, by having succeeded to Lacy in the possession of her charms.'[32] An anonymous versifier crudely remarked that:

> what Lacy's fumbling age abus'd
> Hart's sprightly vigour more robustly us'd.

At all events, the former taught her to dance, the latter to act – and in a remarkably short time Hart and Gwyn were to become a pair in more than the amorous sense. They were the first 'gay couple' of the Restoration theatre – at a time when, of course, the word 'gay' meant light-hearted, vivacious, effervescent.

Nell had probably appeared in early performances of Dryden's *The Indian Emperor*, which was premièred in March 1665, when she was fifteen, though some historians assert that she played, the previous year, in Lacy's *The Old Trooper*. She was extremely fortunate in being taken up by John Dryden, whose *Indian Queen* came out in 1664. By the time he wrote a part with her in mind, four more of his plays had been staged: *The Wild Gallant* (1663), *The Rival Ladies* (1664), *The Indian Emperor* (1665) and *Tyrannic Love* (1669). But it was when she was teamed with Hart that she really began to make her mark. They were successful from the moment they first appeared together. Dryden saw them as Philidor and Mirida in *All Mistaken*, by his brother-in-law James Howard – a low comedy in which most of the entertainment derived from the attempts of a fat courtier, Pinguister, to court a pretty maid (Mirida, played by Nell). Hart rolled about the stage with Nell in his arms, rising occasionally to rush from the stage unbuttoning his breeches in order to deal with the consequences of a purge which someone had given him. Then came another play of Howard's, *The Gay Mounsieur*, and Richard Rhodes's *Flora's Vagaries* – and Dryden adapted Fletcher's *The Chances* for them in 1667. But it was with *Secret Love, or the Maiden Queen*, produced in March 1667, that they had an unqualified success.

The idea of a pair of lovers whose love is sharpened by a degree of witty antagonism had been aired before (not least by Shakespeare, notably in *Much Ado About Nothing*). But it became particularly popular after the Restoration, and its popularity was fired by Hart and Gwyn. *Secret Love* was a tragi-comedy, the plot borrowed from a French piece, in which an introverted Queen is threatened by treachery.[33] The Queen was played by Rebecca Marshall, a colleague in the company, and the play offered Nell, as Florimell, the opportunity to swagger around the stage in breeches, showing off her fine legs – a sort of prototype principal boy.

Secret Love allows us a clear glimpse of a seventeen-year-old Nell. In the second scene a masked maid of honour, Florimell, turns to the courtier Celadon and asks 'What kind of beauty do you like?' Celadon (played by Hart) replies: 'Just such a one as yours.'

Florimell: What's that?

Celadon: Such an oval face, clear skin, hazel eyes, thick brown eyebrows, and hair as you have for all the world . . . A turn'd up nose, that gives an air to your face. Oh, I find I am more and more in love with you! A full nether-lip, an out-mouth, that makes mine water at it: the bottom of your cheeks a little blub, and two dimples when you smile. For your stature, 'tis well, and for your wit, 'twas given you by one that knew it had been thrown away upon an ill face. Come, you are handsome, there's no denying it.[34]

When the actress removed her mask, the truth turned out to be no whit less delightful than Celadon's advertisement – and in Act V, when she appeared 'in Mans Habit' and danced a jig, the whole audience rose to her.

An anonymous writer in *The Manager's Notebook*, a theatrical publication of the early eighteenth century, says that 'she was low in stature, and what the French call *mignonne* and *piquante*, well-formed, handsome, but red-haired, and rather *embonpoint*; of the *enjoué*[35] she was a complete mistress. Airy, fantastic and sprightly, she sang, danced, and was exactly made for acting light, showy characters, filling them up, as far as they went, most effectually.'

Dryden recognised from the first that Nell's greatest attribute was her native wit, on which everyone who met her remarked, and that it could and should be reflected in the parts she played. In *Secret Love* he gave her the opportunity to banter with Hart in a scene which prefigured the more famous passage between Mirabell and Millamant in Act IV of Congreve's *The Way of the World* over thirty years later. The two scenes are so similar that one almost suspects Congreve of having borrowed the idea from Dryden. But at all events, one fancies we can hear the very tone of Nell's voice in the exchange with her real and stage lover as they discuss marriage:

Celadon: As for the first year, according to the laudable custom of new married people, we shall follow one another up into chambers, and down into gardens, and think we shall never have enough of one another. So far 'tis pleasant enough I hope.

Florimell: But after that, when we begin to live like husband and wife, and never come near one another – what then?

Celadon: Why then our only happiness must be to have one mind, and one will, Florimell.

Florimell: One mind if thou wilt, but prithee let us have two wills; for I find one will be little enough for me alone. But how if those wills should meet and clash, Celadon?

Celadon: I warrant thee for that: husbands and wives keep their wills far enough asunder for ever meeting: one thing let us be sure to agree on, that is, never to be jealous.

Florimell: No, but e'en love one another as long as we can; and confess the truth when we can love no longer.

Celadon: When I have been at play, you shall never ask me what money I have lost.

Florimell: When I have been abroad you shall never enquire who treated me.

Celadon: Item, I will have the liberty to sleep all night, without your interrupting my repose for any evil design whatsoever.

Florimell: Item, then you shall bid me goodnight before you sleep.

Celadon: Provided always that whatever liberties we take with other people, we will continue very honest to one another.

Florimell: As far as will consist with a pleasant life.

Celadon: Lastly, whereas the names of husband and wife hold forth nothing but clashing and cloying, and dullness and faintness in their signification, they shall be abolish'd for ever betwixt us.

Florimell: And instead of those, we will be married by the more agreeable names of mistress and gallant.

Celadon: None of my privileges to be infring'd by thee, Florimell, under the penalty of a month of fasting-nights.

Florimell: None of my privileges to be infring'd by thee, Celadon, under the penalty of cuckoldom . . . La ye now, is not such a marriage as good as wenching, Celadon?[36]

One can imagine how well two experienced actors could bring off such a scene; and although Nell had been acting for only a few years, and her technique must have been instinctive rather than conscious, she and Hart made the play successful enough to draw the town. Pepys saw one of the first performances – the King was present, the same evening – and remarked that 'there is a comical part done by Nell, which is Florimell, that I never can hope ever to see the like done again by man or woman . . . so great performance of a comical part was never, I believe, in the world before as Nell doth this, both as a mad girl and then, most and best of all, when she comes in like a young gallant; and hath the motions and carriage of a spark the most that ever I saw any man have'.[37] He especially enjoyed seeing her in drag – it is interesting that so many men, after years of putting up with boy actors dressed in women's clothes, now so frequently seemed besotted with the idea of women dressed as men. About 90 of the 350 or so Restoration plays feature women disguised as boys, many of whom at some point reveal that their masculinity is false by stripping open their jerkins or having a man feel their breasts. In Aphra Behn's *The Younger Brother* (1696) a disguised page, Olivia, is accused of making love to 'his' mistress, and the mistress 'opens Olivia's bosom [and] shows her breasts' to prove she is a girl. Dryden in *The Rival Ladies* (1664) has a scene in which two women are disguised as pages, and after a scene in which they narrowly escape being stripped by robbers, they end up preparing to fight a duel, prevented only when, after they have removed their doublets, one sees 'two swelling breasts! – a woman, and my rival!' and then opens her shirt to display her own bosom.

The actresses, delivering the lines of the playwrights, were not above comparing the favours they could (and did) offer to those which were sold by the boy players of the past. In the epilogue to Killigrew's *The Parson's Wedding*, the actress recalled that:

> When boys played women's parts, you'd think the stage
> Was innocent in that tempting age.
> No – for your amorous fathers then, like you,
> Amongst those boys had playhouse Misses too.
> They set those bearded beauties on their laps,
> Men gave 'em kisses, and the ladies claps.
> But they, poor hearts, could not supply our room. . . .

Even for those men who did not wish, or had not the means, to take advantage of such generous offers, there was no doubt a certain pleasure in the fact that male costume of, say, Rosalind was now filled out by the broad hips and buttocks of a handsome woman rather than merely hanging on the slim body of a boy. Nell had no difficulty in catching the eye of every man in the audience.

The years she spent as a working actress must in some ways have been pleasant enough for Nell, and there is certainly no evidence that she did not enjoy them. Though players were not well paid and when the theatres were closed – which was all too often – there was no salary at all, she was making more money than she was likely to earn in any other work open to her, save outright prostitution. There were perks too – in particular, clothes, including the scarlet cloaks with crimson capes which were worn when the players went to Court, and which marked them out as the King's servants. There is a warrant in existence which granted Nell, Rebecca Marshall and others 'four yards of bastard scarlet cloth and one quarter of a yard of velvet for their liveries'.[38] There was also a great deal of fun to be had, innocent and otherwise. The admiration of the public must have amused and pleased her, especially since among her admirers were men and women of a social class to which she could never aspire. Soon enough her reputation as a player spread among the playwrights, and they began to write parts that would suit her (most playwrights of the period wrote with a particular company, and particular players, in mind). Her range, as an actress, was not great. She was always at her best in comedy, though she played, reluctantly, in tragedy – for instance, in 1664/5, she appeared in Killigrew's *The Siege of Urbino*, and later in Dryden's *The Indian Emperor*, in which Hart played Hernando Cortez and Nell Cydaria, a daughter of Montezuma, Emperor of Mexico.

There was no scope for comedy there, and as she once told her audience, in a prologue:

> I know you in your hearts
> Hate serious plays – as I hate serious parts.[39]

She was not at home with melodramatic dialogue such as:

> Stay, life, and keep me in the cheerful Light;
> Death is too black, and dwells in too much night.
> Thou leav'st me, life, but love supplies thy part,
> And keeps me warm by lingering in my heart . . .[40]

Pepys 'was most infinitely displeased with her being put to act the Emperors daughter; which is a great and serious part, which she doth most basely'; and she got no better as the play continued to run, for he returned to the piece three months later, and still 'Nell's ill speaking of a great part made me mad.'[41]

The play is certainly not Dryden's weakest – but Nell (still only seventeen) was simply not capable of bearing a long, arduous, tragic part, and it is not surprising that she shone rather in the epilogue:

> Last for the ladies, 'tis Apollo's will,
> They should have power to save, but not to kill:
> For love and he long since have thought it fit,
> Wit live by beauty, beauty reign by wit.

The problem Nell had with 'straight' rôles was probably in the main the result of the acting conventions of the time, for while comedy was played naturally, or at least without undue distortion of speech or gesture, tragedy was still played largely in the style that had so irritated Hamlet (and we may guess Shakespeare) a generation earlier: the lines 'mouthed' with much 'sawing of the air' in conventional gestures passed down from actor to actor. Betterton, the greatest actor of his time, wrote a long dissertation on the gestures that should represent each emotion to be expressed on the stage: rage, jealousy, apprehension, rejoicing. He and the best of his colleagues were able to rise above this constraint and impress audiences; but it must have been a great disadvantage to the less gifted, and Nell was certainly no good at it. Had she been allowed to play her few serious rôles as naturally as her comedy parts, she might have been quite as successful in them. But it was to be many years (some would say over 200) before this would become possible.

It would be a mistake to suppose that Nell enjoyed an easy life as an actress. No one could have achieved her degree of success without working for it, and apart from having to pick up a technique without having received any serious training, the day-to-day life of the theatre must have been rather like the most taxing days of provincial repertory theatre 300 years later – or even worse. At ten in the morning (every day except Sunday) there were obligatory rehearsals, and performances every afternoon – and often in the evening, at private theatres or at Court. There were up to sixty productions a year and, since plays were scarcely ever played for more than two or three days, while appearing in one the players were usually attempting to learn at least two more parts, and refreshing themselves in others for revivals. This must have been particularly trying for Nell, who if she could read at all must have read haltingly; presumably she must have employed someone – or persuaded a colleague – to read her parts through to her again and again until she knew them. Other players must have had the same problem, and it is not surprising that it was common for actors to forget their lines or to break down.

Nell obviously had considerable natural talent, and rode it: there is no evidence that she paid particular attention to refining her technique. She may well have been one of those actresses who, the dramatist Charles Gildon complained, came to rehearsals 'too often scarce recovered from their last night's debauch'. She seems to have got on reasonably well with the other actresses of the King's Company – Mrs Hughes, Mrs Knepp and the sisters Marshall, Ann and Rebecca. Peg Hughes acted with the company between 1667 and 1669, then became the mistress of the King's cousin, Prince Rupert. She was no threat to Nell, playing chiefly minor parts. Elizabeth Knepp (or sometimes Knipp) was a singing actress, specially good at speaking prologues and epilogues, and, if we are to believe her friend Pepys, not a great deal better than she should be, for after only a short acquaintance she allowed him to fondle her freely – apart from which her friendships with other gentlemen were sufficiently frequent to make him jealous. It was Mrs Knepp who first introduced him to Nell in January 1667, in the company of a number of friends ('a most pretty woman, who acted the great part, Coelia, today very fine, and did it pretty well; I kissed her and so did my wife, and a mighty pretty soul she is.')[42] Though Knepp was a more likely rival, Nell seems to have got on well with her (they were both lively and gossipy and probably enjoyed each other's company).

Pepys was immediately struck by Nell, off-stage as on. Though he disliked make-up, and urged his wife to have nothing to do with the new fashion of wearing patches of velvet or silk on her face, he did not object to them on Nell; and though he disapproved of her wearing cosmetics off-stage, he clearly found her extremely attractive – and, significantly, so did Elizabeth Pepys. Most people liked her, including her colleagues, though there was a little abrasiveness from time to time between her and the Marshall sisters. Ann seems to have been a thumping wench in the principal boy mode, and the fact that the men in the audience made it quite clear that they preferred Nell's legs to hers made her more than a little irritable; the two women may even have come to blows, or near it. Ann's chief distinction is that she may have been the first actress to appear on an English stage – with the King's Company, as Desdemona on 8 December 1660, an event famously announced by the poet Thomas Jordon:

> I come, unknown to any of the rest,
> To tell you news; I saw the lady dressed!
> The woman plays today, mistake me not –
> No man in gown, or page in petticoat.[43]

In the twentieth century a considerable effort is required to imagine a boy playing Desdemona, Juliet, Cleopatra with any success, though Mark Rylance gave a notable performance in the latter part at Shakespeare's Globe in London in the summer of 1999. The new generation of women actors actually had quite a hard time of it to outdo those performers still remembered by the older generation of theatre-goers. A man who saw Desdemona played by a boy in a performance at Oxford in 1610 spoke of how the young actors 'drew tears not only by their speech but also by their action. Indeed, Desdemona killed by her husband, in death moved us especially when, as she lay in her bed, her face alone implored the pity of the audience.' (Note how even writing after the event, the writer remained so convinced that he described the boy actor as 'she'.)[44] The chief advantage of the women lay in the fact that so many of the boys who had been successful before the Interregnum were now unmistakably men. As Jordan put it:[45]

> Our women are defective, and so sized
> You'd think they were some of the Guard disguised;
> For, to speak truth, men act that are between
> Forty and fifty, women of fifteen,
> With bone so large and nerve so incompliant,
> When you call *Desdemona*, enter *Giant*.

Ann Marshall appears to have been moderately virtuous, but her sister Rebecca was no better than Nell – years later they were to have words on the subject.[46] By then Nell had begun her more successful second career, and could afford to be good-humoured about being called a whore – an insult that was, after all, accurate if ill meant. In their earlier days, however, they were rivals in every sense. Rebecca captured the hearts and purses of a number of prominent men, among them the famous dandy Sir George Hewett. On stage, unlike Nell, she was effective both in comedy and tragedy, making an impression in both: Pepys was an admirer – in 1666 he set her down as 'a pretty good actor', and when she appeared in *Secret Love* the following year, thought it 'impossible . . . ever to have the Queen's part, which is very good and passionate . . . ever played done better than by young Marshall'. He liked her, too, in Shirley's *The Cardinal* and *The Virgin Martyr*. She had a particular success in Beaumont and Fletcher's *The Maid's Tragedy*, in which as Evadne, a king's mistress, she bound and gagged the monarch, recited his sins to him, then stabbed him to death – not a part in which Nell was likely to have succeeded. Later, Rebecca formed a rewarding partnership with Elizabeth Boutell; they appeared together in a succession of plays and became one of the King's Company's major attractions. Interestingly, acting partnerships between woman players were one of the features of the Restoration stage. The idea seems never to have appealed to

Nell Gwyn, though in 1667 she and Mrs Knepp played contrasting cousins in Richard Rhodes's *Flora's Vagaries* (Nell, as Flora, lively and witty, Knepp as Otrante timid and shy).

If she was friendly enough with the women of her own company, Nell felt under no obligation to be specially kind to rivals at the Duke's Theatre, and while she was appearing, in April 1667, in *All Mistaken, or the Mad Couple* by James Howard, she shot off a poisoned dart in the direction of the popular Mall Davis, then playing in an adaptation of Fletcher's *The Noble Kinsmen*, in which she had a song, 'My lodging it is on the cold ground . . .' written, perhaps especially for her, by Davenant:

> My lodging it is on the cold ground,
>   And very hard is my fare,
> But that which troubles me most is
>   The unkindness of my dear;
> Yet still I cry, O turn, love,
>   And I prithee love turn to me,
> For thou art the man that I long for,
>   And alack what remedy.

The early theatre historian John Downes famously recorded that 'all the women's parts [were] admirably acted – chiefly Celia, a shepherdess being mad for love, especially singing several wild and mad songs – "My lodging it is on the cold ground", etc. [Mall Davis] performed that so charmingly that not long after it raised her from her bed on the cold ground to a bed royal.'[47]

Mall (her real name was Mary), the date of whose birth is unknown, but who presumably was more or less Nell's exact contemporary, was said to be the daughter of a Wiltshire blacksmith, though Pepys reported a rumour that she was 'a bastard of Colonel Howard, my Lord Berkshire, and that he doth pimp to her for the King, and hath got her for him'.[48] She had joined the Duke's Company in 1662 when she was almost a child, a 'pretty girl' as Pepys noted, and her physical attraction together with a real talent for dancing soon made her extremely popular – indeed, it seems likely that the King's Company set Nell up as a rival to her (rather than the other way around, as has been suggested). She was never as popular as Nell – but her dancing seems to have been better. Pepys certainly thought it so. When she was put on the stage to announce the coming attractions, she was dressed as a boy and given a jig to dance, simply to delight the groundlings and drum up custom.

Perhaps irritated by her rival's success, both on-stage and with the King, Nell persuaded Howard to write a pastiche for her:

> My lodging it is on the cold boards,
>   And wonderful hard is my fare,
> But that which troubles me most is
>   The fatness of my dear.
> Yet still I cry, O melt, love,
>   And I pray thee now melt apace,
> For thou art the man I should long for
>   If 'twere not for thy grease.

The song had originally poked fun at Nell's old friend and lover John Lacy, who had grown decidedly plump; but the new verse unmistakably drew attention to Mall Davis's fuller figure – especially since Nell took the opportunity to imitate Mall's voice. She also displayed her own slim and beautiful legs, so superior to her rival's. The whole performance caused a considerable furore, and it has even been suggested that some of Mall's admirers attempted to have Nell beaten up. But Mall was a good-natured sort, and did not take the fun particularly amiss. She and Nell were two of a kind and were to find themselves sharing a lover soon enough.

That lover – the King – delighted in them both not merely as additions to his cast of mistresses, but as delightful women totally uninterested in influencing him in any other way than perhaps to enrich themselves materially. Matters of state were no matters for them. Years later, the anonymous librettist of an opera performed before Charles (see p. 166) wrote lines for Venus and Adonis that were strongly suggestive of the contrast between Nell and Mall on one side of the bed, and Barbara and Louise on the other – lines that were even more ironical as the part of Venus was sung by Mall herself:

Venus	I seldom vex a lover's ears
	With business or with jealous fears . . .
Adonis	Yet there is a sort of men
	Who delight in heavy chains
	Upon whom ill usage gains
	And they never love till them.
Venus	Those are fools of mighty leisure
	Wise men love the easiest pleasure.
	I give you freely all delights
	With pleasant days and easy nights

Both women had their charms, and we might guess that Nell did not have the voice (or perhaps the musical talent) to sing the leading rôle in an opera. However, as a comedienne she excelled.

What – apart from a natural talent for the stage, especially in comedy – made Nell so attractive? She stepped upon the stage with a minimum of training from Hart and Lacy, learning her lines presumably by rote and able by sheer force of beauty and character to take the audience in the palm of her hand. She had an excellent carrying voice, which endeared her to the playwrights whose lines were all too frequently lost in the babble of a rarely completely attentive audience. But above all, what engaged the audiences was a natural pert sensuality, which combined with what was clearly a natural ability to perform. Imagine an actress with the personal magnetism of the young Vanessa Redgrave and the Cockney chirpiness of the young Barbara Windsor, and one might be very near the mark.

Clearly, she was pretty (rather, perhaps, than beautiful), with the interesting combination of red-brown hair, bright blue eyes, very white, even teeth – and the smallest feet, several intimate observers suggested, in the country. She laughed readily, had a quick tongue, and above all an enormous sense of fun and the ability to flirt deliciously from the stage with members of her audiences. Her first biographer remarked on this as perhaps her prime advantage – 'her great power lay in speaking an epilogue and exposing any characters of vanity with a striking air of coquettishness and levity'.[49] Pepys's description of her as 'pretty, witty Nell' has become a cliché, but wit is always seductive – and unusual in a girl still in her mid-teens. The diarist was only one of her early admirers, but he was delighted, one May morning while walking to Westminster, to see 'pretty Nelly standing at her lodgings-door in Drury-lane in her smock-sleeves and bodice, looking upon one – she seemed a mighty pretty creature'.[50] No one in London, it seems, was likely to dissent from that view.

CHAPTER FOUR

Nell's Merry Parts

An excellent play, and so well done by Nell, her merry
part, as cannot be better done in nature, I think.

Samuel Pepys, Diary, *25 March 1667*

Charles's serious interest in Nell probably did not begin until 1668, by
which time his relationship with Barbara had become rather more lively
than was entirely comfortable. The years since his marriage had
confirmed her as his *maîtresse en titre*, but had also begun to confirm his
relationship with the Queen as, in its way, a devoted one. She had had
her difficulties, not all of them emotional; while she saw him showering
gifts upon Barbara, she herself seemed always to be short of money –
she complained at one time that of the £40,000 due to her as an
allowance, only £4,000 had been paid; on another occasion she had to
postpone for three months a visit to Tunbridge Wells because she could
not afford the journey; on another, when her doctors recommended
that she take the waters at Bourbon, she could only afford to go to Bath.

She was continually under observation – the entire country hoped
for an heir – and in 1663 a pregnancy was rumoured. Charles was
delighted and attentive. It was a false alarm, but when shortly
afterwards she fell seriously ill with 'a spotted fever accompanied by
sore throat'[1] the King continued to devote his time to her; he was
seen in tears at her bedside, and his care for her was said to have
helped her recovery much more positively than anything her
physicians did for her. (Given the sort of treatment usually meted out
by physicians to their patients, this is very likely to have been the
case.) At all events, she recovered, and was well enough to be seen
with Charles at the opening of Parliament in March 1664.

Her sickness was as nothing to the sickness that smote the nation
the following year, when the plague descended on London – the last

of a number of ferocious plagues which had troubled the city in 1563, 1593, 1603 and 1625. It was on 7 June that Pepys, walking down Drury Lane, saw two or three houses marked with a red cross, 'Lord have mercy' scrawled on a nearby wall. From then until the end of the year the city was in terror, with 10,000 deaths in each of its ninety-seven parishes – and 7,000 even in the small, relatively remote village of Stepney.

A student, writing to his tutor at Clare College, Cambridge, described what he found in London when he reached the city on 18 July:

Blessed be the Lord I got to London safe on Wednesday by eleven of the clock, and there is but very little notice took of the sicknesses here in London though the bills[2] are very great. There died threescore and eighteen in St Giles in the fields since the bill, and five in one hour in our parish since. It spreads very much; I went by many houses in London that were shut up, all over the city almost. Nobody that is in London fears to go anywhere but St Giles's. They have a bellman there with a cart; there die so many that the bell would hardly ever leave ringing and so they ring not at all. The citizens begin to shut up apace; nothing hinders them from it for fear of the houses breaking open – my father's has been shut up about a week – but there is hardly an house open in the Strand, nor the Exchange. The sickness is at Tottenham High Cross, but Mr Moyse would not have you let his son know. It is much at Hoddeston . . . I saw them as I went in the road lie in a small thatched house, and I believe almost starved, so great a dread it strikes into the people . . . On Wednesday night such news came from Hampton Court. The sickness is at Richmond, and we believe the King will not reside there long. Thus with my humble service to you and Mr Blithe Jun., I rest your obedient servant Sam: Herne.[3]

The playwright Thomas Dekker described a previous pestilence, but his account is one of the most vivid:

All her inhabitants walk up and down like mourners at some great solemn funeral, the City herself being the chief mourner.

The poison of this lingering infection strikes so deep into all men's hearts that their cheeks, like cowardly soldiers, have lost their colours; their eyes, as if they were in debt and durst not long abroad, do scarce peep out of their heads; and their tongues, like physicians ill-paid, give but cold comfort. By the power of their pestilent charms all merry meetings are cut off, all frolic assemblies dissolved, and in their circles are raised up the black, sullen, and dogged spirits of sadness, of melancholy, and so, consequently, of mischief. Mirth is departed and lies dead and buried in men's bosoms; laughter dares not look a man in the face; jests are, like music to the deaf, not regarded; pleasure itself finds now no pleasure but in sighing and bewailing the miseries of the time. For, alack! What string is there now to be played upon whose touch can make us merry? Playhouses stand like taverns that have cast out their masters, the doors locked up, the flags, like their bushes, taken down – or rather like houses lately infected, from whence the affrighted dwellers are fled, in hope to live better in the country.[4]

Among those who fled from 'the purple whip of vengeance' (as Dekker called the infection) were most of the city's actors. On 5 June, the Lord Chamberlain issued a proclamation closing all theatres, and the Court, the Parliament and most of society left London – so there was nothing to keep the players there. Naturally, since she had a connection with Oxford, Mrs Gwyn suggested that as a place of refuge, and Nell accompanied her there, together with Hart. Many of the members of the King's and Duke's theatres followed when the King decided to make the city the centre of Court life during the emergency. The Parliament also sat there. For safety's sake, Charles forbade all public entertainments, so there was no employment for Nell and her colleagues. Though at Christmas the danger seemed to be subsiding and the embargo was lifted, there seem to have been no theatrical performances, and the actors must have been impatient to return to London.

The Queen went with the King to the country – to Salisbury and then to Oxford, where in February 1666, she miscarried. This was not regarded as a total misfortune; at least it proved that she was capable of conceiving. By that time the King had returned to Hampton Court (in January) and rode into his capital the following month, closely followed by the other refugees. Grass was growing in the streets, houses and public buildings had been neglected and in some cases pillaged. The city was soon humming as workmen put things to rights – among them, Killigrew's King's Theatre. Pepys and a couple of friends walked over to the building after dinner one day and found it

> all in dirt, they being altering of the stage to make it wider . . . My business was to see the inside of the stage and all the tiring rooms and machines; and indeed it was a sight worth seeing. But to see their clothes and the various sorts, and what a mixture of things there was, here a wooden leg, there a ruff, here a hobby-horse, there a crown, would make a man split himself to see with laughing – and particularly Lacy's wardrobe. . . But then again, to think how fine they show on the stage by candle-light, and how poor things they are to look now too near-hand, is not pleasant at all. The machines are fine, and the paintings very pretty.[5]

'The machinery' – contrived to enable the scenery to move smoothly on and off stage, and to lower and raise both set and actors from above or beneath the stage – was now the most modern that could be installed, but it is unlikely that a great deal of money was spent on making life more comfortable for the actors. There were possibly a couple of single dressing-rooms, of which Nell may have commanded one. But whenever we hear of visitors 'going round', the actors and actresses seem to be crowded into one or two large rooms, and with no fireplaces, so that in winter, while the audiences sat dressed in all their finery, with cloaks and surcoats and gloves, the actresses, who always displayed their shoulders and most of their breasts, must have been freezing. No doubt there was gradual improvement: in 1667 the Lord Chamberlain approved the provision of 'a dressing room with a chimney in it' for the sole use of Ann Quin (née Marshall) – though even a generation later the celebrated Mrs Bracegirdle was extremely proud of having a dressing-room with a sea-coal fire to keep her warm in winter.

Fate had not finished with London. On 2 September 1666 a fire started in Pudding Lane and burned for four days and nights, razing much of the city – but providentially sparing the theatre district and that part of London around Drury Lane where Nell lived. Neither she nor anyone else anywhere near the city can have been unaware of it: smuts and ashes, pieces of burned paper and linen were scattered for miles around, and smoke obscured the sun even as far away as Oxford, where 'the sunshine was much darkened, the moon was darkened by clouds of smoke . . .'[6] The fire had its effect on the theatres. For no very comprehensible reason, performances were forbidden until October, when the Duke's Theatre reopened with Sir George Etherege's *The Comical Revenge, or Love in a Tub* – a piece which had an immediate success, and introduced Etherege to society and to the actress Elizabeth Barry, by whom he had an illegitimate daughter.

The King's Theatre opened five weeks later – during a sharp cold snap that froze the Thames – with a revival of Beaumont and Fletcher's old play *The Maid's Tragedy*. (Killigrew may have thought that a celebrated, indeed notorious semi-pornographic scene which it contained would appeal.) It was given for only one evening, and was followed by James Howard's *The English Monsieur*, which Pepys enjoyed on its opening night. The women, he thought, 'do very well, but above all, little Nelly, that I am mightily pleased with the play, and much with the house, more than I ever expected and very fine women'.[7]

In this not specially good play Nell played Lady Wealthy, a good-natured, rich widow living with Wellbred, played by Hart. The parts were clearly written for them, with plenty of badinage, and some good lines, including one which cannot have failed to get a laugh for Nell: 'This life of mine can last no longer than my beauty, and though 'tis pleasant now – I want nothing while I am Mr Wellbred's mistress – yet if his mind should change I might e'en sell oranges for my living, and he not buy one of me to relieve me.'

Nell now had a number of rôles at her command, and while she may not have been considered the best actress on the contemporary stage – she still failed to please in straight, and much less in tragic, rôles – she was almost certainly the most popular. Pepys was delighted to know her (though, alas, not in the Biblical sense) and took every opportunity for even the mildest familiarities: he went round after a performance of John Fletcher's *The Humorous Lieutenant* in January 1667, congratulated Nell on her performance as Celia, and kissed her, going home pleased with himself, 'specially of kissing of Nell'. What Mrs Pepys thought of all this – and she was with him at least on that occasion – he does not record.

Nell's career must now have seemed secure. She triumphed in Dryden's *Secret Love*,[8] which the King enjoyed so much that he arranged for her to be provided with particularly handsome costumes for a command performance in April – including a pair of 'rhinegraves', or breeches slashed to the upper thigh. Pepys may not have seen her in that costume, but he continued to return to the play again and again: 'the more I see, the more I like [it], and is an excellent play, and so well done by Nell, her merry part, as cannot be better done in nature, I think'.[9] As a tribute to her success as Florimell, Beaumont and Fletcher's *The Knight of the Burning Pestle* was revived, and a special epilogue written for her. Next came Sir Robert Howard's *The Surprisal*, an indifferent play which even Nell could not rescue from failure; then James Howard's *All Mistaken*, with the all-star cast of Nell, Charles Hart and John Lacy – the play in which Nell so successfully scored a comic point at the expense of Mall Davis.[10]

But now there was a short break in Nell's theatrical career. In the spring of 1667 the Dutch, with whom the King had been quarrelling because by their energetic trading throughout the world they 'do hinder and destroy us in our lawful course of living, hereby taking bread out of our mouths',[11] suddenly brought off a startling coup. On 12 June 1667, in one of the most spectacular attacks ever mounted in English waters, their Admiral Michiel de Ruyter sailed his fleet up the Medway, cut the chain meant to protect English shipping, and fired as many ships as he could reach, then captured the *Royal Charles* – the very ship on which the King had returned to England at the Restoration – and towed her away. All theatres were immediately closed (for all the good it could have done; closing the theatres seems to have been an instant reaction to any national emergency).

Nell found herself, once more, out of work – and in some financial difficulty. Happily, by this time more important admirers than Pepys had come upon the scene. Surely one of them could help her, for the right consideration? She turned first to a new young acquaintance, the nineteen-year-old John Wilmot, Earl of Rochester.

Rochester was one of the most fascinating characters of his time. Young though he was, he had already distinguished himself as a soldier in the Dutch war, and spiced his reputation with feats of debauchery sufficient to be remarkable in one so relatively young. He once claimed to have been drunk for five years at a stretch, though bearing in mind Shakespeare's lines about drink being a provoker of lust but a disabler of performance this may be something of an overstatement, considering his reputation as a lover.

Rochester has been dismissed as a mere drunken brute, only mildly accomplished as a wit. He was more than that. He was, for instance, a considerable poet. It is certainly the case that some of his poems reach such depths of lubricity that the only word to describe them is pornographic – it has only been possible to publish some of them within the past twenty years or so. Yet his best poems are fine: his ode 'Upon Nothing' ('Nothing! Thou elder brother ev'n to shade . . .') is surely one of the most remarkable of the age; 'The Mistress' has fine verses; and the remarkable 'Song of a Young Lady to her Ancient Lover' is extraordinarily tender and understanding. He was also an adept satirist, who better than any other writer captures – though in the crudest terms – the sexual fashions of his time.

At the Restoration, the twelve-year-old Rochester wrote and dedicated a poem to King Charles, and was rewarded by a pension of £500 and – two years later – the gift of a tour of the Continent after his graduation from Wadham College, Oxford, with a Master's degree. He was accompanied on that excursion by a distinguished Scots physician, Sir Andrew Balfour, who during the course of their travels taught his ward to drink deep. Back in England, Rochester was advised by the King to marry a certain Elizabeth Malet, 'the great Beauty and Fortune of the north', with £2,500 a year. When she proved reluctant, Rochester, no doubt prepared to justify his action by pleading his monarch's command, simply kidnapped her, waylaying her grandfather's coach at Charing Cross, dragging her from it and into a coach and six, and rattling off in the direction of Uxbridge, leaving her kinsman Baron Hawley in a fury. The Baron complained bitterly to the King, and since he was not only an MP but a Gentleman of the Bedchamber to the Duke of York, Charles had to take notice. He had Rochester arrested and sent to the Tower. After a short while the prisoner appealed to the King on the grounds that 'passion was the occasion of his offence', and was released.

In 1665, still only seventeen, Rochester sailed on the *Royal Katherine* as a volunteer against the Dutch, and saw action, proving himself (the Earl of Sandwich reported to Charles) 'brave, industrious and of useful parts'. On 1 January 1667, a London newsletter reported that 'This morning the Earl of Rochester was married to Miss Malet, Lord Hawley's grand-child.' We need not be too surprised that he won her round: he was clearly an enormously attractive man – 'the delight and wonder of men, and the love and dotage of women, with a wit that could make even his spleen and his ill-humour pleasant', as his friend Robert Wolseley said. The guardian was clearly more reluctant than the lady.

The married couple settled at Adderbury, in Oxfordshire, Rochester's ancestral home. He was, however, a town man. Aubrey wrote of him that 'in the country he was generally civil enough, he was wont to say that when he came to Brentford the devil entered into him and never left him till he came into the country again'.[12]

Marital difficulties almost immediately arose. Rochester's wife did not care for town, while he preferred it, and had the excuse that, appointed a Gentleman of the Bedchamber, he had to attend on the King at Whitehall – theoretically for one week in every quarter, but actually for considerably longer. He also took his seat in the House of Lords, which he frequented from time to time, and leased a house in Lincoln's Inn Fields 'next to the Duke's Playhouse in Portugal Row'. Lady Rochester, aware of his taste for actresses, cannot have been pleased at that piece of news, and they quarrelled.

It is worth pointing out that while he and his wife were no doubt basically incompatible, he did love her:

Give me leave to rail at you,
I ask nothing but my due;
To call you false, and then to say
You shall not keep my heart a day.
But alas! Against my will
I must be your captive still;
Ah! Be kinder then, for I
Cannot change, and would not die.[13]

He did not, however, allow sentiment to interfere with extramarital pleasure, and lost no opportunity for a tumble with any willing woman he admired – and few were unwilling.

So, by 1667 he was already celebrated, and a constant member of the group of young men around the King, mostly younger than Charles, and licensed to amuse him. When not in attendance on the King, 'the Wits', as they were known, spent their time roistering about the town – Henry Jermyn, Lord Buckhurst, John Sheffield, Earl of Mulgrave, Harry Killigrew, Sir Charles Sedley and the playwrights Etherege and Wycherley. They were all great lovers of the arts, but at the same time devoted to dissipation. We should pay some attention to Buckhurst and Sedley in particular: Charles Lord Buckhurst, later Earl of Dorset and of Middlesex (Nell always alluded to him as 'my Lord Dorset') was four years older than Rochester, a fellow MP, and a fellow Gentleman of the Bedchamber. He too was a poet as well as a courtier – one of his lyrics, allegedly written on the eve of a great naval battle against the Dutch, fought on 3 June 1665, still holds its place in the anthologies:

To all you ladies now at land,
    We men, at sea, indite.
But first would have you understand
    How hard it is to write:
The Muses now, and Neptune too,
We must implore to write to you –
    With a fa, la, la, la, la.

In Restoration year he was elected MP for East Grinstead, but was more interested in the arts; he was a patron of Samuel Butler and

William Wycherley, and was said to be 'the best bred man of his age'. In his youth he had led an extremely racy life. He was a toper who could not hold his drink without becoming foul-mouthed and violent – and was actually on one occasion charged with manslaughter after he, his brother Edward and another MP, Sir Henry Bellasis, had fatally wounded a tanner they said they suspected of being a highwayman. Whether the matter came to trial, and what happened if it did, is obscure; at all events, they were released – possibly on the King's intervention.

Sir Charles Sedley, known as 'Little Sid'[14] because of his small stature, was the author of several plays, and several of his poems were set to music by Purcell. He was only marginally less objectionable than Buckhurst, and was eager to join in any drunken prank. He, Buckhurst and Sir Thomas Ogle caused a riot at the Cock Inn in Bow Street, Covent Garden one evening when they shouted pornographic verses and abuse from the balcony of their rooms until a crowd gathered. Sedley then stripped to the buff and, a wineglass in one hand, urinated on the people beneath while the others mimed various erotic postures from Aretino. The crowd understandably objected and began throwing stones and trying to break into the inn. The three gentlemen as a result found themselves before the Lord Chief Justice, and Sedley was fined £500. On other occasions, they managed to escape – and even to shift the blame to others. In October 1668, Pepys speaks of Sedley and Buckhurst 'running up and down all the night, almost naked, through the streets; and at last fighting, and being beat by the watch and clapped up all night; and the King takes their parts; and the Lord-chief-justice Keeling hath laid the constable by the heels to answer it next sessions; which is a horrid shame'.[15]

Buckhurst, Sedley, Rochester – indeed all the Wits – took a keen interest in the theatre. Rochester himself wrote a not particularly good play, *The Rehearsal*, and was a close friend of the playwright Aphra Behn and the model for the hero of her play *The Rover* (1677). When Nell turned to him for advice when the theatres were again closed he might well, had he not been rather too newly married, have taken her under his wing. As it was, he seems to have suggested that she invite Buckhurst to entertain her. Charles Hart was still her lover, but was poor and in no position to protest – and in any event was now enjoying the attentions of Barbara Villiers, of whose muscular embraces, it was said, the King had begun to tire.

Nell seems to have had no difficulty in kindling a flame in Buckhurst. It is said that she inflamed his passions when he saw her in Howard's *All Mistaken, or the Mad Couple*, in which she had an excuse to reveal her legs, and did so with enthusiasm. As he wrote, later, of another woman:

> All hearts fall a-leaping whenever she comes,
> And beat day and night like my Lord Craven's drums.[16]

He accepted her advances – if indeed that is how it was – and took her off to Epsom. On 12 July, an acquaintance told Pepys that 'my Lord Buckhurst hath got Nell away from the King's Theatre, lies with her and gives her £100 a year, so as she hath sent her parts to the house and will act no more'.[17] Ever after, she referred to him as her Charles I.

Why Epsom? Why not? Only fifteen miles from London, it was the equal of Tunbridge Wells and even Bath as a fashionable place at which to take the waters. Half a century previously a farmer called Henry Wicker had dug a shallow well to water his cattle, which resolutely declined to drink the water that bubbled forth. Human beings, however, rapidly discovered that the strong-tasting mineral water was good for all sorts of ailments, impregnated as it was 'with a bitter purging salt, now in common parlance called Epsom salt'.[18]

Within three years, the fortunate Mr Wicker had surrounded his spring with a wall and built a shed 'for the protection of invalids', and by the 1660s it was common for doctors to advise patients to take the waters – the Domestic State Papers are full of applications from the civil servants of the time for leave of absence for that purpose. Quite apart from any medical attributes of the water, the fashionable seized the excuse to make Epsom a place of recreation, and the village soon possessed every modern convenience, including regular coach traffic to and from the capital, and up-to-date means of correspondence, for (as the *London Gazette* announced) the post went every day 'to and fro betwixt London and Epsom, during the season for drinking the waters'.

Thomas Shadwell's comedy *Epsom Wells* (1672) – which Sedley may have helped to write – portrays it as a place for the fashionable, but also unquestionably for the dissolute. The play opens with Bisket, 'a comfit-maker, a quiet, humble, civil cuckold', praising the waters as a cure for a hangover, and Cuff, 'a cheating, sharking, cowardly bully' drinking them for the same reason, 'to wash away claret'.

The day after hearing that Nell was at Epsom, Pepys decided – 'only for air', he tells his diary – to take his wife to taste the waters. By a strange coincidence when he and Mrs Pepys arrived, and after drinking ('I did drink four pints and had some very good stools by it') applied for a room at the King's Head, they found that 'my Lord Buckhurst and Nelly is lodged at the next house, and Sir Charles Sedley with them, and keep a merry house. Poor girl, I pity her; but more the loss of her at the King's House.'[19]

Pepys's pity sprang no doubt from his dislike of the Wits and his disapproval of Buckhurst and Sedley in particular. He not only admired but clearly liked Nell, and possibly – though goodness knows he was no Puritan – disliked the thought of what the two rakes would require of her. A touch of envy is also probable; and his regret at not being able to see her on the stage for the present is clearly sincere.

It does not take a great deal of imagination to envisage what went on in the house next to the King's Head. Buckhurst was not known for sexual discretion – indeed, he himself claimed:

> My love is full of noble pride
> And never will submit
> To let that fop, discretion, ride
> In triumph over it.[20]

No doubt the house was indeed 'merry', and no doubt Buckhurst got his £100 worth – and very possibly Sedley, too, though he occasionally left the other two alone. On 5 August, for instance, he dined with Lord Robartes in his house nearby. The Countess of

Warwick was also present, and noted the occasion in her diary: it was 'much trouble to see him for fear he should be profane. But it pleased God to restrain him: yet the knowledge I had how profane a person he was troubled me to be in his company.' It may be that the Countess's notorious piety troubled Sedley equally; in any event he returned to the merry house, where any troilism that took place was probably very enjoyable. Nell, though still only seventeen, was no innocent, and knew what she had let herself in for; if Buckhurst and Sedley were on occasion extremely coarse, they were also (when not so drunk as to be incapable) fun to be with. Apart from the pleasures of love, they rode out almost every day, and both Sedley's wife Catherine and his young daughter apparently called at the house on several occasions. It would perhaps be going too far to suggest that Catherine, the daughter, was influenced by what she saw or heard at Epsom; but she must surely have watched Nell's career with interest, and it may not be entirely irrelevant to note that she herself became the mistress of James, Duke of York, and ended her life as the Countess of Dorchester.

While Nell, Buckhurst and Rochester were cavorting, her other friend, Buckingham, and his protégée Barbara Villiers were doing their best to dispose of the Lord Chancellor, Lord Clarendon. Barbara persuaded Charles to order Buckingham's release from the Tower, where he was allegedly languishing because of a silly business of the King's horoscope being cast (see p. 89). It was not an easy task, and she had eventually to nag the King: 'If you were not a fool you would not suffer your business to be carried on by fools that do not understand it, and have your best subjects and most able servants imprisoned,' she told him.[21]

Once released, Buckingham regained his positions as Gentleman of the Bedchamber, Privy Councillor and Lord Lieutenant of the West Riding, and was soon encouraging Barbara to support him in urging the King to recall Parliament and form a standing army that would make him independent of the Commons. The idea was anathema to Parliament, and the resulting storm of rumour and speculation became so hysterical that the King swiftly recanted, made Clarendon a scapegoat, and dismissed him. Clarendon was impeached for high treason, fled the country and for the rest of his life insisted that 'the Lady and her party' had been responsible for his downfall.

Meanwhile, Nell, as ever delightfully uninterested in politics, reappeared on stage back in town. Orange Mall told Pepys that Buckhurst had quarrelled with Nell and thrown her out, swearing that 'she hath had all she could get of him', that she was destitute, that Hart now hated her, and that in short she was ruined. Her earliest biographer says that 'She found but little comfort in the embraces of this fickle, luxurious, malicious nobleman; at one time he was all fondness, rapture and good-nature, at another time sullen, discontented, and sometimes cruel . . . sometimes he was whole weeks without holding any commerce with her, and introduced abandoned creatures to her acquaintance, at whom she had always an aversion; and he only introduced them that he might mortify her by taking them next night into his arms.'[22]

This does not sound right, and if there was a quarrel it was soon made up. She and Buckhurst may have had words – goodness knows they were both high-spirited enough, and Nell is said to have spent his money too freely, and perhaps may have paid a little too much attention to Sedley: three in a bed are not invariably comfortable. But they remained friends.[23] And if Orange Mall was jealous, or repeating the jealous words of the other actresses (and it is at this time that Nell had her little spat with Rebecca Marshall, who called her 'Buckhurst's whore'),[24] Nell, once more pleasing the public, had the last laugh.

Interestingly, among Orange Mall's other gossip was the allegation that Nell had 'lost Lady Castlemaine, who was her great friend'. Here is a hint that Nell was closer to the Court and the King at this time than one might have suspected. Her rôles continued to be as good as they had been before her much discussed excursion to Epsom, and no doubt then, as now, a little lubricious publicity did the box office no harm. She played in Dryden's *The Indian Emperor* and Robert Howard's *Surprisal* (in 'a serious part, which she spoils', Pepys thought), in Beaumont and Fletcher's *A King and No King* and Richard Rhodes's *Flora's Vagaries*. Pepys saw her in this, but fails to comment on the play, recording instead the fact that Mrs Knepp took him and his wife into 'the women's shift' or dressing-room, where

Nell 'was dressing herself, and all unready; and is very pretty, prettier than I thought'.[25]

Nell also played Bellario in a revival of John Fletcher's old play *Philaster*, another breeches part, in which she was always much admired. She seems to have settled down to her career again. But the episode with Buckhurst had unsettled her. For the first time, she had lived as the wealthy aristocracy lived – a great deal more comfortably than she, herself could afford. She had eaten well and dressed well, begging or borrowing from her wealthier women friends or perhaps even from the theatre wardrobe, holland chemises with their sleeves exposed, the sleeves threaded with ribbon, and heavily boned corsets to support and raise the breasts in the extreme *décolletage* of the time. It was not difficult to acquire a taste for these things, and it was time, she decided – urged on no doubt by her friendly rival Mall Davis, for they were now close – to find a rich . . . what? – lover? – protector? – even, if the worst came to the worst, husband?

And at this moment came the news that King Charles was taking the Court to Tunbridge Wells for the waters in the hope, it was said, that with their help he could get the Queen with child.

CHAPTER FIVE

Love's Theatre, The Bed

Leave this gaudy, gilded stage
From custom more than use frequented,
Where fools of either sex and age
Crowed to see themselves presented.
To love's theatre, the bed,
Youth and beauty fly together.

Earl of Rochester, from 'Leave this gaudy, gilded stage . . .'

It was in 1606 that Dudley, 3rd Baron North, suffering from an
undiagnosed illness, was walking in a clearing in the woods of Lord
Bergavenny's Eridge House at Tunbridge Wells when he noticed
something odd about the Sun's reflection on a pool of water. The only
other place where he had seen the surface of water gleaming with
similar iridescent patches had been at Spa, in the Low Countries,
where enormous numbers of sickly people drank it as a cure for almost
every possible ailment. Lord North tasted the Tunbridge water: it had
the same strange taste as that at Spa. The following year he invited
himself again to Eridge House and stayed for some time, regularly
drinking the water. News of his allegedly improved health got about,
and within weeks other Court invalids began to crowd the district.

Lord North lived to be eighty-five, and his illness, whatever it was,
continued to plague him until the end of his long life. But seizing his
opportunity, a certain Dr Rowzee published a treatise on Tunbridge
water, recommending large doses for almost every illness, and laying
down rules for imbibing it: one should drink it before breakfast, as early
as possible in the morning – and the larger the quantity taken, the more
complete the cure. He hesitated to describe in detail the ingredients of
the waters, but his colleague Dr Madan, some years later, explained that
they were 'impregnated with a chalcanthous or vitriolate juice which with

its sulphureous particles irritates and moves the belly to a blackish excretion' – and went on to warn that 'frequent drinking thereof blackeneth the tongue; because this member, being of a spongy substance imbibes some sooty sulphureous minims into its porosity, occasioning this tincture'. He went further, in a splendidly obscure diatribe:

> The waters, with their saponary and detersive quality, clean the whole microcosm or body of man from all feculencey and impurities. No remedy is more effectual in hypochrondrical and hysterick fits by suppressing the anathymiasis of ill vapours, and hindering damps to exhale to the head and heart. In reference to the number of glasses, you may make it either odd or even; though some who are of opinion that all things are composed of number, prefer the odd before the even; and attribute to it a greater efficacy and perfection especially in matters of physic. . . .'[1]

North, with the help of Rowzee and Madan, made the reputation of Tunbridge Wells, which was enormously enhanced when Queen Henrietta Maria, wife of Charles I, visited in 1629 to recover her health after a miscarriage.

The crowds who flocked to take the waters saturated the little town, and soon two villages sprang up expressly to house the invalids, imaginary and otherwise – Southborough, on the Tunbridge road, and Rusthall, in the opposite direction. Even these could not accommodate everyone, and visitors who could not find lodgings in cottages there or in the surrounding countryside camped in tents on Bishop's Down (later known as Tunbridge Wells Common).

In 1638 a handsome promenade was laid out where ladies and gentlemen could stroll in the shade of an avenue of elms and take their ease protected a little from the heat of the long summer days that stretched before them after their dawn drinking. This walk, the Pantiles, became the centre of social life in the town. Substantially, Tunbridge Wells was now the town that Nell Gwyn knew, and that Philibert de Gramont, the French Ambassador to Charles's Court, described:

> Tunbridge is . . . the rallying-point, when the time comes to take the waters, of all that is fairest and most gallant in both sexes. The

company there is always numerous but always select, and, since those whose motive in visiting it is the quest of amusement always considerably outnumber those who have been brought there by motives of necessity, the whole atmosphere is redolent of distraction and delight. Constraint and formality are banished; intimacy ripens at the first acquaintance; and the life led there is generally delicious.

Accommodation is provided by clean, comfortable little houses, standing apart from one another and scattered over the country within half a league's distance of the Wells. Here, at the place where the Wells are, the visitors gather every morning. This is a spacious avenue, bordered by shady trees under which they stroll while taking the waters. Along one side of it runs a lengthy range of booths, garnished with all kinds of jewellery, laces, stockings and gloves, and at which gambling goes on as at a fair; along the other the market is established, and, as everybody comes to choose and bargain for his own provisions, nothing offensive is ever displayed. But little village-girls, fresh-skinned and yellow-haired, with fair white linen, small straw hats and neat shoes, sell poultry, vegetables, fruit and flowers. You may live at Tunbridge Wells as highly as you please; large sums are staked at play; and the tender commerce flourishes.[2]

Rochester knew all about 'tender commerce', and left a vivid versified picture of his recollections of Tunbridge Wells,[3] of rising at five in the morning and riding to take the waters at

> The rendezvous of fools, buffoons and praters
> Cuckolds, whores, citizens, their wives and daughters.

He goes on, in his satirical poem, to describe the society of the Pantiles in a bitterly sardonic tone. His sketch of the place and the people who visited it is well worth quoting at some length:

> A tribe of curates, priests, canonical elves,
> (Fit company for none besides themselves) . . .

Were got together; each his distemper told,
Scurvy,[4] stone, stranguary; some were so bold
To charge the spleen[5] to be their misery,
And on that wise disease brought infamy.
But none had modesty enough to 'plain
Their want of learning, honesty and brain,
The general diseases of that train.
These call themselves ambassadors of Heav'n. . . .

. . . now were come (whitewash and paint being laid)
Mother and daughter, mistress and the maid,
And squire with wig and pantaloon display'd.
But ne'er conventicle, play or fair
For a true medley with this herd compare.
Here lords, knights, squires, ladies and countesses,
Chandlers, Mum-bacon-women,[6] sempstresses
Were mixt together; nor did they agree
More in their humours than their quality.
Here waiting for gallant, young damsel stood,
Leaning on cane, and muffled up in hood;
The would-be wit whose business was to woo,
With hat remov'd, and solemn scrape of shoe,
Advanceth bowing, then genteelly shrugs.
And ruffled foretop into order tugs.
And thus accosts her: 'Madam, methinks the weather
Is grown more serene since you came hither.
You influence the heav'ns – but should the sun
Withdraw himself to see his rays outdone
By your bright eyes, they would supply the morn
And make a day before the day be born.'

With mouth screw'd up, conceived winking eyes
And breasts thrust forward, 'Lord, Sir,' (she replies)
'It is your goodness and not my deserts
Which makes you show this learning, wit and parts.' . . .

Tired with this dismal stuff, away I ran
Where were two wives, with girl just fit for man –
Short-breathed, with pallid lips and visage wan.
Some curtsies past, and the old compliment
Of being glad to see each other spent,
With hand in hand they lovingly did walk
And one began thus to renew the talk:

'I pray, good madam, if it may be thought
No rudeness, what cause was it hither brought
Your ladyship?' She soon replying, smiled,
'We have a good estate, but have no child –
And I'm informed these wells will make a barren
Woman as fruitful as a coney-warren.'

The first returned, 'For this cause I am come,
For I can have no quietness at home –
My husband grumbles though we have got one –
This poor young girl – and mutters for a son –
And this grieved with headache pains and throes
Is full sixteen, and never yet had those.'[7]

She soon replied, 'Get her a husband, madam.
I married at that age, and ne'er had had 'em –
Was just like her. Steel-waters[8] let alone –
A back of steel will bring 'em better down,
And ten to one but they themselves will try
The same means to increase their family.'

Poor, foolish fribble, who by subtlety
Of mid-wife, truest friend to lechery,
Persuaded art to be at pains and charge
To give thy wife occasion to enlarge
Thy silly head! For here walk Cuff and Kick,[9]
With brawny back and legs and potent prick
Who more substantially will cure thy wife

84

Nell Gwyn, after a portrait by Lely.

Barbara Villiers (also known as Mrs Palmer), the Countess of Castlemaine and the Duchess of Cleveland was said to be 'by far the handsomest of all King Charles's mistresses and . . . perhaps the finest woman in England in her time'. Mezzotint by Chaloner Smith after a portrait by Lely.

Charles's taste was for women with more beauty than Catherine of Braganza, but she came with a dowry of £300,000 in cash and the cities of Tangiers and Bombay. She proved an understanding Queen, and their love for each other survived his numerous affairs. Engraving by William Faithorne after a painting by Dirck Stoop, 1662.

Small, with tiny feet, chestnut hair and hazel eyes, Nell Gwyn evidently retained her beauty – and her firm, white bosom – after giving birth to her two sons. Madame Ellen Gwinne and her two sons, Charles, Earl of Beaufort and James, Lord Beauclaire, c. *1679. Mezzotint by Chaloner Smith after a painting by Lely.*

Louise de Kéroüalle, fair-skinned and dark-haired, with large sad eyes, captivated the King from the moment he set eyes on her; romantic and idealistic, she was a connoisseur of painting and poetry, about which she knew little. Her 'prodigal and expensive pleasures' (Evelyn) took the form of clothing and the furnishing of her grand apartments in Whitehall. Mezzotint by Chaloner Smith after a portrait by Henri Gascar, c. 1675/8.

The famous Bohemian engraver Wenceslaus Hollar, appointed 'His Majesty's Designer', published this print in 1660. The Covent Garden piazza is centre right, and Drury Lane ran diagonally down from Holborn, at the top of the map, to join the Strand at the bottom. The large open space of Lincoln's Inn Fields is on the right.

A magnificent print by Richard Gaywood commemorated Charles II's entry into London before his coronation. His brother, the Duke of York, is seen on horseback on the right. John Evelyn described in his Diary how Charles entered London 'with a triumph of over twenty thousand horse and foot brandishing their swords and shouting with unexpressable joy. The ways were strewn with flowers, the bells were ringing, the streets were hung with tapestry. And the fountains were running wine.'

A painting by the Danish artist Hendrick Danckerts of St James's Park and the Palace of Whitehall. The Banqueting Hall is on the left, and King Charles's favourite 'canal' on the right.

The stage of the Duke's Theatre in Lincoln's Inn Fields, which was managed by Sir George Davenant, during a performance. The theatre was originally a tennis court, and was used by the Duke's Company until November 1671, when they left for the new theatre in Lincoln's Inn Fields.

The Duke's Theatre in Dorset Gardens, into which the Duke's Company moved in 1671, was the most luxurious of all Restoration theatres. Inset are the Davenants, father and son.

The stage of the Red Bull Theatre in Clerkenwell (traditionally said to have been the theatre outside which Shakespeare held horses' heads for the patrons). Clandestine performances were held there during the Interregnum, and after the Restoration Killigrew's King's Company performed there for a time. This (engraving by William Herbert and Robert Wilkinson of the frontispiece to a collection of drolls by Francis Kirkman, published in 1672) is one of the very few representations of theatre interiors during Nell Gwyn's time.

Inside of the RED BULL Playhouse.

The Red Bull Playhouse stood in a plot of ground lately called 'Red Bull Yard' near the upper end of St John's Street Clerkenwell, and is traditionally said to have been the Theatre at which Shakespeare first held gentlemen's horses. In the civil wars it became highly celebrated for the representation of Drolls, to a collection of which pieces published by Francis Kirkman in 1672, this view of it forms a frontispiece. The figures brought together on the stage, are intended as portraits of the leading actors in each Droll. The one playing Simpleton is Robert Cox, then a great favorite, of whom the publisher thus speaks in his preface. 'I have seen the Red Bull Playhouse which was a large one, so full, that as many went back for want of room as had entred: Robert Cox, a principal actor and contriver of these pieces, how have I heard him cryed up for his John Swabber, and Simpleton, the Smith: In which latter, he being to appear with a large piece of Bread & Butter on the stage I have frequently known some of the female spectators to long for it.' The above print may be regarded not only as highly curious for the place it represents, but as a unique specimen of the interior economy of our ancient English Theatres.

A possibly spurious playbill for a performance in April 1663. One of the players was 'Major' Michael Mohun, who performed with Nell Gwyn.

When Charles II came to the throne, he had a mane of curly black hair, but in only three years turned 'mighty grey', and thereafter had his head shaved and wore a series of black wigs, growing heavier and thicker as he aged. This portrait is by William Sherwin.

And on her half-dead womb bestow new life.
From these, the waters got their reputation
Of good assistants unto generation.

Nothing was simple where the Court was concerned, and removing to the country in the heat of July 1667 was quite a performance, involving a train of great lumbering coaches carrying the Queen and her Portuguese attendants, accompanied by many others on horseback. Where they all stayed is uncertain: the Queen, and the King when he arrived, seem likely to have been installed at Mount Ephraim House, built on one of two hills overlooking the town – the other was Mount Sion (the names had been given them, unsurprisingly, by Cromwell's men). The lesser courtiers presumably put up at any available cottages, and perhaps in tents and pavilions on Bishop's Down.

All sorts of rumours about the Queen had been circulating recently – connected, of course, with her persistent inability to provide the King with a son. There was naturally serious concern about this, and some theologians had actually gone so far as to recommend that polygamy might be legalised, at least in the case of His Majesty, in order that a legitimate heir should be provided.[10] (The British Ambassador in Lisbon was much embarrassed when the Queen of Portugal asked him whether this could possibly be a serious proposition.) Meanwhile, it was said that Catherine was going to retire to a nunnery; Charles was going to divorce her because she had made a secret vow of chastity;[11] Buckingham had been instructed to kidnap her and escort her to some remote place of imprisonment so that the King could divorce her for desertion. (The Pope, it seemed, would be quite happy to accede to such a proposition.)

But here she was with the King at Tunbridge Wells, and apparently the couple were on perfectly amiable terms. What the Queen thought about the reputation of the place is not recorded. The French Ambassador to Charles's Court was in no doubt about its equivocal reputation. 'Well may they be called *les eaux de scandale*,' he wrote a month after the Queen's visit, 'for they have nearly ruined the good name of the maids and the ladies (those who are there without their husbands). It has taken them a whole month and for some more than that to clear themselves and save their honour; and it is even reported that a few of them are not quite out of trouble yet. For which cause the Court will come back in a week; one of the ladies of the Queen stays behind and will pay for the others.'[12] The Queen must have been quite as aware of the sexual shenanigans as the French Ambassador – yet she ordered that Court etiquette need not be observed while she was at the Wells, and set about contriving a series of entertainments to keep the King happy: balls and banquets, at some of which the behaviour was certainly less than formal.

According to de Gramont, it was the Queen who invited actors from both the King's and Duke's Companies to entertain the Court while it was in residence at Tunbridge Wells. So, in the intervals between appearances at their London theatres the actors took the road south on several occasions at the turn of the year, and the King was delighted when Peg Hughes, one of Nell's colleagues at the King's Theatre, set her bright eyes at Prince Rupert, his more than middle-aged cousin, and brought him down – though he had such *gravitas* and was so feared and respected that even Charles smothered the temptation to make fun at his expense. De Gramont, writing home to Paris, felt under no such restriction, and commented that the Prince had bid 'an entire farewell to all mathematical instruments and chemical speculations: sweet powder and essences were not the only ingredients that occupied any share of his attention'.

The second interesting consequence of the actors' visits occurred one afternoon early in January, when Mall Davis, appearing before the King and Queen and the whole Court, danced a jig so inflammatory that the Queen walked out. Barbara, almost as outraged, followed her. A few minutes later, the King also left the room – with Mall. A fragment of verse by Rochester may not have been written at this time, but is highly apposite:

> Leave this gaudy, gilded stage
> From custom more than use frequented,
> Where fools of either sex and age
> Crowd to see themselves presented.

> To Love's theatre, the bed,
> Youth and beauty fly together –
> And act so well, it might be said
> The laurel there was due to either . . .[13]

In January 1668, the gossips of the playhouses heard that Mall was retiring from the stage: Mrs Knepp told Pepys that she 'is for certain going away from the Duke's House, the King being in love with her; and a house is taken for her and furnishing and she hath a ring given her already, worth £600'. She added that 'the King did send several times for Nelly, and she was with him, but what he did she knows not . . .'.[14] A few days later, Pepys's wife and her friend Mrs Pierce agreed that Mall:

> is the most impertinent slut . . . in the world, and the more now the King doth show her countenance and is reckoned his mistress, even to the scorn of the whole world, the King gazing on her, and my Lady Castlemaine being melancholy and out of humour all the play, not smiling once. The King, it seems, hath given her a ring of £700, which she shows to everybody, and owns that the King did give it her. And he hath furnished a house for her in Suffolk Street most richly . . . which is a most infinite shame. . . . But Pierce says that she is a most homely jade as ever she saw, though she dances beyond anything in the world.[15]

Slut and homely jade she may have been, but Charles was evidently pleased with Mall. Theirs was not a brief association, for she was to bear him a daughter in 1673.[16] Apart from the women of the streets to whom he sometimes resorted, she was probably the coarsest of his mistresses, and satisfied one side of his sexual nature. In time he was to give her another house, in St James's Square, and a pension of £1,000 a year.

Her abrupt elevation to the King's bed was not especially surprising, but it seems not merely to have been a matter of his suddenly fancying her. She was very probably put in his way by the Duke of Buckingham, a close friend of the King who had already been busily ingratiating himself with Barbara Villiers on the grounds that she might bring him even more influence at Court than he already had.

George Villiers, 2nd Duke of Buckingham, was forty years old in 1668. He had virtually been an adopted son of Charles I, educated at Trinity College, Cambridge, and an enthusiastic member of the Royalist army from the beginning of the Civil War, in which he served under Prince Rupert. Charles II, in exile, gave him the Order of the Garter and made him a member of the Privy Council. Already with a reputation as a libertine, he sought a second reputation in the cannon's mouth, and quarrelled with the King when he declined to make him general-in-chief of the army. He quarrelled, too, with most of Charles's ministers – he was a considerable political intriguer and eagerly ambitious, and in 1652 was reported to be keen to marry the widowed Princess of Orange (the Queen protesting that she would tear her daughter in pieces with her bare hands before allowing her to marry an irreligious intriguer such as Buckingham).

By 1654 Buckingham and the King were completely at odds: Buckingham criticised his monarch far too freely, and there were also financial problems between them. Then in 1655 it was reported that the Duke had been secretly to Dover to confer with one of Cromwell's men about the possibility of returning to England and securing the reversion of his sequestered estates. Suddenly, two years later, he did return to England, planning to marry the only daughter of the Parliamentarian general Sir Thomas Fairfax. No matter that Mary Fairfax was promised to the Earl of Chesterfield – that the banns had actually been published; Buckingham, when he wanted to be, was irresistible, and when Mary met him she fell instantly in love. They were married. Cromwell, however, was deeply suspicious of Buckingham and ordered his arrest. Fairfax generously appealed on behalf of his son-in-law, and for a while he was allowed to live privately; but with typical impatience he declined to remain at home and, while venturing out to visit his sister, was arrested and sent to the Tower.

In 1659 he was released, having given his word not to assist Charles II in any attempt to regain the throne. The following year his personal fascination triumphed once more when Charles returned to London.

His charm and wit rescued him from many a difficult situation: and there can be no doubt that it was considerable. One acquaintance described him as 'the finest gentleman of person and wit I think I ever saw'.[17] Another described him to Alexander Pope as 'the most accomplished man of the age in riding, dancing and fencing. When he came into the presence chamber, it was impossible for you not to follow him with your eye as he went along, he moved so gracefully.'[18]

Returned to favour, Buckingham carried the orb at the coronation and was appointed a Gentleman of the King's Bedchamber. During the following six or seven years, his estates were returned to him, and, reputed to be the richest man in England, he served the King well, though Clarendon, Charles's Lord Chancellor, remained his enemy, and prevented his achieving high office. But Buckingham was a confidant of the King, and one of the cabal[19] chosen by him in 1667 as intimate advisers.

In 1663, Buckingham was extremely interested in trying to get a pretty, fifteen-year-old French girl into the King's bed, hoping to influence Charles through her;[20] but he had no success, and shortly was out of favour once more as the result of a public brawl with the Marquis of Dorchester – the two men went at it hammer and tongs, the Duke tearing Dorchester's wig from his head while Dorchester 'had much of the Duke's hair in his hand'. Both were sent to the Tower. Released, Buckingham was swiftly in trouble again, being found in possession of the King's horoscope – always a dangerous matter; not only that, but it seems that the astrologer had suggested that Buckingham himself might one day be king.[21] His arrest was ordered, but he gave himself up. After a short stay in the Tower, his charm once more won his freedom and he returned to his place in Court.

Now, in 1667, he turned his attention once more to replacing Barbara Palmer, now Lady Castlemaine, with another mistress whom he might more easily manipulate. Mall Davis and Nell Gwyn came to mind, as did another young woman, Jane Roberts – a more obscure actress who like Mall danced a lively jig, and of whom it was said that it would be 'hard to find one with limbs more brawny, conscience more supple, or principles more loose; all these extreme qualifications for a lady of pleasure'.[22]

Jane Roberts seems to have performed only one private jig for the King; Mall was more successful; Nell even more so. Whether it was at Tunbridge Wells that Charles first took the latter to bed, we shall never know; it seems likely – but at all events the episode was not long delayed. His taste for beauty and vivacity would not have allowed the prime possessor of both to escape him for long, though it may be that Mall was enough for him during his visits to the Wells. It may, incidentally, have been here that Nell played her notorious practical joke on her friend: knowing that Mall had an appointment with the King one evening, she spiked her drink with an emetic, with immediate and tumultuous results.

It has been suggested that Nell did not sleep with the King at Tunbridge Wells because 'she was enjoying her life as an actress too much at that stage to want to risk pregnancy and early retirement'.[23] Conception was of course an occupational hazard for all prostitutes of the period, of whatever degree of reputation or technique. Common whores could turn to those fallible methods of contraception available to them; one cannot imagine the King being specially concerned about such things – nor would it be likely that his mistresses would rush from his bed to the washbasin or the douche. (Certainly he was not concerned to take any precautions when sleeping with Barbara; neither was she – she was pregnant almost every year during their affair.) Bearing the King's child was a passport to a reasonably – sometimes unreasonably – generous pension and a certain position in society, possibly even a title. Nell would have been perfectly aware of this; she had had a taste of the high life and was eager to climb even further. It would by no means have been a calamity to become pregnant by Charles, though she may certainly not have been specially eager for it – yet.

The early history of contraception is obscure, but women had taken precautions of one kind and another for at least 2,000 years. Though it was not until the end of the seventeenth century that scientists actually discovered that seminal fluid carried spermatozoa, the conviction that semen was connected with pregnancy had existed for millennia: the Egyptians used sponges and other barriers (including crocodile dung), rather in the manner of a tampon, and all sorts of leaves, roots and herbs were used to prepare allegedly contraceptive ointments and liquids.

On the relatively rare occasions when men were determined to make a serious effort to avoid getting their wives or mistresses pregnant, *coitus interruptus* was the most common form of contraception; often, of course, it failed – and in any case a woman could not force a man to practise it. By the middle of the seventeenth century the condom certainly existed: the Italian anatomist Fallopius claimed to have invented it in the 1550s as a protection against syphilis, though his device was a truncated one – a little cap made of linen which was placed over the glans, the foreskin pulled over it to keep it in place (if you were circumcised, hard luck). The condom as we know it appeared rather later, made of sheep's gut or sometimes fish skin; it was not stocked in brothels until the eighteenth century, when a Mrs Phillips seems to have had a monopoly in London, supplying 'ambassadors, foreigners, gentlemen, and captains of ships &c going abroad'.[24]

But whatever Nell's hopes or fears about conception, it was very clear to London society – or that part of it which was interested – that by the spring of 1668 the King and she were on extremely familiar terms. (There was a distinct hint in the fact that Buckhurst had been sent to France on some negligible diplomatic excuse – 'a sleeveless errand' as Dryden drily put it.) The degree of their familiarity is demonstrated in the anecdote which has been repeated so often that it has become folklore – but it rings true, the behaviour of everyone concerned in it being highly characteristic. It seems that the King and the Duke of York went to see a revival of Etherege's *She Would if she Could*, and that Nell was entertaining a young Villiers, one of Buckingham's relatives, in a neighbouring box. Let her first anonymous biographer take up the story:

His Majesty saw her, and that very night possessed her. . . . As that monarch had an aversion to his robes of royalty, and was encumbered with the dignity of his state, he chose frequently to throw off the load of kingship and consider himself as a private gentleman. Upon this occasion he came to the play *incog.* and sat in the next box to Nell and her lover. As soon as the play was finished, His Majesty, with the Duke of York, the young nobleman and Nell retired to a tavern together, where they regaled themselves over a bottle, and the King showed such civilities to Nell that she began to understand the meaning of his gallantry.

The tavern-keeper was entirely ignorant of the quality of the company; and it was remarkable that when the reckoning came to be paid, his Majesty upon searching his pockets found that he had not money enough about him to discharge it, and asked the sum of his brother who was in the same situation: upon which Nell observed that she had got into the poorest company that ever she was in at a tavern. The reckoning was paid by the young nobleman, who that night parted both his money and mistress.[25]

Bishop Burnet reports that Buckingham told him at this time that 'when Nell was first brought to the King, she asked only £500 a year' in recognition of her favours. This was by no means an outrageous request, certainly when compared to what he was still spending on Barbara, in whom he had completely lost any erotic interest – it was less than the income of an average knight of the realm.[26] It seems the King thought it too much, however, and in any event Nell remained for the time being a busy professional actress. She took over, for Killigrew, Mall Davis's rôle in *The Man's the Master* (a play the producer had translated from the French), Sir Charles Sedley wrote *The Mulberry Gardens* for her (both the King and Queen attended the première), and – with Hart – she appeared in Dryden's *An Evening's Love, or, the Mock Astrologer*, set in modern Spain: an Englishman, Wildblood (Hart) pretends to be an astrologer in order to seduce Donna Jacinta (Nell, as a Spanish lady), who to test him pretends to be a Muslim called Fatyma. Pepys thought the play 'very smutty'. Nell also played in *The English Monsieur*, Beaumont and Fletcher's old play *Philaster, or Love Lies a-Bleeding*, and Sir Robert Howard's *The Committee*. That she made a success (again with Hart) in *Philaster* is confirmed by the fact that when the play was revived in 1695, a prologue declared:

> This good old play, *Philaster*, cannot fail –
> But we young actors, how can we prevail?
> Philaster and Bellario, let me tell ye,
> For these bold parts we have no Hart, no Nelly,
> Those darlings of the stage . . .

Though Pepys disapproved of it, it was *An Evening's Love* that was a particular success with the King. The cast included Mohun and Mrs Knepp – all-star, indeed – and Charles must specially have relished one speech of Nell's (as the heroine of the piece, Donna Jacinta): an ordinary lover, she said, was only good 'to be admitted to pass my time with while a better comes; to be the lowest step in my staircase for a knight to mount upon him, and a lord upon him, and a duke upon him, till I get as high as I can climb'. A touch of *lèse-majesté* there, surely – but Dryden and Nell were allowed that. The King was amused.

While still a professional actress, Nell spent a considerable amount of time with her royal lover between September 1668 and the spring of 1669. She was virtually absent from the stage except for speaking a prologue or two and taking a small part in Shirley's *The Sisters* in December 1668. In spring 1669 the King went to see her play Valeria in Dryden's *Tyrannic Love, or the Royal Martyr* (Hart and Peg Hughes were also in the cast). It was a tragedy, Nell stabbing herself in the last act – but her death would not do to end the play, and she sprang from her bier:

> Hold! Are you mad, you damned confounded dogs?
> I am to rise to speak the epilogue.

Dryden had some fun with this, and so did the actress for whom he wrote it:

> I come, kind gentlemen, strange news to tell ye:
> I am the ghost of poor departed Nelly.
> Sweet ladies, be not frightened – I'll be civil –
> I'm what I was, a harmless little devil . . .

To tell you true, I walk because I die,
Out of my calling in a tragedy.
Oh, poet! damned dull poet, who could prove
So senseless, to make Nelly die for love.[27]

Actors spoke directly to their audiences in the prologues and
epilogues written for them – and were outspoken and satirical enough
to delight everyone who heard them. Everyone, that is, except the
Puritans, who found them lascivious and wanton – unsurprising when
Nell's lover Hart, for instance, virtually invited the men in the
audience to come round to the dressing-rooms after the performance
of Wycherley's *The Country Wife* in 1675 and take their pick of the
actresses:

We set no guards upon our tiring-room,
But when with flying colours there you come,
We patiently, you see, give up to you
Our poets, virgins, nay our matrons too.

Nell never gave out such an all-embracing invitation, but by now
her intimacy with the King was complete; they met with increasing
frequency. Charles, it appears, quite as often visited her as having her
brought to him at Whitehall. Her position was almost formal: when
Charles's sister came to England she paid Nell the compliment of
bringing her a considerable number of quite valuable gifts. Nell
repaid the compliment by satirising the dress of the Princess and her
attendants (see p. 101). Henriette-Anne brought, as a lady-in-waiting,
a personable young woman called Louise René de Penancöet de
Kéroüalle, a member of a poor but ancient family who had been at
the French court for some little time – long enough to have her name
scandalously linked with that of the young Comte de Sault, son of the
Duc de Lesdigiuères. He may not in fact have been her lover, but the
association was certainly not entirely free from scandal. The Duc de
Saint-Simon, in his memoirs, suggests that Louise's parents 'intended
her to be [Louis XIV]'s mistress, and she obtained the place of maid-
of-honour to Henriette of England. Unfortunately for her, Mlle de la

Vallière was also maid-of-honour to the princess, and the King gave her the preference.'[28]

Charles, then, may have been the second monarch on whom Louise set her ambition, and in the second case she was more successful. She had, according to Evelyn, 'a childish simple and baby face'[29] that immediately appealed to Charles, as did her low, musical voice – and when his sister left for home, Charles made an attempt to persuade her to leave Louise behind. The story is that Henriette-Anne sent her lady-in-waiting to fetch her jewel box, and opening it offered anything it contained to her brother as a parting gift, whereupon Charles took the young girl's hand and said that she was the only jewel he wished to keep beside him. But his sister knew just what that would mean, and took Mlle de Kéroüalle safely back to France.

Fate, however, then stepped in, for Minette (as Charles called his sister) was taken ill and died of peritonitis only a few days after returning to France. A month later the King sent the Duke of Buckingham to Paris, partly to convey his respects to Louis and his thanks for messages of condolence on Minette's death, and partly on a diplomatic mission. He may have mentioned Louise de Kéroüalle to Buckingham; but whether he did or not, others certainly spoke to the Duke of her, for there were plans in France to take advantage of the King's taste for women, and provide him with a French – and a Catholic – mistress. The Marquis de Saint-Maurice, French Ambassador to Duke Charles Emmanuel II of Savoy, wrote in a dispatch that Buckingham 'has taken with him [to England] Mlle de Kéroüalle, who was attached to her late Highness; she is a beautiful girl, and it is thought that the plan is to make her mistress to the King of Great Britain. He would like to dethrone Lady Castlemaine, who is his enemy, and his Most Christian Majesty would not be sorry to see the position filled by one of his subjects, for it is said the ladies have great influence over the mind of the King of England.'[30]

Indeed, although Louise had been devoted to Henriette-Anne – as had all her servants – and was said to be contemplating entering a nunnery, Buckingham persuaded her to accompany him to London, where, it was understood, she would become the King's mistress. How much the success of the proposition may be put down to

Buckingham's powers of persuasion (though perhaps also to the persuasion of French agents), and how much to Louise's ambition is debatable; her subsequent behaviour suggests that she was not averse to the idea. It has been suggested that Buckingham virtually offered her the throne, suggesting that the King's marriage was to all effects over. She is unlikely to have taken that proposition seriously, but she must certainly have believed that she could become the *maîtresse en titre*, and thus perhaps the most important and influential woman in England. At all events, she decided to travel to London with Buckingham.

The journey did not start well. Buckingham took her as far as Dieppe, and then went on alone to London, unaccountably neglecting to arrange a passage for her. She remained in Dieppe, bored and angry, for over a month until a ship was sent for her, and by the time she reached London she had taken an understandable dislike to Buckingham, which was to last her lifetime.

Meanwhile, Barbara had to all effects been dethroned. The King had tired of her; perhaps he even began to take Andrew Marvell's view:

> Paint Castlemaine in colours that will hold
> Her, not her picture, for she now grows old . . .[31]

She was twenty-seven in 1667, when the poet suggested that she was an old woman reduced to seducing her servants. She was certainly not (nor had she ever been) an angel. Among her lovers was Nell's partner, Charles Hart: Pepys heard from one of his actress friends, Frances Davenport, in 1668, that 'my Lady Castlemaine is mightily in love with Hart . . . and he is much with her in private, and she goes to him and doth give him many presents'.[32] Frances told him that Becky Marshall had introduced Hart to Barbara in revenge for the King's favours to Mall Davis, of which Becky was jealous.

In January 1669 Barbara was created Duchess of Cleveland, Countess of Southampton and Baroness Nonsuch. That last title went with one of the finest houses in England, Nonsuch, near Ewel, in Surrey, which was built by Henry VIII and completed by the Earl of

Arundel. Loved by Queen Elizabeth I, and of the utmost magnificence, it actually belonged to Henrietta Maria, now the Queen Mother. Barbara cherished it so dearly that she sold all its furniture and hangings and simply left it to rot, turning the park into farms. All that is now left of the house are some ragged foundations where it once stood. She certainly did not want for anything; Charles made her a generous allowance. All her debts were paid, and she had an income in the region of £30,000 a year. But her influence, and her position, depended entirely on her retaining his favour.

From the beginning, she had been cordially disliked not only by that minority who disapproved of the King's loose living and of the general licentiousness of most of the men who surrounded him, but also by those who believed that she exercised too much political influence over Charles. That influence was less considerable than was commonly thought, but she certainly made her views known to him, and they may have had some effect. Clarendon particularly disliked her – so much so that he could barely bring himself to pronounce her name – and was hated in return. She seized the opportunity, eventually, to contribute to his downfall when, in 1667, everyone turned against him, his windows were broken by the crowd, and he was finally dismissed and exiled. Barbara was seen in her aviary at Whitehall, wearing a smock and 'joying herself at the old man's going away'.[33]

But she herself was slighted by many of the Court ladies inside the walls of the Palace and insulted by members of the public outside – even physically accosted, on one occasion, by masked men who compared her to Edward IV's mistress, Jane Shore, and warned that, like her, she might well end up as a slighted corpse thrown upon a dung-hill.

None of the criticism of her, or of his own private peccadilloes, much impressed the King – and the children Barbara bore him drew them closer together: Charles liked children, and was always happy to romp with them. For a considerable period after his marriage, he had remained close to Barbara, and those about the Court – in particular the servants – who were eager to curry favour with him, tended to favour her in any matter where her interests collided with those of the Queen.

Eventually, the Queen concluded that some kind of accommodation with her husband's mistress was necessary, and brought herself to be civil and even pleasant to her. It may also have been the case that she recognised that Barbara made Charles happy in a way with which she could not compete, and liking and coming to love him, accepted the situation.

It seems that the King, in recognition of his wife's surrender, originally agreed that as long as the Queen accepted Barbara as at the very least on a level with the other Court ladies, he would not grant her rooms at Whitehall. If he did make such a promise, it did not last long. But Barbara turned out to be her own worst enemy: established at Whitehall, she began to rule the roast with an enthusiasm that soon began to upset even the King. His advisers soon objected to her interference, and in particular to the establishment at Court of various placemen of hers in positions if not of power, at least of influence: her friend Sir Henry Bennet became Secretary of State, and Sir Charles Berkeley, Privy Purse. Pepys took exception to the fact that 'my Lady Castlemaine's interest at Court increases and is more and greater than the Queen's. That she hath brought in Sir H. Bennet and Sir Ch. Berkeley; but that the Queen is a most good lady and takes all with the greatest meekness that may be.'[34] And again, the King was 'himself following his pleasures more than with good advice he would do – at least to be seen to all the world to do so' with 'his dalliance with my Lady Castlemaine being public every day, to his great reproach. And his favouring of none at Court so much as those that are the confidants of his pleasure, as Sir G. Bennet and Sir Ch. Berkeley – which good God put it in his mind to mend before he makes himself too much condemned by his people for it.'[35]

Barbara had always had a volatile temper and a tendency to tell the King what he should and should not do. And she was also notoriously unfaithful: on one occasion, it was said, the King called unexpectedly to see their children, and on his way in perceived a lover escaping through a downstairs window. He was more amused than offended, and seems rather to have admired his mistress's insatiable sexual appetite. Among her lovers was the playwright Wycherley. The story there is that Barbara went up to him one day in the park and saluted him with the words: 'Wycherley, you are the son of a whore.' This was actually an allusion to a song in his *Love in a Wood*, but was forward enough to interest the playwright, whom she found to be as sexually voracious as she herself. He was soon making assignations with her at the house of Mary Knight, a well-known *bona roba*, and – allegedly – satisfying them both before leaving. The King, hearing about this, went one night to the house, and passed Wycherley on the stairs. Barbara, hastily adjusting her dress, professed to have been alone, meditating on the religious significance of Easter, at which Charles remarked, 'Ha! – and I suppose that was your confessor I met going downstairs.'

Though he clearly did not worry himself about Barbara's infidelity, obvious disrespect was another matter – as was any attempt to gull him. One of the last straws was Barbara's pregnancy by Henry Jermyn, a gentleman of no morals whatsoever. He was a short, bowlegged man, generally considered one of the ugliest in London – but also the best-endowed. (The rumour was that, admiring Barbara, he had greeted her one day straight from his bath, rather too negligently swathed in a towel.) Charles may not have known whose child she was bearing, but was certain it could not be his, 'he having not lain with her this half year' (as Pepys was told by the Lord Chamberlain's secretary). Indeed, the Lord Chamberlain's secretary told Pepys that the King now so disliked Barbara that he would rather masturbate than entertain her: 'for a good while the King's greatest pleasure hath been with his fingers . . .'[36]

Barbara was determined to pass the baby off as the King's. When Charles demurred, 'God damn me! but you shall own it!'[37] she told him. It should be christened in the Royal Chapel at Whitehall and publicly acknowledged, or she would hurl it to the floor in front of the King and dash out its brains.[38] This, with all the other irritations and incidents, was more than enough. Barbara was given her *congé* and ordered to move out of her apartments in the Palace of Whitehall. 'Madam,' said the King (according to Barbara's own report) 'all that I ask of you for your own sake is, live so for the future as to make the least noise you can, and I care not who you love.'[39] The news of Louise's arrival must have made the position even clearer to her.

By now, Nell seems frequently to have mounted as high as she would climb – not only to the King's bedroom, but to a private dressing-room at the theatre, on whose playbills she now appeared as 'Mrs Ellen Gwyn', respected by her colleagues and by the public for whom her notorious private life did not in the least detract from her appeal as an actress. She was quite as respectable as any player could hope to be. Having already moved from the Cock and Pie tavern, where she had rooms during her early days in the theatre, to a house in Newman's Row, she now took rooms in one of the most fashionable quarters of London – Lincoln's Inn Fields, originally laid out under James I by Inigo Jones, and now with its own imposing square of houses, each with its own little courtyard. Lord Sandwich had rented a house there six years earlier, in 1664, for £250 a year, a very solid rent indeed; we can guess who paid Nell's rent.

Tracing the sites of Nell Gwyn's various houses has been something of a hobby for her biographers over the years, but because the whole Drury Lane and Holborn area has so radically altered it is impossible to be sure of anything in that location. The original streets which by the beginning of the twentieth century had become rickety slums were swept away with the development of Kingsway and Aldwych, and even the superimposition of modern maps over old fails to tell us precisely which old streets lay under the modern ones. The Cock and Pie was rebuilt in 1891 but then vanished under the new development, and Bush House now covers much of the ground with which Nell would have been familiar, including Maypole Alley, which originally led from the tavern past the house of the astrologer William Lilly and the great maypole which had been re-erected at the Restoration, and down to the Thames.

In the autumn of 1670, Dryden's *The Conquest of Granada* was produced – by which time Nell (on 8 May) had given birth to Charles's son: as one gossip put it, 'one that belongs to the King's Playhouse was brought to bed of a boy in her house in Lincoln's Inn Fields, next to Whetstone Park – the King's bastard'.[40]

Dryden's new piece was a substantial one, in no fewer than ten acts. Nell appeared as Queen Almahide, Hart as her lover Almanzor, and the popular veteran Kynaston as her jealous husband Boabdalin.

Rebecca Marshall took in a virtuoso part as the seductress Lyndaraxa, and Dryden wrote the small part of Almahide's servant Esperanza for an inexperienced young actress, Anne Reeves, who was – or shortly became – his mistress. The play became the source of some contention among the more serious playgoers of the time, who wondered what things were coming to when the mistress of the King, who had just borne him a bastard son, could be cast as a virtuous queen falsely accused of adultery.

Nell's confinement had done nothing to reduce her chirpiness, and though her part was basically a serious one she got peals of laughter and rounds of applause as, dressed in an enormous cartwheel hat and a broad belt, she spoke a prologue poking fun at the dresses worn by the retinue of the King's sister, Henriette-Anne, the Duchesse d'Orléans – then visiting London to propose a treaty by which the King would become a permanent ally of France (in return for very considerable annual funds from that country) and would remove many of the repressive anti-Catholic laws. Her dress, satirising the huge hats and broad waist-belts of the visitor's male attendants, was also a comment on the current productions at the Duke's Theatre, where the actors were much given, it seems, to outrageous costumes and funny hats.

What Pepys found particularly 'smutty' about the play is now difficult to see – though there were certainly some candidly erotic songs, and a 'Zambra Dance' in Part I, which may have been mildly outrageous. The play itself is an extremely interesting one, and with discreet cuts (for it is certainly very long) might well bear revival, with its frank sexual innuendo balanced by some imposing poetry, fine wit and a fascinating test for the leading characters, caught between the exigencies of reality and an abstract devotion to purity and religion.

Its first production, however, cannot have impressed the audience by an air of high seriousness, and the sight of the noble hero, played by Nell's former lover, apparently struck dumb and incapable of action at the mere sight of her, gave rise to some unfortunate giggling. And what could be made of Nell – *Nell!* – delivering an impassioned plea for purity? Almanzor was more in line with her emotions when he argued that he would give an age of purity for a moment of passion:

> Praise is the pay of Heav'n for doing good;
> But Love's the best return for flesh and blood.[41]

At all events, the play was a considerable success, and there is no doubt that Nell played a considerable part in ensuring that success. In February 1671, there was a performance at Court, and on the following day the text was published; Dryden was now unquestionably recognised as the finest playwright, and perhaps the finest poet, of the age. His place in society was assured when he took Barbara, now Duchess of Cleveland – and retired from the royal bedchamber – as his mistress.

Almahide seems to have been the last original part Nell learned for the stage, and though she continued to appear for a while,[42] she had clearly now decided to devote herself entirely to her monarch. Her increasingly sound position in the King's favour led her on to a more satisfactory and prestigious address: 79 Pall Mall. Lord Scarsdale had bought it from Sir William Coventry, and was living there contentedly; but Nell, having rejected a smaller house nearby (which was only leasehold) set her eye firmly on it. From what we know of it, it sounds a thoroughly pleasant house, not too large and not too small, with two floors of rooms for Nell, most of them to be furnished for the kind of entertaining she would do there; and three upper stories for servants. The house had a garden which gave onto the royal gardens and rose at its southernmost end to a small hillock from which there was an uninterrupted view of St James's Park. No doubt prompted by the King, Scarsdale complacently moved out of his house, and Nell moved in – and on Christmas Day 1671, bore there her second child by the King, another son, christened James after the Duke of York. Sixteen years later, she would die in the same house.

CHAPTER SIX

From Whore to Whore

Restless he rolls about from whore to whore,
A merry monarch, scandalous and poor . . .

Anon

One day in March 1671, the author and diarist John Evelyn, talking with the King about some work an architect friend of his was doing for His Majesty at Windsor, strolled with him through St James's Park 'where', he wrote in his diary, leaving tactful gaps where Charles's name should have been, 'I both saw and heard a very familiar discourse between   and Mrs Nellie, as they called an impudent comedian, she looking out of her garden on a terrace at the top of the wall, and   standing on the green walk under it: I was heartily sorry at this scene. Thence the King walked to the Duchess of Cleveland's, another lady of pleasure and curse of our nation.'[1]

It was a scene that has been often reproduced on stage, in film, and in a notoriously popular romantic painting by a forgotten Victorian painter, C.M. Ward, which may be seen in the collection of the Victoria and Albert Museum in South Kensington: Nell, rather more conventionally pretty than seems actually to have been the case, with her finger to her cheek and a fan negligently dangling from the other hand as the King looks darkly up at her, his two dogs at his feet – and Evelyn making a disapproving face in the background.

The King much enjoyed St James's Park, and a swift walk through it and then on to the top of Constitution Hill (named incidentally after the King's daily constitutional, when he was in town) left his companions panting behind him. The park had until comparatively recently been an untidy, marshy and rather unhealthy place. (James I had experimented with crocodiles there, but they had not taken.) Charles I's queen, with her French taste, had laid it out more formally around a long lake with a little island on which water birds could nest, and hung cages with parrots and cassowaries along what became known as Birdcage Walk.

Charles cared for the park both emotionally and practically. When the lake waters began to fall, he paid £1,700 to bring water from Hyde Park, and added interest to the view by providing two gondolas, complete with homesick (and underpaid) gondoliers. A wall was built around the area, but it had always been, and remained, an extremely unsavoury place, especially after dark, when prostitutes of all ages and both sexes were readily available and where (as Rochester put it, with his usual elegance) nightly beneath the shade of the trees

> Are buggeries, rapes and incests made.
> Unto this all-sin-sheltering grove
> Whores of the bulk[2] and the alcove
> Great ladies, chambermaids and drudges,
> The rag-picker and heiress trudges,
> Car-men, divines, great lords and tailors
> Prentices, poets, pimps and gaolers,
> Footmen, fine fops, do here arrive,
> And here promiscuously do swive.[3]

The terrace of which Evelyn spoke was at the end of the garden of Nell's new house at 79 Pall Mall, where she was setting herself up in enormous style, going about town in the expensive carriage she had acquired, to buy furniture and bibelots. Though not specially interested in wealth for its own sake, she enjoyed making a show, and no doubt the house was a-bustle with men mounting wallpaper on canvas and nailing it to battens, and hanging the best rooms with damask, velvet and brocade in the vivid colours favoured at the time. Tapestries, which were not especially expensive, hung where drafts were likely to be most fierce. Perhaps she went in for gilt leather – the King had his royal yacht hung with it, and Nell certainly used it in a handsome sedan chair. The main rooms in the house were already finely panelled, but Nell may have had to use pine or deal for any new work, since the price of oak had become very considerable.

The bedroom was probably one of the finest rooms in the house – for at least one very obvious reason. The bed was certainly elaborate enough (see p. 196) and with a close-stool beside it; Charles's own was a fine padded one, the fabric matching that of his bed, and Nell would have wanted him to have an equally comfortable convenience when he spent the night with her. A couple of fashionable carved wooden black boys very possibly held candelebra on each side of a table or two, one of them a dressing-table entirely covered in rich fabric.

Life, as she bustled about, must have seemed very good indeed. If she had given up the plaudits of the playhouse, she had done so not only in order to be 'on call' for His Majesty at any hour when he felt in need of her attentions, but also for the very good reason that she no longer needed to act; she was as financially secure as any dependant on the King could claim to be, and unless she in some way seriously antagonised him and fell out of favour, nothing, she believed, could shake her position. Evelyn might complain in his diary, and some sour courtiers might even do so in public (Sir John Coventry MP, who had once lived at the house in Pall Mall, crassly asked the House of Commons 'whether the King's pleasure did lie among the men or among the women who acted'), but Nell was not touched by their criticism.

Apart from the pleasant luxury of her new house, which grew more sumptuous by the day, she was also thoroughly at home in the Palace of Whitehall, although she seems never to have had apartments there – unlike Barbara, who had moved into the Palace in April 1663 and was maintained there in some state. Barbara had demanded residence as a right; she saw herself as only a step below the Queen in rank. Nell never perceived herself in such terms. At home she could welcome Charles informally, and with as little ceremony as possible. In the Palace, she would have felt constrained to behave herself like a lady, which was never her strong point.

Nothing now remains of the great, rambling Palace of Whitehall except the splendid Banqueting Hall and some cellars, and though it would certainly be interesting if it did, we have probably not lost anything of particular beauty. In the time of Charles II the Palace was a maze of over 200 rooms, and in plan was much like London in miniature: narrow corridors, instead of streets, darted to all points of the compass, ending in a small courtyard here, a blank wall there, a concealed entrance in one direction, a bedroom in another. As a French correspondent put it, 'It contains nothing resembling a palace unless it be the building called the Banqueting House. The remainder is an accumulation of badly built houses not constructed to be joined together.'[4]

When the King returned to his capital, the Palace was empty and echoing – no one had used it since the death of Oliver Cromwell two years previously, and when the government had tried to sell it in order to pay its soldiers, there were no takers. The walls were bare of Charles I's great art collection, which had been sold and dispersed by the Commonwealth, the interiors pillaged of fine furniture, the tennis courts and cockpit used as a theatre were derelict, the gardens overgrown, the bowling green wrecked by moles and weeds.

Some preparations had been put in hand for the monarch's return – 'necessaries to be provided for the King's Household' – the furnishing of a bedroom, for instance, 'a rich bed to be of velvet, either embroidered with gold or laced, lined with cloth of silver or satin . . .'[5] The King immediately set about some renovation (characteristically one of the first pieces of work put in train was the restoration of the Cockpit Theatre). Within a few months of his return he had spent £1,200 on refurnishing the royal apartments, though it was to be two years before his bedroom was as he wanted it, with a handsome black and white marble floor and chimney-piece and giant eagles surmounting a bed, the hangings of which were supported by twin golden cherubs.

However splendid the Banqueting Hall (the ceiling magnificently painted by Rubens, paid over £3,000 by the King to depict the glories of his Restoration), however splendid his bedroom (its ceiling decorated by Charles's official Court Painter Michael Wright), the rest of the Palace was a smelly disgrace, and Charles throughout his life was ambitious to raze it to the ground. Indeed, it must have seemed far from fit for a King, and visitors who knew the grandeur of Versailles were aghast at the whole muddled maze where the courtiers were forced to live cheek by jowl with their servants – scullions and Ladies of the Bedchamber, corn cutters and rat-killers, sempstresses and saddlers and fishmongers and mat-layers, the Master of Tents and the Cormorant Keeper, the Falconer and the Surveyor of Stables, all hugger-mugger.

The Palace was remarkably accessible. It was cut in two by a main road – the road from Charing Cross to Westminster. (The present Whitehall and Parliament Street follow its route exactly.) The main part of the Palace lay between this road and the river, and two gates arched across from it to the smaller part, where the Cockpit, the Tilt-Yard and Horse Guards lay. Privileged visitors (including Pepys) could enter the Palace by the Holbein Gatehouse; visiting dignitaries, or those on State business, usually entered by the Great Gate, just north of the banqueting house; those who delivered goods or were on less important errands came in through two gates further to the north, though many provisions came by river, and were unloaded at Scotland Dock.

The King and Queen usually entered the Palace by the Privy Stairs, which led from the river straight into their private apartments. They thus looked out onto the Thames, the city's main artery of communication, teeming with life. Less fortunate inhabitants had to make do with the light offered by windows giving onto little courtyards or light wells with blank walls. One, however, had a particularly privileged set of rooms – the ubiquitous Mr Chiffinch, purveyor of young flesh to His Majesty. His chambers were tucked neatly between the King's and Queen's, and Catherine learned to look the other way while

> England's Monarch in his closet lay
> And Chiffinch stepped to fetch the female prey.[6]

Chiffinch's mother-in-law, a Mrs Nunn, was the Queen's laundress, while Mrs Chiffinch herself was chief sempstress, with an uncommonly large annual salary of £1,200. (Chiffinch was paid a total of over £10,000 within a few years, from funds tactfully and silently disbursed, usually from the Secret Service accounts.) It is difficult to believe that

Catherine did not know that her sempstress's main duty was to assist Chiffinch in obtaining young women for Charles, and getting them without undue fuss into his bedroom, not many feet from the Queen's own. Among them was one of the Queen's own maids of honour, Winifred Wells, who had 'a physiognomy of a dreamy sheep' – but at least did not have a long journey to the King's bed.

When Nell, on what seem to have been rare occasions, came to Whitehall she did not enter by the river entrance, but walked or took a chair from Pall Mall across what has become Horse Guards Parade, came in by the King Street gate – very near Barbara's lodgings! – and thence into the stone gallery originally built by Henry VIII and now housing what remained of the royal picture collection, together with new pictures Charles II was buying. From there she made her way to the King's private apartments. When the King went out into the park to exercise his dogs and feed the ducks, he usually went by the Stone Gallery – or by the Long Matted Gallery above it – an informal way of leaving the Palace.

It seems possible that Charles was a little wary of encouraging Nell to visit him at Whitehall. She always declined to behave like the lady she wasn't, and was quite capable in an excess of high spirits of escaping from the bedroom and finding her way into the apartments of the Earl of Lauderdale, the Countess of Suffolk, the Earl of Bath, or any other of the courtiers whose rooms were near the King's own. This might have amused the King, but there were limits.

Louise de Kéroüalle, who had moved into the Palace of Whitehall, was another matter. Properly raised, she knew how to behave. In 1671 the King finally managed to take her virginity – something of an event, for alone, as far as we can know, among Charles's mistresses, she came to his bed a virgin. She was, of course, a Catholic, but that was no safeguard against seduction, and indeed there had been rumours in France that 'La Belle Bretonne' (as they called her there) had been the mistress of Louis XIV. However, she was a good girl, if an ambitious one, and what we know of her suggests that her ambition was not to become Charles's mistress but his wife. Louis and some of his ministers would have been delighted by this, but in any case were determined to make use of her politically.

The idea of a royal marriage was never seriously on the cards. Even had Queen Catherine died (and Louise's correspondence with the French Ambassador, Colbert de Croissy, suggests that she believed that the Queen was in bad health), Charles would not have married a little French nobody: there were bigger and more advantageous fish in the sea. But there was no problem in taking the lower, shallower step. Charles was intensely susceptible to the ladies, and Louise had the advantage of being handsome, innocent, vulnerable – and of course accessible. A painting by Gascar shows her toying with a white dove, her skin almost as white as its feathers, set off by intensely dark, long ringlets and equally dark eyes – with no sign of the cast which Nell later saw (and named her 'Squintabella'). Though she had been twenty-one when Charles first saw her, she still looked extremely young, with a little round, plump, innocent face (he called her 'Fubbs' because of the plumpness of her cheeks).

The King's courtship was unusually protracted. De Croissy wrote to Versailles reporting that Charles went to see Louise at nine every morning, never staying less than an hour – sometimes two – and that in the evening he was often seen bending over her chair as she played cards, making sure that any money she lost was replaced in her purse.

Some Englishmen were inclined to favour her. Lord Arlington, it appeared, was naively impressed by her apparent lack of interest in politics: she was, he said, clearly not of a mischievous disposition, and was a gentlewoman – and it was far better that the King should form a liaison with her than with 'actresses and suchlike unworthy creatures, of whom no man of quality could take the measure'. The Countess of Arlington, a Dutchwoman given to serious intrigue, collaborated with de Croissy in inviting Louise to stay at Euston Hall, her house near Thetford in Sussex, during October 1671, while Charles was enjoying the racing at Newmarket. 'As the inclination of the King for Mlle de Kéroüalle . . . is increasing daily, I doubt not that he will often come to visit us.'[7]

He did. By the end of October the King had travelled to Euston three times, and spent several hours with his friend. As de Croissy tactfully put it, 'since she has not been wanting, on her side, in all the gratitude that the love of a great King can deserve from a beautiful girl, it is believed that the attachment will be of long duration and that it will exclude all others'.[8] The diarist Evelyn, ever the puritan, was more forthright:

> It was universally reported that the fair lady was bedded one of these nights, and the stocking flung after the manner of a married bride; I acknowledge that she was for the most part in her undress all day, and that there was fondness and toying with that young wanton; nay, t'was said I was at the former ceremony, but 'tis utterly false, I neither saw nor heard of any such thing while I was there, though I had been in her chamber and all over that apartment late enough, and was myself observing all passages with curiosity enough. However, 'twas with confidence believed that she was first made a *Miss*, as they call these unhappy creatures, with solemnity at the time, &c.[9]

There had for a while been considerable uneasiness at the French court, lest Louise should not manage to capture the King. In September de Croissy had told Louis that while dining at the French Embassy Louise had suddenly felt nauseous and had to leave the table, and Louis rejoiced – Charles must have got her with child. That was a false alarm. But nine months after her visit to Euston, Louise gave birth to Charles Lennox. Louis sent his congratulations to her, via de Croissy: His Majesty would be pleased if she would maintain herself in the good graces of the King.

Once Charles's mistress in fact, Louise began to exert all her charms and all her sagacity to consolidate her position. She was adept at bursting into tears if she did not get what she wanted – at which the King, embarrassed, invariably gave in. Nell would have despised such a trick, and added 'the weeping willow' to the list of nicknames she had for 'Mrs Carwell' as she called Louise – so did everyone else; Kéroüalle was beyond most English tongues. But the ploy clearly worked: Louise acquired a suite of twenty-four rooms in the Palace of Whitehall, with sixteen attic rooms for her servants. Evelyn was taken one morning by the King into her bedroom, 'where she was in her morning loose garment, her maids combing her, newly out of her bed'. 'That which engaged my curiosity', he wrote in his diary, was the rich and splendid furniture of this woman's apartment, now twice or thrice pulled down and rebuilt to satisfy her prodigal and expensive pleasures, [which] Her Majesty's do not exceed . . . Here I saw the new fabric of French tapestry, for design, tenderness of work and incomparable imitation of the best paintings, beyond anything I had ever beheld; some pieces had Versailles, St Germans and other palaces of the French King, with hunting, figures and landscapes, exotic fowl and all to the life rarely done – then for Japan cabinets, screens, pendule clocks, huge vases of wrought plate, tables, stands, chimney furniture, sconces, branches, braseras &c., they were all of massive silver, and without number, besides of His Majesty's best paintings . . . Lord, what contentment can there be in the riches and splendour of this world, purchased with vice and dishonour?[10]

It would in fact have required little effort to contrive a room more richly decorated than the Queen's; the only secular item there was an illuminated clock at her bedside. Other ornaments consisted of second-rate religious pictures, devotional texts, and a stoup of holy water.

Having finally seduced Louise – or been seduced by her – the King continued to pay her his attentions, in tandem with Nell, who he set up in a house at Newmarket, convenient for the races; he also brought Louise there from time to time, and the two mistresses can scarcely have avoided meeting. Later, they were both entertained at Windsor, Nell in a house said to be connected to the Castle by an underground passage (though why such a subterfuge should have been thought necessary has never been explained).

There was general amusement at the fact that Charles should run two such dissimilar mistresses at the same time. Madame de Sévigné[11] found the situation delightfully amusing:

Kéroüalle saw well her way, and has made everything she wished for come to pass. She wanted to be the mistress of the King of England; and behold, he now shares her couch before the eyes of the whole Court. She wanted to be rich; and she is heaping up treasures, and making herself feared and courted. But she did not foresee that a low actress was to cross her path, and to bewitch the King. She is powerless to detach him from his comedian. He divides his money, his time and his health between the pair. The low actress is as proud as the Duchess of Portsmouth, whom she jeers at, mimics, and makes game of. She braves her to her face, and often takes the King away from her, and boasts that she is the best loved of the two. She is young, of madcap gaiety, brazen, debauched and ready witted. Since Kérouälle has become a favourite, Gwyn insists upon the King owning her son as his.

This is how she argues: 'That hoity-toity French duchess sets up to be of grand quality. Every one of rank in France is her cousin. The moment someone over there dies she orders a suit of deep mourning. Well, if she's of such high station, why is she such a jade? She ought to be ashamed of herself! If I were reared to be a lady, I'm sure I should blush for myself. But it's my trade to be a doxy, and I was never anything else. The King keeps me; ever since he has done so, I have been true to him. He has had a son by me, and I'm going to make him own the brat, for he is as fond of me as of his French miss.' This creature holds her own in an extraordinary manner, and embarrasses and disconcerts the new-fledged duchess.[12]

Wherever the writer heard the reported conversation, it certainly rings true. That was Nell's ground, and she stood firmly upon it. Evelyn was less understanding and less sanguine. When he looked in at Newmarket on his way to London from Euston, he found a ménage 'more resembling a luxurious and abandoned rout than a Christian Court; the Duke of Buckingham was now in mighty favour, and had with him here that impudent woman the Countess of Shrewsbury [she being Buckingham's mistress, Anna Maria Brudenell, who Nell liked and often entertained] with his band of fiddlers, &c.'[13]

When Louise gave birth to her first son she was made Duchess of Portsmouth, Countess of Fareham and Baroness Petersfield. Young

Charles was to receive the Garter and to become Earl of Southampton, and her other sons by Charles were to be equally ennobled – the second as Earl of Euston, the third as Lord George Fitzroy; her two daughters received a grant of the royal arms.

Though Nell was sufficiently well off – astonishingly so, considering her low birth – and though she never hankered after the glory of a title (not for the likes of her and Mall Davis), she would not have been human if she had not felt her nose a little out of joint, nor if she had not relished the fact that of all Charles's mistresses, Louise was the only one to be heartily disliked by the vast majority of his subjects, chiefly because of her Catholicism. King Louis hoped that the new mistress would be able to persuade Charles to turn Catholic, to effect a reconciliation with Rome and restore England to the true religion; and as a bonus, to arrange the marriage of the heir to the throne, the recently widowed Duke of York, to a Frenchwoman of his choosing.

Charles's attitude to the Catholic Church had always been both equivocal and guarded. While on the run during the Civil War, hidden at Moseley Old Hall in the company of Father John Huddleston and invited to pray at a secret chapel in the house, he had told the priest: 'If it please God I come to my crown, both you and all of your persuasion shall have as much liberty as any of my subjects.'[14] It was not going to be as easy as that. Certainly in the Declaration of Breda, in 1660, the King promised to search for a 'tolerant' religious settlement, but left the details to the Convention Parliament, which did a number of things – fixing the King's income and returning confiscated estates to him and to some bishops, for instance – but considered religious compromise impossible. The Cavalier Parliament was sturdily Anglican throughout the eighteen years of its life, and time and again renewed its determination to compel conformity, insisting in the Corporation Act of 1661 and the Act of Uniformity of 1662 that all civil servants and clergymen should take oaths of allegiance and non-resistance to the Crown, and recognise the King's supremacy in the Church. Almost one-fifth of all clergy lost their livings as the result of this Draconian policy, and were barred from setting foot within five miles of their old parishes. All dissenters were prohibited from holding services.

As the King fully recognised, though many of his subjects were on the side of Parliament a very considerable minority objected vigorously to the repressive anti-Catholic legislation. Indeed, the various forms of repression were a significant embarrassment to Charles, whose prominent advisers were by no means all enthusiastic Anglicans. None of the members of the Cabal were Anglicans, and two were Roman Catholics. But the whole religious problem was a tightrope on which it was enormously difficult for Charles to keep his balance. When in the Treaty of Dover, in 1670, he allied himself with Catholic France against Protestant Holland, he was rewarded by considerable funds from King Louis XIV. A secret clause in the Treaty offered him an even larger sum if he openly declared himself a Catholic – but this was always impossible, and the idea (apparently fostered by King Louis) that Louise could ever have 'converted' him was even more ridiculous. Even had the circumstances been more favourable, the King would never had been influenced in such a matter by a mistress.

In another attempt to be more tolerant, he pressed in the Declaration of Indulgence (1672) for the lifting of penalties imposed on nonconformists, but Parliament openly rebelled, and refused to vote any money for war against Holland unless the Declaration was abrogated. Rather than promoting freedom of religious belief the King was forced to approve the Test Act of 1673, which barred from public office everyone but Anglicans. This affected his brother James, Duke of York, who was forced to resign from the Admiralty.

James was by then a Catholic. He had probably been converted as early as 1669, although he was not officially received into the Catholic Church until early in 1672.[15] Charles asked him not to declare himself publicly, and he went on attending Anglican services until 1676. Louis, unable to take advantage of the conversion of the heir, concentrated instead on finding him a good Catholic wife. James had seduced and secretly married Anne Hyde, daughter of the Earl of Clarendon, but the marriage had ended with her death in 1671, and it was certainly the case that he was looking about for a second wife. A number of women about the Court were of a mind to assist him. De Croissy wrote in a dispatch that 'all the belles of the

Court bedeck themselves in order to make a conquest of the Duke of York'.[16] He suggested to Louis that it might well be possible to incline the Duke's affections towards a suitable Frenchwoman, the suitability being in direct proportion to the marriage settlement. The Duchesse de Guise was much favoured: recently widowed, she had been pregnant three times within two years which, together with her great wealth, would surely commend her to a man anxious for an heir?

The Duke was not persuaded. He was quite happy with his sixteen-year-old mistress, the daughter of Sir Charles Sedley, the dissolute poet; she was scrawny and pale and had a decided squint, and herself wondered why he was so fond of her. No one else could understand it, either – least of all Louise, who pressed the French King to recommend either Marie Eléonore or Marie Françoise de Lorraine, the daughters of the Duc d'Elbœuf, as a wife for James. Louis still favoured the Duchesse de Guise, and Louise had to write to France very forthrightly, pointing out that it was perhaps not good policy to recommend an elderly, plain widow to a man who was clearly enjoying the company of a sixteen-year-old girl. She had already been exercising herself on behalf of the d'Elbœufs, sending to France for their portraits and displaying them prominently in her rooms (they were indeed two very pretty girls). She had some success. De Croissy pointed out to Louis that she 'has exerted herself . . . with so much ardour to cause one of the *demoiselles* d'Elbœuf to be preferred to anyone else, that no one will now listen to the praises of the Duchesse de Guise. Yesterday, in the King's chamber, Mlle de Kéroüalle drew me aside and told me that the Duke of York would have preferred Mlle d'Elbœuf even if he had found me much less encouraging; and she begged me not to offer any opposition to this marriage, and even to make it known that it would not be disagreeable to your Majesty.'[17]

It was not to be: both d'Elbœuf girls ended up as nuns, and James married another young girl, the fifteen-year-old French Catholic Mary of Modena (whom he chose in preference to her thirty-year-old aunt, whose hand he was also offered). As might have been expected, England was not happy at this marriage with 'a daughter of the

Pope', and the King was so disturbed by public unrest that he consulted an astrologer[18] on the best way to deal with the House of Commons. Louise tactfully put away the portraits of the d'Elbœufs, and sent Louis a message congratulating him on arranging the marriage with Mary.

The British public greeted the news of Louise's ennoblement as Duchess of Portsmouth about as enthusiastically as they celebrated James's marriage. Another Catholic had been honoured. Moreover, her new title seemed to mean nothing to the people around her, many of whom were as virulent against her as the general public. She found one morning, pinned to her door, the couplet:

> Within this place a bed's appointed
> For a French bitch and God's anointed

and the anonymous balladeers had a field day:

> Who can on this picture look
> And not straight be wonder-struck
> That such a speaking dowdy thing
> Should make a beggar of a King?
> Three happy nations turn to tears
> And all their former love to fears.
> Ruin the great, and raise the small,
> Yet will by turns betray them all.
> Lowly born and meanly bred
> Yet of this nation is the head,
> For half Whitehall make her their court
> Tho' th'other half make her their sport . . .
> False and foolish, proud and bold,
> Ugly, as you see, and old,
> In a word, Her mighty Grace
> Is whore in all things but her face.[19]

It is difficult to find, anywhere, a pleasant reference to Louise: no one – except of course the King – had time for her; and the fact that she had been added to the monarch's stable of mistresses led to some of the most virulent anonymous attacks on him. By no means all of them were anonymous, though it has never been conclusively settled whether Rochester or Marvell wrote the most venomous of them, attacking not only Louise but Charles himself, virtually accusing him of being a dirty (and almost impotent) old man:

> Restless, he rolls about from whore to whore,
> A merry monarch, scandalous and poor.
> To Carwell the most dear of all thy dears
> The sure relief of thy declining years;
> Oft he bewails his fortune and her fate,
> To love so well, and to be lov'd so late;
> For when in her he fettles well his tarse[19]
> Yet his dull graceless buttocks hang an arse.
> This you'd believe, had I but time to tell ye,
> The pain it costs to poor labourious Nelly,
> While she employs hands, fingers, lips and thighs
> E'er she can raise the member she enjoys.[20]

If the men and women about the Court did not use quite such forthright language, at least in public, they were for the most part no fonder of Louise. James disliked her intensely; Lady Sunderland, who had been a fellow guest at Euston, gave it as her opinion that for 500 guineas Louise would sell anyone; the 7th Earl of Pembroke (who was her son-in-law, having married her younger sister, Henriette) suggested that she should be hung upside down at a street corner, her skirts raised to show the source of her power.

She could protest as much as she liked, but the general malignancy was unshakeable – and indeed unanswerable, for as Nell Gwyn asked, if she was so respectable, why was she a whore? Even her allies had turned against her, disliking her continual assertions that she knew best about everything. De Croissy wrote to Louis: 'I own I find her on all occasions so ill-disposed for the service of the King, and showing such ill-humour against France (whether because she feels herself despised there, or whether she is merely capricious) that I really think she deserves no favour of His Majesty.' This in answer to her request – transmitted via King Charles – that King Louis should grant Louise the French estate of Aubigny. After considerable hesitation, Louis agreed, but granted Aubigny to the Duchess of Portsmouth only with reversion to any child of King Charles whom he might appoint to succeed her. She did not, therefore, become a French Duchess – and she badly wanted a French title to add to her English one (much inferior, as she thought).

Her *annus horribilis* was not over, for at the end of that same year – 1673 – the Comte de Ruvigny, appointed Ambassador in succession to de Croissy, wrote to Arnauld de Pomponne, the French Foreign Minister: 'While the King [Louis] wins new provinces, the King of England has won the pox, which he has conscientiously passed on to the Duchess of Portsmouth. She has been consoled for this troublesome present by one which is very much more to her tastes. She has had a pearl necklace worth four thousand pounds and a diamond worth six thousand, with which she is so pleased that I doubt not that at the same price she would not object to another attack.'[21]

However Louise got the pox – and it was probably not from Charles, who made her a present merely to cheer her up – Nell did not go into mourning at the news: it would be pleasant to have the field to herself. She delightedly took full possession of it through her talent for mimicry; she had Louise's languid look to a T. One day, just before Louise went off to Tunbridge Wells for the cure, they met at Whitehall. Nell was, on this occasion, rather splendidly dressed, and Louise made the mistake of congratulating her on growing rich: she was fine enough to be a queen. 'You are right, madam,' said Nell, 'and I am whore enough to be a duchess.'

Louise left London accompanied by Dr Frazier, who specialised in venereal disease. Arriving at Tunbridge Wells, she discovered that the house she had rented was occupied by a dowager who declined to give way to her – Lady Worcester remarked that Louise might outrank her, but titles which were the result of prostitution were not recognised in polite society. Louise had to turn away and take refuge at Windsor. It had been a decidedly difficult year.

CHAPTER SEVEN

Pleasant Days and Easy Nights

I give you freely all delights
With pleasant days and easy nights.

Anon., from 'Venus and Adonis'

Louise recovered from the pox with reasonable speed. 'The French disease' or 'the great pox' had been a scourge in England for a century. It had been given the former name because it was believed to have originated in France; in fact it very possibly came to Europe from Haiti, brought by Columbus's crew. It had certainly been known in Italy as early as 1530, when the physician, poet, astronomer and geologist Hieronymus Fracastorius named it *syphilis* in a poem, *Syphilis sive morbus Gallicus,* in which he described its symptoms in graphic rhyming couplets. The mercury cure for the disease had first been suggested by the German alchemist and physician Paracelsus in the 1520s, and consisted of the application of mercury ointments and pills, and the administration of mercury enemas. The idea was to expel corrupt matter from the body, so the cure included intense heat treatment from hot stoves or in hot baths. The application of the mercury (often in very high doses) was extremely painful, and it was often said with some accuracy that the treatment was worse than the disease. The advice of astrologers was less painful, and based on the proposition that the pox was caused not by sexual contact but by the presence of the planet Saturn in the sign Aries, which affected the whole of mankind.

It is an open case whether Charles II ever suffered from syphilis. Reason would suggest that he must have; the number of his sexual partners and the fact that at least two of them are known to have had the disease at some time makes it probable. Few men escaped, for few took any precautions. (Indeed, few knew that such precautions were necessary.) There is some slim anecdotal evidence – not only the suggestion that he had given Louise venereal disease, but the allegation made many years after his death – that Nell Gwyn died from syphilis, given to her by the King. But no doubt Chiffinch would have been as careful as possible to ensure that the girls he provided for the King were clean, and there is no evidence in the household accounts of the purchase of mercury necessary for treatment.[1] So the best guess is that Charles was extremely lucky.

The treatment, if unpleasant, was efficacious; by the summer of 1675 Louise was once more regularly seen about the Court. The King, perhaps because he felt sorry for her trial, now created her son Duke of Richmond – though her pleasure was somewhat lessened by the fact that Barbara's second son, Henry Fitzroy, already Earl of Euston, was at the same time to become Duke of Grafton, which meant that Barbara might with some justice demand that he should take preference over Louise's boy, unless, of course, the former's son was created Richmond before Fitzroy became Grafton (since precedence depended on the date of creation). Barbara made considerable efforts to achieve this desirable result. Hearing that Charles's Lord Treasurer and Chief Minister, the Earl of Danby – who must seal the patents – was about to leave London to take the waters at Bath, she instructed her lawyer to go to his house at dawn with young Fitzroy's patent. Louise, however, heard that Danby had changed his mind and was going to leave London at midnight – several hours earlier. Her lawyer handed her son's patent to Danby as he was getting into his coach, and the result was that the Duke of Richmond took precedence over the Duke of Grafton, to his mother's fury.

Nell was not particularly pleased to hear the news of her rivals' sons' enoblement. She was singularly lacking in ambition for herself, but she did not see why Louise's and Barbara's bastards should have titles while her own children remained commoners. There are a number of good stories about the methods she allegedly adopted to remedy the situation, perhaps the best of which was first told by an early historian:[2] the King appeared one day at her house in Pall Mall, and Nell, greeting him, hollered down the hall 'Come here, you little bastard, and say hello to your father!'

Charles swept the little boy up into his arms, and rebuked Nell for insulting the child.

'Why, Sire, Your Majesty has given me no other name to call him by,' she replied, boldly. Later that year – 1676 – the boy was made Baron Headington and Earl of Burford, and eight years later Duke of St Albans.

In another story, Nell is alleged to have held the child out of a first-floor window by the heels and threatened to drop him unless he was given a title; the King, thinking fast, cried 'God save the Earl of Burford!' – probably the first place that came into his mind, though it is interesting that in 1694 the boy was to marry Diana de Vere, daughter of the Earl of Oxford, whose ancestral home was not far from Burford.

All this bandying about of titles irritated some people and amused others. The poet Andrew Marvell was one of the former:

> The Misses take place, and advanc'd to be Duchess
> With pomp great as queens in their coach and six horses:
> Their bastards made Dukes, Earls, Viscounts and Lords.
> And all the high titles that honour affords.

Many people were outraged at the amount of money the King was spending on his mistresses – though the fact is that no one can have known with certainty just how much. The three of them, Barbara, Louise and Nell (and we cannot assess the amount of money spent on, as it were, casual labour), now each had pensions of £10,000 a year settled on them. But this did not mean, of course, and overwhelmingly in the case of the two former, that that represented their total income. Barbara received present after present and £3,000 a year for each of her sons. The extent of her gambling and the expense of her household suggests very considerable wealth indeed; Louise had been granted wine licences that brought her in £10,000 a year, and is said to have received in one year the astonishing sum of £136,668.

Nell came third as far as the accumulation of wealth was concerned. She did not enjoy one-tenth the income of either Louise or Barbara, but the evidence is that she also did extremely well out of the King (which meant, of course, the country). According to the account of her silversmith, John Coques, she spent £1,700 on furnishing her bedroom alone. He charged £1,135 3s 1d for ornamenting her silver bedstead with eagles and crowns and cupids, and a representation of Barbara Cleveland's lover, the acrobat Jacob Hall, dancing on a silver rope.[3] The walls of one of the rooms – perhaps the bedroom? – were entirely lined with mirrors. She clearly enjoyed silver for itself as well as for its value: she had excellent silver plate (some of it was once stolen, and she offered a reward in the columns of the *London Gazette* for its return), and even the andirons in her fireplace were of silver. Silver bibelots stood about the house – sugar boxes, pepper and mustard pots, silver bottles, a gold hourglass. She had nothing against expensive jewellery, and once paid £4,000 for a pearl necklace which had belonged to the actress Peg Hughes, sometime Prince Rupert's mistress. She also commissioned a fine sedan chair, which cost £34 11s: 600 gilt and 600 'coloured and burnished' nails were used inside, while another 3,400 gilded nails must have almost covered the exterior, leaving room, however, for five gilt sprigs decorating the roof, a 'rich gilt hasp' for the door, and a glass window costing £2.

Evidently she did not take her own chair everywhere, for an account with a chairman called William Calow shows him carrying her 'to Mrs Knight's and to Mrs Cassell's[4] and to Mrs Churchill's for 4s, on another occasion charging 7s 6d for waiting outside a house for seven hours, and again for 'carrying one Lady Sanes to ye play at Whitehall, and waiting' – 2s 6d. (Nell regularly took a side box at the Duke's Theatre and shared them with friends.)

A number of other bills and accounts have survived, some for such ordinary expenses as cleaning a warming-pan or buying ale, oats, beans and oranges, and some for rather more luxurious goods such as 'a French coach', huge mirrors, white satin petticoats, scarlet satin shoes covered with silver lace, white and red satin nightgowns, and 'a fine lanskip fan' – presumably a fan with a landscape painted on it.

She kept a large household – eight servants, a steward and a secretary (the more necessary since she was unable to write). This was not inexpensive: maids could be had for between £3 and £5 a year;

footboys earned rather less, but a first footman took £10. A coachman could earn £8, and a housekeeper, good chambermaids and waiting-women, about the same. A good cook would certainly cost £10 or more a year. All these servants would also have their keep. Nell's mother lived with her, too, and though she rented a house for her sister, where she and the King occasionally met when he wished to vanish temporarily from the eyes even of Chiffinch and his like, Rose was often with her. She lived extremely well, spending a great deal on food and drink. (Her mother's consumption of spirits, alone, cost her a considerable sum; Mrs Gwyn was a notorious drunkard, though the accounts of an apothecary also record the purchase of julep, plasters, glysters and cordials for 'old Mrs Glyn'.)[5]

Apart from her annual allowance from Charles, she received for a time £10,000 a year or more from the Secret Service fund. The *Calendar of Treasury Books* shows a payment of £1,000 in March 1675, and £500 on a number of occasions, 'which is not to be accounted any part of her allowance'. Charles slipped her at least £2,500 between December 1674 and April 1675 as 'bounty'.

Nell continued to reign as the most popular of the three mistresses. The ordinary people of London never lost the affection and admiration they had felt for her as a popular actress. After her retirement from the stage, she continued to go to the theatre as a spectator, and was enthusiastically welcomed by the house. In 1674 and '75, for instance, she went to see *Macbeth, Hamlet, King Lear* and *The Tempest* – the latter no fewer than four times. Killigrew had put her on the free list at the Drury Lane Theatre, and the Treasury paid for her box at Davenant's theatre.[6]

She was not particularly interested in scoring points off her rivals, though she unhesitatingly put them down when they appeared to her to be a touch too pretentious. When the Duchess of Cleveland drove about town with 'a coach and six horses', she acquired a large wagon and six oxen, donned a blowsy dress, and drove past the Duchess's house cracking a whip and shouting 'Whores to market!' As we repeatedly hear, she did not find the term especially pejorative. A story goes that her coachman got into a fight one day because – as explained to Nell – he had heard her described as a whore. She simply laughed and said that, after all, it was an accurate description. (The coachman, however, was having none of it: 'You may be called a whore,' he said, 'but I will not be called a whore's coachman.') Both senior mistresses from time to time protested at her squibs, but Charles found her far too amusing to take offence on their behalf. He and James still regularly visited Nell at her house in Pall Mall, where her supper parties were famously entertaining, with music and gambling and gossip going on until the early hours. She kept a generous table, too – goose and duck, hare and partridge, chicken and rabbit – and as the King mounted the stairs she made sure that his favourite pigeon pie was ready for him. (He sometimes ate a dish of it in bed.)

All her old friends gathered around her – Rochester, Buckhurst and the rest of the Wits. She kept them in order, once slapping Buckingham's face soundly after (according to the French Ambassador) he had tried to fumble her. Some of Buckingham's escapades were beyond her intervention, as when he, Etherege and another reprobate got into trouble in Epsom: 'They were tossing some fiddlers in a blanket for refusing to play, and a barber, upon the noise, going to see what the matter [was], they seized upon him, and, to free himself from them he offered to carry them to the handsomest woman in Epsom, and directed them to the Constable's house, who demanding what they came for, they told him a whore, and he refusing to let them in, they broke open his doors and broke his head and beat him very severely.'[7]

The amount of gambling which went on was very considerable. This was strictly speaking illegal. In 1664 gaming had been prohibited, to put an end to 'the debauch of many of the younger sort, both of the Nobility and Gentry . . . to the loss of their precious time and the utter ruin of their Estates and Fortunes'.[8] But who cared about that? All three mistresses loved cards – cribbage, gleek, and basset in particular, the latter a variant of faro, which had come to England from Venice. When French guests were present, they played faro itself, or *trente-et-quarante*. Nell is said to have lost £1,400 at one session of play with Hortense Mancini (see p. 127); Barbara lost almost £10,000 one evening, and in gold, of course, for no banknotes yet existed. Hortense was said to be specially good at faro, and on one evening she was rumoured to have won £8,000 from Louise and £5,000 from Nell. The sums are outrageous, but even ordinary people, if they had any money at all, gambled it with remarkable freedom. Working men would bet £3 or £4 at an afternoon's cockfighting. The King did not share this taste, and seems to have looked on somewhat bemused at his mistresses' profligacy; he could not understand a passion for gambling, and never himself staked more than £5, though he occasionally covered his mistresses' losses.

If gambling was a major part of the evening's pleasure when one or other of the royal ladies held a party, there was also wine and song. The King loved music, and nurtured his own string band; he also enjoyed songs to the guitar. Nell's familiarity with the King was greater than he allowed with anyone else – not only because he so much enjoyed her refusal to give herself airs, but because she treated him as a close friend, never hesitating to say the first thing that came into her head. Colley Cibber describes how she had commissioned a group of singers to entertain the King and his brother, and His Majesty warmly applauded them.

'Then, Sir,' said Nell, 'to show that you do not speak like a courtier, I hope you will make the performers a handsome present.'
The King, after feeling in his pockets, said he had no money, and asked the Duke if he had any.
'I believe, Sir, not above a guinea or two.'
'Odds fish!' cried she, making bold with His Majesty's favourite oath, 'what company am I got into!'[9]

On another occasion, when the King was complaining (as he often did) of being short of money, she suggested that he should bribe the House of Commons with a feast of French *ragoût*, Scotch collops and a calf's head – meaning that he should get rid of the Duchess of Portsmouth, the Earl of Lauderdale and the Countess of Sunderland (the latter two irritating thorns in the King's side). Her barbs usually struck home, and she was afraid of nothing. When the King asked her, as a personal favour, to invite the Countess of Shrewsbury to the birthday party she was giving in his honour, she firmly declined with the words 'One whore at a time is enough for you, Sir.'

Sometimes she played practical jokes, but her humour was so much in Charles's own line that he never took offence. Famously, she once (so the Venetian Ambassador said) went fishing with the King at Hampton Court, and took the precaution of carrying with her a basket of fried fish and attaching them to his line. It has been suggested that he was so pleased by the joke that he rewarded her by commissioning the famous Lely portrait of her with the pet lamb. Her talent to amuse gave her considerable influence, and it is perhaps fortunate that she took no interest in politics, and thus never really antagonised any of the King's ministers. There are only one or two cases in which she seems to have tried to use her influence. While she was generally popular, and applauded when she appeared in public, she became aware that the cliques who met in the coffee houses of the city were on the whole antagonistic to her. Her old friend and mentor Dryden told her that the problem lay with the Green Ribbon Clubs, instigated by the Earl of Shaftesbury, who disapproved in principle of all the King's mistresses. She persuaded the King – it really does seem that she was personally responsible – to issue a Proclamation (at Christmas 1675) for the Suppression of Coffee Houses on the grounds that 'many tradesmen and others do therein misspend much of their time, which might and probably would otherwise be employed in and about their lawful callings and affairs' and moreover that it was in the coffee houses that 'divers false, malicious and scandalous reports are devised and spread abroad to the defamation of His Majesty's Government, and to the disturbance of the peace and quiet of the realm'.[10]

It was never going to succeed; the coffee houses were too popular – and after all, as an anonymous scribbler suggested,

Coffee-houses shall stay free
You get no pox from D'Arcy's tea.[11]

Nell could well have afforded to ignore the petulant political cliques who met in the coffee houses. She could not afford – any more than Barbara or Louise could – to ignore another phenomenon that now appeared on the scene: and phenomenon is the word to describe Hortense Mancini, Duchess of Mazarin.

On 4 January 1676, the then French Ambassador in London, the Comte de Ruvigny, wrote to the French Foreign Minister, Arnauld de Pomponne, informing him that the Duchesse de Mazarin had arrived in London dressed *en habit de cavalier*. She brought with her five male and two female servants, and Mustapha, a small black boy who took all his meals with her, and whose sole duty was to prepare her coffee.

Hortense Mancini, Duchesse de Mazarin, the Italian niece of the late Cardinal Mazarin, who in 1642 had succeeded Richelieu as chief minister of France, was one of the great and notorious beauties of Europe. When she was fifteen, in 1660, the Cardinal had attempted to marry her either to King Pedro II of Portugal or King Charles of England; but for various reasons neither was interested, despite the fact that it was taken for granted that the Cardinal would leave his niece his enormous fortune, a supposition that might have been expected to commend her especially to the impecunious Charles.

Just before his death the following year the Cardinal saw Hortense married to Armand Charles de la Porte, Marquis de la Meilleraie, who at the Cardinal's request King Louis made Duc de Mazarin. The Duc, who had a naturally religious and puritan streak, was unprepared for so beautiful and naturally flirtatious a wife, and within a very short time became virtually mad with jealousy. Other men might have delighted in her expressive sensuality; he regarded it as a sinful manifestation of irreligious lust, and it so distressed him that he attempted to remove all signs of sexuality from the Palais-Mazarin, taking a hammer to the genitalia of nude male statues and daubing with paint those pictures of women that he found too revealing. He also issued strict orders that no women should be permitted to milk the cows on his estates, the action being far too suggestive. Seeing the prettiness of his daughters, he toyed with the idea of having all their teeth extracted, lest they should be a temptation to men. Fortunately, he was persuaded to reject the idea.

His notion of religion was quite as curious as his notion of sexuality. When fire broke out in one of his houses he let it burn on the grounds that his servants should not obstruct the will of the Almighty; and to give the Creator's will unobstructed rein he would cast lots each morning to determine what rôle each servant should play – so that yesterday's chef would be today's bedmaker, and the groom of last week, this week's valet. His guests occasionally found this disconcerting.

At last the Duc's jealousy became insupportable: if he saw Hortense speaking to a servant, the man was immediately dismissed; if a male visitor called at the house more than twice, he was permanently refused entry; her favourite maids were dismissed lest they should be helping her to plan intrigues. Even his relatives became strangers, because they showed signs of sympathising with Hortense in what was quickly becoming an extremely disagreeable marriage.[12]

Eventually, Hortense brought an action against the Duc before the Cour des Enquêtes of the Parliament of Paris, planning to remove herself for the time to the Abbey of Chelles, a pleasantly liberal nunnery. Her husband instead dispatched her to the extremely strict Convent des Filles de Sainte-Marie, near the Bastille. There, she seems to have made the nuns' lives a misery by a number of practical jokes, including putting ink in the holy water stoups, running through the corridors with her dogs yelling hunting cries, and pouring water through the floorboards of her room so that it fell onto the beds of the nuns in the room below. They petitioned the King to remove the Duchess forthwith, and she was sent to Celles – whence her husband followed with a troop of cavalry, attempting to kidnap her. He failed, and the Cour des Enquêtes sympathetically ordered that she should continue to live at the Palais-Mazarin while the Duc moved to the Arsenal – his official residence as Grand Master of the Artillery.

Hortense feared, however, that she would be kidnapped and very possibly killed. In June 1668 she persuaded the Chevalier de Rohan to pose as her lover, and with the help of her brother, the Duc de Nevers, disguised herself as a man and fled from Paris on horseback for the Court of Charles IV of Lorraine. He gave her a troop of horse to escort her to Geneva. Thence she went on to her sister Marie's home in Milan. (Charles, when he heard, remarked to the Queen, 'I see wives do not love devout husbands!')[13]

At Milan it soon became clear that while Rohan had only pretended to be her lover, his equerry, one Couberville, actually filled that position. Her sister's husband, the Constable Colonna, distressed by Hortense's lack of taste, had Couberville arrested and imprisoned and forced her to accompany his family first to Sienna and then to Rome. There she, infuriated by their interference in her romantic life, left them and took refuge with an aunt, the Mother Superior of the Convent of Campo-Marzo, thus trumping the efforts of her husband, who was petitioning the Pope to have her sent to another, no doubt less agreeable, convent.

But there was no rest for the wicked – for that was how the Mother Superior regarded Hortense on discovering that she was pregnant by her imprisoned lover. Hortense was dismissed from the convent and settled into the Palazzo Mancini, which Mazarin had left to her brother. There, completely unabashed by her situation, she began to lead an adventurous social life in Rome, making no attempt to conceal her pregnancy, nor indeed allowing it to interfere with her general enjoyment of life. She succeeded despite her condition in provoking a duel between two admirers.

In the autumn, short of money, she prepared to return to Paris, but hearing that her husband was preparing to kidnap her *en route*, she turned about and went back to Rome. There she found Marie highly discontented with her husband, and the sisters decided to abscond. After an adventurous escape from Italy, they made their way to Marseilles and planned to go on to Paris, but again the Duc's men were on their trail, and they split up, Hortense making for Savoy, where the Duke Charles Emmanuel II set her up in a castle and supported her in great style. She repaid him generously, and in a manner that quickly became notorious.

Alas, in the summer of 1675 the Duke died, and his widow suggested that Hortense might move on. We do not know quite why she decided to try her luck at the Court of Charles II, but at all events she immediately left Savoy – dressed once more (it was increasingly her wont) in men's clothing, plumed hat and peruke. Accompanied by twenty servants, she rode to Amsterdam, embarked for England, and having landed at Torbay set out for London and St James's Palace, where she had been promised a set of rooms by her cousin, the Duchess of York, formerly Mary Beatrice of Modena.

A former British Ambassador to France, Ralph Montagu, an ambitious middle-aged man married to the wealthy Countess of Northumberland but living with a mistress, hoped to use Hortense to forward his political ambitions. The Duchess of Portsmouth, he told her, was plump and poxed, and the position of *maîtresse en titre* was open to bidders. The Comte de Ruvigny reported to King Louis that he considered Hortense – though she was thirty years old – by far the most beautiful woman in England: already every man spoke of her with admiration, every woman with jealousy. It was assumed, not improbably, that she would set her cap at the King, and that he would be unable to resist her. All eyes were upon Louise and Nell. (Barbara had immediately retired to Paris, where she usurped the position of a Madame de Bretonvilliers and settled down as mistress of the Archbishop of Paris.)

Edmund Waller announced the coming fight between Hortense and Louise:

> When through the world fair Mazarin had run,
> Bright as her fellow-traveller, the Sun,
> Hither at length the Roman eagle flies,
> As the last triumph of her conquering eyes.
> As heir to Julius, she may pretend
> A second time to make this nation bend;
> But Portsmouth, springing from the ancient race
> Of Britons, which the Saxon here did chase,
> As the great Caesar did oppose, makes head,
> And does against this new invader lead . . .
> Dressed to advantage, this illustrious pair
> Arrived, for combat in the list appear.
> What may the fates design! – for never yet
> From distant regions two such beauties met.[14]

Nell went into ironical mourning, anticipating the death of Louise's relationship with the King. Indeed, the Duchess was once more not having a good year. Ruvigny observed that she looked pale and ill, and though this may in the first instance have been the result of a miscarriage, she became increasingly agitated at what she perceived to be a change in the King's attitude to her. When, as usual in autumn, she went with the Court to Newmarket, instead of finding that Charles had provided a house for her, she had to rent one – and the only accommodation available was outside the town, which made it difficult for her to see him as regularly as she would have liked.

Louise was also short of money. (A steward had defrauded her of a large sum.) But then, so was Hortense, who had not yet become Charles's mistress, and so felt unable to ask him for any help other than to support her appeal to King Louis for an increase in the annual pension of 24,000 livres she was receiving from her husband. Charles wrote to Louis suggesting that he should instruct the Duc de Mazarin to increase his wife's income by 34,000 livres. Louis, however, owed Mazarin a considerable sum himself, and found it impossible to comply.

Charles was now well acquainted with Hortense – partly because he visited the Duchess of York regularly during her confinement, and almost always found her friend at her bedside. Ruvigny was soon reporting to Louis that Hortense had a secret understanding with the English King. Something of a puritan at heart, the Ambassador found the idea of conspiring to assist Hortense into the King's bed extremely embarrassing, and Louis, inferring this from his reports, replaced him as Ambassador with Honoré de Courtin, an extremely agreeable and sophisticated man. Although he carried with him a letter from the Duc de Mazarin inviting Hortense to return to France, where a protracted visit to the Abbey of Montmartre would be good for her soul, de Courtin saw quite clearly that there would be a far greater advantage to be obtained from Hortense's promotion to Charles's bed than from her return to her husband; he played his cards accordingly. He wrote to Louis advising him strongly to persuade Hortense's husband to increase her allowance and permit her to remain in England; at the moment, he said, she felt that the

French King was unsympathetic to her, 'so that it is to be feared that if she obtains any influence here, she will not employ it as your Majesty might desire'.[15]

Courtin's eagerness for Louis to support Hortense was not based on any particular enthusiasm for the lady; he simply wanted the Italian woman to be sympathetic to France and her King. He knew how unpopular Louise was, and he also knew that the Earl of Danby was anxious to diminish French influence in Europe. The replacement of a Frenchwoman by an Italian in the King's bed would be a potent symbol of France's diminished interest, but at least Louis should make an attempt to ingratiate himself with her.

Just as Nell had not been particularly worried at the advent of Louise, she greeted the arrival of Hortense only with mild interest. The Italian might be a beauty, but after all she had put herself about (her reputation as a beauty was only equalled by her reputation for promiscuity), so she had no advantage over Nell where respectability was concerned and she was five years older. The King was still seeing Nell regularly, was still giving her presents in addition to her pension, and had promised to pay proper attention to her children – as indeed he did, making young Charles (now Baron Heddington and Earl of Burford) an allowance of £1,000 a year. Moreover, her parties were a great deal better and more eagerly attended than the ones Hortense had begun to give at her new house in St James's Park.

It was Louise who suffered. She simply did not know what to do, as it became clear that after only four months Charles was becoming more and more attached to Hortense. He had been seen standing in the park at night, gazing wistfully up at the Italian's bedroom window. Eventually, in a temper, Louise left London at the end of May 1676 for Bath, to take the waters. Charles (he did, after all, have a conscience) visited her once or twice, but when he got back to town he usually dined with Nell, then returned to Westminster, changed for bed, waited until his servants had retired, dressed again and went on to Hortense's, where he frequently stayed until dawn. It is reasonable to suppose that not all the time was spent discussing Anglo-French relations.

Returning to London, Louise was heartened by the fact that Charles took the trouble to go to meet her, and decided to throw the party of the century, ostensibly to honour the French Ambassador. She spent over £3,000 on food and drink. Louis XIV's personal chamber orchestra played for her guests – the first number she requested was 'Mate me con mirar, mas no me mate con zelos' ('Make me die of grief, but not of jealousy'). The King attended the party, but when the Ambassador called on her the following day he found Louise profoundly depressed; she had realised that though her party had been a wonderful evening for the guests, it had done nothing to persuade anyone that Hortense was not the coming woman or that her own reign was not substantially over. Nell had told everyone that she was going to arm herself from head to foot in order to repel a rival infuriated by the attentions the King had been paying her, but Louise was too distressed and irritated to bother about anyone but Hortense. (She was further upset by the fact that she had contrived to fall and injure an eye – whereat Nell put it about that she was trying to give herself black eyes like Hortense's.)

One useful coup of Hortense's was a contrived friendship with the fifteen-year-old Anne, Countess of Sussex, Barbara's elder daughter by the King who, married and pregnant, was probably a little frightened and in need both of reassurance and entertainment. She soon insisted on seeing her Italian 'aunt' every day. The girl's apartments were right above the King's at Whitehall. They had been occupied by her mother, and a private staircase connected the two sets of rooms. The King, mounting the stairs to see his daughter, frequently found Hortense with her. By the end of July, Courtin was drily telling Louis that:

> the King goes nearly every day to visit Madame de Sussex, whom Madame de Mazarin is nursing. I happened to be there the day before yesterday when he came. As soon as he came in Madame Mazarin went and whispered to him with a great air of familiarity, and she kept it up all the time the conversation was general, and never called him 'your Majesty' once. At the end of a quarter of an hour His Britannic Majesty sat on the end of the bed, and as I was alone I thought it proper to retire. But I remain convinced that it is not without foundation that the most enlightened

courtiers believe that the King their master desires to profit by his opportunities.[16]

Soon, no one was in doubt that Charles was indeed profiting by his opportunities. Nor could he be blamed, at least on the grounds of taste: Hortense, with her indeterminately coloured but handsome eyes and her splendid raven hair, was worthy of the most discriminating bed. She was also 'different' – not least in what appears to have been a taste for both sexes: Saint Evremond, the French moralist and political refugee, remarked in a poem drily welcoming her to England that 'each sex provides its lovers for Hortense'. Apart from sexual innuendo, with his love of dogs Charles probably enjoyed the company of Boy, Little Rogue and Chop – maybe they were themselves on friendly terms with the King's dogs, the white bitch Fymm and the black lurcher Gypsy. Charles must also have been on nodding acquaintance with Jacob (Hortense's starling), Pretty (her parrot), her canary and white sparrow. Hortense enjoyed food as much as the King did, and enjoyed riding, hunting and swimming too, though it appears that this last was exercise as much for Mustapha as for Hortense – he was required to enter the water with her and support her as she attempted the breaststroke.

Now, it was being said that the only time Hortense was not at the King's side was when he was taking his bath. In the interest of keeping her an enthusiastic friend of France, Courtin was soon beseeching Louis to help her out of her financial difficulties on the grounds that she was now installed as Charles's favourite, and indebtedness to France would be no bad thing. However, the Ambassador seems to have found the whole situation somewhat confusing. Though the King had become Hortense's enthusiastic lover, she certainly had not replaced all other women in his favour. Though he saw her often, he seemed to pass more nights with Nell than with her, and while his attitude to Louise was now rather that of a husband than a devoted lover, he had certainly not dismissed her, and used his trick of appearing to retire to bed and then rising to make his way to the Italian's rooms as a means of keeping Louise happy, or at least of not insulting her too obviously.

The situation was complicated when the King's son-in-law, the Earl of Sussex, took against Hortense and demanded that his wife see less of her. Perhaps he suspected them of a more passionate friendship than was the case. Both Barbara and Louise naturally encouraged his view of the disreputable Italian, and when Hortense and Anne caused a scandal by going down into St James's Park in their dressing-gowns and demonstrating their skill in fencing (a pastime they had taken up) the Earl, naturally hot-tempered, took his wife off to Hurstmonceaux Castle, leaving Charles without his former convenient excuse for regular meetings with Hortense.

Nell was perfectly sanguine about the Hortense affair, but as ever found it difficult to curb her sense of mischief, and on one occasion Courtin was regaled, after Louise had paid her respects and left, by a description of the three mistresses' taste in underclothing – Louise's was always grubby, Hortense wore none at all, while she . . . Nell lifted her petticoats, one after the other, showing each to be neat and whiter than white. No doubt Courtin enjoyed the display, but it was not particularly lascivious: petticoats were meant to be seen, and were often very elaborately embroidered, sometimes with gold or silver thread. The interesting thing is, perhaps, the fact that Nell was proud of the scrupulous cleanliness of her underwear – a reaction, very possibly, to the poverty of her youth. Cleanliness was costly.

Though Courtin supposed that in all England it would be impossible to get together in one room three women who were more obnoxious to one another, it was soon clear that Charles's mistresses had decided toleration was the only possible resolution of an untidy and rather tiring situation. They were seen together at the opera, descending the main staircase hand in hand, and in January 1677 all met to exchange New Year's gifts – Nell distributed chocolates which, having heard the story of Mall Davis and the doctored sweets, the others probably tasted with care.

Nell had no difficulty in being friendly with the other two (if she could never resist the occasional jibe); Hortense, in triumph, could afford to be generous; it was Louise whose nose was most out of joint, and it must indeed have required a major effort to tolerate Hortense's extravagant display of newly acquired riches – footmen who wore so much lace that it obscured their coats, extravagant clothes, entertainment on a grand scale.

Hortense now settled down happily as one of His Majesty's regular bedfellows, and was given a markedly prominent position on some social occasions: at the opening of Parliament in February 1677, for instance, she was 'in a very prominent position raised above all the other ladies'. She put herself about a little – and the King winked at this; he understood enough about women's sexuality by now to know that expecting an enthusiast such as she to restrict herself to intermittent nights with him was perfectly unreasonable. As a result, her rather adventurous life in Chelsea was unrestricted – though he did put a stop to a spirited affair with the Prince of Monaco when it became so notorious that he feared he was being regarded as a cuckold. He simply declined to pay her allowance (of £4,000 a year) until she gave the prince his *congé*.

A great many people, including Louise, were pleased to hear of Hortense's temporary dismissal. From the beginning they had been at one with Andrew Marvell in wondering:

> That the King should send for another French whore
> When one already hath made him so poor . . .

and shared the opinion of the balladmongers on Hortense's character:

> Thy well-known merits claim that thou shouldst be
> First in the glorious roll of infamy.
> To thee they all give place, and homage pay,
> Do all thy lecherous decrees obey;
> Thou Queen of Lust, the bawdy subjects they . . .
> For what proud strumpet e'er could merit more
> Than to be anointed the Imperial Whore? . . .
> Thou sea of lust, that never ebb does know,
> Whither the rivers of all nations flow.
> Lewd Messaline was but a type of thee,
> Thou highest, last degree of lechery.

For in all ages, except her and you,
Who ever sinned so high, and stooped so low? . . .
Nor does old age, which now rides on so fast,
Make thee come short of all thy lewdness past;
Tho on thy head grey hairs, like Etna's snow,
Are shed, thou'rt fire and brimstone all below . . .[17]

Hortense's hair was far from grey; but one must allow for hyperbole – after all, equal vituperation was being poured on Louise:

Who can on this picture look
And not straight be wonder-struck
That such a speaking dowdy thing
Should make a beggar of a King?
Three happy nations turn to tears
And all their former love to fears.
Ruin the great, and raise and small,
Yet will by turns betray them all.
Lowly born and meanly bred
Yet of this nation is the head,
For half Whitehall make her their court
Tho' th'other half make her their sport . . .
False and foolish, proud and bold,
Ugly, as you see, and old,
In a word, Her mighty Grace
Is whore in all things but her face.[18]

Another scribbler portrayed Louise rising from bed to consult her glass in order

To varnish and rub o'er those graces
You rub'd off in your night embraces,
To set your hair, your eyes, your teeth
And all those powers you conquer with –
Lay trains of love, and State intrigues
In ponders, trimmings and curl'd wigs

until Charles

> Knows not what to do
> But loll and fumble here with you.
> Amongst your ladies, and his chits,
> At cards and Councils here he sits.
> Yet minds not how they play at either,
> Nor cares not when 'tis walking weather.
> Business and power he has resigned
> And all things to your mighty mind . . .[19]

All this was in strong contrast to the general attitude to Nell, whose personality remained as delightful as ever. As late as 1680, when she went to the play at the Duke's Theatre and a drunk shouted a coarse remark, the entire audience rose to her defence, and 24-year-old Thomas Herbert, three years later to become the 8th Earl of Pembroke, drew his sword and threatened to kill the offender.

For most of 1677 only Charles and Nell seem to have been completely tranquil. If Louise was happy because, for the time at least, Hortense seemed to be out of the way, and if the latter was somewhat disconsolate (partly, perhaps, because alone among the King's chief mistresses, she had not given him a child), Nell was perfectly at ease in the knowledge that Charles was still most at his ease with her. ('I hope I shall have your company at night, shall I?' she once called out to him in public, at Newmarket; and usually, she did.) And the King himself? He had Nell; he regarded Louise more or less as a wife; he had the company of the Queen, who he adored and who adored him; and Hortense would no doubt come at his call should he require a little additional entertainment. As usual, in his private life, he enjoyed the best of all possible worlds.

CHAPTER EIGHT

Friends and Acquaintances

You never appear but you gladden the hearts of all that have the
happy fortune to see you, as if you were made on purpose to
put the whole world in good humour.

Aphra Behn

The Duke of Buckingham, who since they first met had remained
Nell's close acquaintance – 'friend' is not perhaps quite the word –
was in the news in the spring of 1677. For ten years he had been to
the fore in politics, and after Clarendon's fall from grace in 1667 had
become virtually Charles's first minister. 'The King is now fallen in
and become a slave to the Duke of Buckingham, led by none but
him,' an acquaintance told Pepys.[1] There was a great deal of animosity
against him in various quarters; his reputation was to say the least
shaky. Bishop Burnet remarked that he 'had no principles of religion,
virtue or friendship' and that 'pleasure, frolic or extravagant diversion
was all that he laid to heart'.

His chief attributes were charm and wit. Though his private life was
always scandalous, he was nevertheless highly regarded by those for
whom his pleasant personality outweighed his lack of principle; for
them, though indeed he was 'notoriously and professedly lustful' he
was 'yet of greater wit and parts, and sounder principles as to the
interest of humanity and the common good than most lords in the
Court'.[2] Dryden described him in his satirical poem *Absalom and
Achitophel*[3] as:

> A man so various, that he seem'd to be
> Not one, but all mankind's epitome:
> Stiff in opinions, always in the wrong;
> Was everything by starts, and nothing long;

But, in the course of one revolving moon,
Was chemist, fiddler, statesman and buffoon.
Then all for women, panting, rhyming, drinking,
Besides ten thousand freaks that died in thinking.

A lover of the theatre, Buckingham had admired Nell from the first moment he saw her on the stage. In the epilogue of his *The Chances* he complimented her on her ability to please the crowd and gain applause – applause so enthusiastic that authors, standing in the wings and overhearing it, believed the audience must be applauding them rather than a mere player:

The author dreads the strut and mien
Of new prais'd poets, having often seen
Some of his fellows, who have writ before,
When Nell has danc'd her jig, steal to the door,
Hear the pit clap and with conceit of that
Swell, and believe themselves the Lord knows what.

Nell, though hard-headed enough, was as much under Buckingham's spell as anyone else – their relationship was not necessarily platonic, at least before she committed herself to his monarch; and his interest in the theatre, his career as a dramatist, gave them much in common. She appreciated his sense of humour; herself an excellent mimic, she was delighted when he naughtily coached Lacy in an impersonation of Dryden, mocked in his play *The Rehearsal.* She laughed at his half-serious ambition to get rid of the Queen and marry Charles to someone through whom he could have more influence. His feud with the Duke of York was potentially more serious and thus more dangerous; he and James had little love for each other, and Buckingham at one time believed that the Duke had plans to have him assassinated. Nell, a friend of both, encouraged neither in their bickering.

In 1674 Buckingham was attacked by both Houses of Parliament. The Earl of Shrewsbury petitioned for redress against the scandal of the Duke's association with his wife, the ravishing Anne Maria

Brudenell. The Duke later fought a duel[4] with and killed the Earl over his intrigue with the Countess. (Their bastard child had been buried in Westminster Abbey under the title of the Earl of Coventry.) The Commons voted to ask the King to remove Buckingham from 'all employments held during His Majesty's pleasure, and from his presence and councils for ever'. Even for the devil-may-care Duke, things had gone too far, and for the sake of his political career he appeared to reform, was regularly seen at church (with his wife, which was something of a surprise), and even began to pay some of his debts. His imperfect sense of tact led him to fall foul of the King when he suggested that Charles should release from gaol all those courtiers at present imprisoned for misdemeanour, including Rochester and Etherege, who had recently been locked up for that stupid escapade during which they had attacked a Constable whose house they had mistaken for a brothel (see p. 124). He also argued, with Lord Shaftesbury, that as the House of Commons had not met for over a year, it could be regarded as dissolved, and added, in a speech in the Lords, that in any case the Commons should be dissolved rather than prorogued from month to month. Precedent was not necessarily a good thing: 'Acts of Parliament are not like women, the worse for being old.' His proposition was defeated by a large majority, and when he and three other peers declined to apologise for what was regarded as their ridicule of the House of Lords, they were themselves arrested and imprisoned in the Tower.

When the news reached Nell that Buckingham was in the Tower, she immediately, 'with Middlesex, Rochester and the merry gang . . .',[5] began working for his release. Buckhurst describes how he visited Rochester in his cell; in the letter[6] he describes Nell as 'the best woman in the world . . . and, at this time, the discreetest' (very true: she was always the most discreet of Charles's mistresses). She spoke to Charles on Buckingham's behalf, and passed on to the prisoner the King's reaction. Buckingham, heartened, wrote to his old and royal friend:

I am so surprised with what Mrs Nelly has told me, that I know not in the world what to say . . . What you have been pleased to say to Mrs Nelly is ten thousand times more than ever I can deserve. What has made this inclination[7] more violent in me than perhaps it is in other people, is the honour I had of being bred up with your Majesty from a child, for those affections are strongest in men which begin in their youngest years. And therefore I beseech your Majesty to believe me when I say that I have ever loved you more than all the rest of mankind . . . I wish that all the curses imaginable may fall upon me, if I tell you a lie to free my life . . .[8]

The Duke was released. It was not the last favour Nell was to do him; later, she was to help him financially, when she was comfortably off and he was almost destitute. If there had been any romance between them, it was by now over – not only because she was, as far as we know, faithful to Charles, but perhaps because though he retained his charm and wit, Buckingham was physically a spent force. His teeth had fallen out (he wore a false set), he was raddled and unhandsome, and no longer seemed to care either for his appearance or for hygiene. The truth was that, to put it crudely, he stank. Nell advised him at one point to put a little money aside 'to buy him new shoes, that he might not dirty her rooms, and a new periwig that she might not smell his stink two storeys high when he knocks at her outward door'.[9] The door was none the less always open to him. Indeed, it seems that he even spent some time living in Nell's house – or so the Lord Chancellor, Boyle, believed, for he told an Irish correspondent that Buckingham's 'present favour and allowance to have his lodgings in Madame Nelly's house . . . doth not a little contribute to the jealousies and dissatisfactions of the people'.[10] (One can't imagine why he should have thought so; there is little or no evidence that 'the people' were ever antipathetic to Nell.)

She still had a great deal of fun in the Duke's company. His talent for mimicry matched her own – their joint impersonation of the generally disliked Earl of Danby and his wife enlivened many an evening, and 'the King looks on with great delight, which has been a fat prognostic unto some'.[11] (Danby and his wife were great partisans for Louise, and had firmly advised Charles against ennobling Nell.)

Though the King, and Nell's other friends, were privileged to see her repertoire of impersonations at evening parties, it seemed a waste that the public should be deprived of them. This, at all events, was what writers such as Dryden, Etherege, Wycherley and Aphra Behn said. What they would have liked was for her to return to the stage in one of their plays – Behn's *The Rover*, Etherege's *The Man of Mode* (with its wicked portrait of Nell's other noble friend the Earl of Rochester as 'Sir Fopling Flutter') or Dryden's *All for Love*. If she liked, Dryden said, she could take as long as a year to learn her part, provided she would agree to play – but she declined, partly, it has been suggested,[12] because she hoped soon to become a Duchess. But she never seems particularly to have enjoyed performing in the theatre, and there was no reason to return to the boards. She did not need the money; she did not want the applause – or, one may guess, the hard work. And despite her lack of a title, she was socially as secure as anyone in her position could hope to be. She was able to choose her friends from any strata of society. And she did so without fear or favour. Her relationship with James, Duke of Monmouth, Charles's son by Lucy Walter is another illustration of her invariable determination to choose her own associates, whatever the personal or political consequences. And there must have been times when Charles was a little uneasy at her rapport with his son. He liked Monmouth well enough, but embarrassment about the succession – or more particularly about public feeling on that matter – was never far away from his mind.

There had always been rumours that Charles and Lucy had been secretly married, and that therefore Monmouth was the legitimate heir to the throne. An enormous amount of energy has been spent, over the years, in attempting to confirm or disprove the allegation. The truth is that a marriage can neither be conclusively proved nor disproved; there is simply no evidence on either side. What cannot be denied is the fact that the King was absolutely determined, until his dying day, to say or do nothing that could legitimise his eldest son's claim to the throne. His heir was his brother James, and that was that.

Nell liked Monmouth, and felt some sympathy for him. 'Young Jemmy was a fine lad', as the popular song had it, and was certainly just the lad to appeal to Nell: handsome, attractive, courageous, and like herself more than a little hot-headed – he had only to think of an idea, or have one suggested to him, to insist on putting it immediately into action. He was a regular visitor to 79 Pall Mall when he was in town. Barillon, the French Ambassador, told his King that 'the Duke every night sups with Nelly, the courtesan who has borne the King two children, and whom he daily visits'.

Nell knew Monmouth's faults as well as anyone: she christened him 'Prince Perkin' – an allusion to Perkin Warbeck, the pretender to the English throne who had claimed to be Edward V's brother – and stood no nonsense when his pride rose too high. On one occasion when he called her 'ill-bred' she merely asked coolly 'was Mrs Barlow better bred than I?' 'Mrs Barlow', of course, had been Lucy Walter, his mother. Monmouth may have regarded her an ally who would help him curry favour with his father. She knew perfectly well that he was a subject on which she could not sway the King, who was never going to accede to Monmouth's demands that he should admit marriage with his mother, and thus legitimise him. But while she never raised that particular matter with Charles, on a personal level, loyal as always to those she liked, she never stopped discreetly trying to bridge the increasing gap between the King and his son. Occasionally they met at her house, and were coolly civil to each other, but after one meeting had ended less than civilly, Charles told Nell frankly that he would see Monmouth hanged at Tyburn before he was given the right to sit on the throne; and when the young man finally stood on the scaffold, like Perkin Warbeck before him, he admitted that his father had 'indeed told him he was but his base [i.e., illegitimate] son'.

The Earl of Rochester was another old friend with whom Nell always kept in touch. He took her side in most things, and particularly in her skirmishes with Louise. He published, anonymously, 'A Pleasant Battle between Two Lapdogs of the Utopian Court', in which Nell's British mutt sees off Louise's Catholic pooch:

> The English lap-dog here does first begin
> The vindication of his lady, Gwyn;
> The other, much more Frenchified, alas,
> Shows what his lady is, not what she was.

Rochester was, like Buckingham, a great deal of fun, and his sense of humour was also never far from Nell's. When on one occasion he went a little too far, and Charles dismissed him from Court, he set up a stall on Tower Hill, dressed himself in a great cloak covered in stars, and calling himself Alexander Bendo dispensed astrological advice and cosmetics to passing women, treating the prettiest to special intimacies and promising in his advertisements that 'they who will do me the favour to come to me, shall be sure to find me from three o'clock in the afternoon till eight at night, at my lodgings in Tower Street, next door to the sign of the Black Swan, at a goldsmith's house'. Nell is said to have passed these bills around among her acquaintances, and the Earl was not short of company. Unlike some others, she was not particularly outraged (or, one may guess, surprised) to hear that her friend had been seen running naked through Woodstock Park with Lord Lovelace and some other cronies – just frisking, they told the authorities, just frisking. And at Christmas, she presented him at a party as the enchanter Bendo in a double act with Thomas Bushell, a celebrated black magician, prognosticating trouble from hot-tempered courtiers during the New Year 1678. Two years later he was to die, worn out by the ravages not only of venereal disease, but of the awful treatment prescribed for it. In his funeral oration, the Reverend Robert Parsons described the Earl as 'a martyr to sin'.

The year 1678 started well for Nell – apart from a burglary which deprived her of some of her silver – with the complimentary dedication to her of a book[13] by Robert Whitcom, who spoke not only of her 'delicate body . . . every limb about you an exact symmetry and pleasing proportion' but went on to praise nature for being 'lavish of her allurements in wantonly strewing them about your wealthy face, and to complete the fabric [ennobling] it with that brisk air and graceful mien which certainly she has given you a patent for, since none could ever acquire it but yourself', and finally and perhaps even more pleasingly (if less convincingly) commended her 'great mind and illustrious troop of sublime thoughts'. His was not the only compliment of the new year. Thomas Duffet, an indifferent dramatist, dedicated *The Spanish Rogue*, 'appropriately, the most indecent of his plays',[14] to her in similarly adulatory terms: 'Nature almost overcome by art, has in yourself rallied all her scattered forces, and on your charming brow sits smiling at their slavish toils, which your and her envious foes endure; striving in vain with the fading weak supplies of art to rival your beauties, which are ever the same and almost incomparable.' More interesting is what follows: his praise of her for her kindness to one and all, 'as if doing good was not her nature but her business'. Few disagreed with that.

Aphra Behn, always her friend, dedicated *The Feigned Courtesans* to her, assuring her that 'besides all the charms, and attractions, and powers of your sex, you have beauties peculiar to yourself – an eternal sweetness, youth and air which never dwelt in any face but yours. You never appear but you gladden the hearts of all that have the happy fortune to see you, as if you were made on purpose to put the whole world in good humour', and went on to tell her that when she spoke 'men crowd to listen with that awful reverence as to holy oracles or divine prophesies, and bear away the precious words to tell at home to all the attentive family the graceful things you uttered . . .' Nell must have giggled on reading this as much as Aphra laughed when writing it.

One must make allowances for hyperbole, but Nell was certainly good-humoured enough. No one really disliked her – even the two rival mistresses were in the end seduced by her affability. She could be generous when the mood took her: when the King led a fund in aid of the people of Wapping whose homes were consumed by a serious fire, she gave £100. But she never made money, unlike Louise or Barbara, by pretending that she had any special influence with the King or by asking any special favours from him. Attempts were occasionally made to use her as a means of approach to him; and it was perhaps partly because they failed that there were occasionally attempts to introduce new, young, mettlesome beauties who might take her place as Charles's favourite provider of light entertainment.

In the summer of 1678, Henry Saville, one of the 'merry gang', wrote to Rochester with the news that Lady Elizabeth Harvey, a bitchily witty elderly woman who pretended to be Nell's friend, was actually plotting to get a Mrs Jane, or Jenny, Middleton into Charles's bed. Mrs Middleton was at that moment said to be the most beautiful woman in England (these highly rated beauties rode a sort of merry-go-round for the favour of connoisseurs), and to have refused an offer of £1,500 to sleep with the then French Ambassador, Philibert de Gramont. Lady Harvey, Saville said, was

> working body and soul to bring Mrs Jenny Middleton into play. How dangerous a new one is to all old ones I need not tell you, but her Ladyship, having little opportunity of seeing Charlemagne[15] upon her own account, wheedles poor Mrs Nelly into supper twice or thrice a week at W.C.'s[16] and carrying her with her; so that in good earnest this poor creature is betrayed by Her Ladyship to pimp against herself; for there her Ladyship whispers and contrives all matters to her own ends, as the other might easily perceive if she were not too giddy to mistrust a false friend.'[17]

Nell was not as naive as Saville thought; she knew perfectly well what Lady Harvey was up to, and was perfectly confident that it mattered not a whit whether Charles fancied Mrs Middleton or not. If he wanted to take Mrs Middleton to bed, *tant pis* – it would not affect her position in the least. Rochester hurried to write to her advising her to 'take your measures just contrary to your rivals, live in peace with all the world, and easily with the King. Never be so ill-natured as to stir up his anger against others, but let him forget the use of a passion, which is never to do you good . . .'[18] The advice, we may be sure, was superfluous. Nell looked on with more amusement and interest than rancour at Charles's extramural flirtations, and showed no apprehension at all at the prospect of possible rivals, real or imaginary. She had showed no anxiety when everyone started talking about a more than ordinarily beautiful young French actress who appeared at Whitehall with a travelling group of French players in December 1677. Saville thought that the pretty young thing had 'more beauty and sweetness than ever was seen upon the stage since a friend of ours left it', and it was generally believed that the King had his eye on her. The 'friend', Nell, smiled, completely without jealousy – and as it happened, the King was contented merely to look and admire.

For a biographer, one of the most interesting events of 1678 occurred in June, when Nell sat down to write – or rather, to dictate – a letter. She never succeeded in learning to write more than her name, though at one time she seems to have tried, for one of her friends passed on to another the message that 'Mrs Nelly presents you with her real acknowledgements for all your favours, and protests she would write in her own hand but her wild characters she says would distract you.'[19] Her character, her zest for life and for gossip, nevertheless come through in the few pieces of her correspondence that have survived, even though the handwriting is that of a secretary, probably James Booth, who worked for her for some years.

It is worth quoting this earliest surviving letter at some length. It was addressed to her friend Laurence or 'Lory' Hyde, Lord Clarendon's younger son, a brother-in-law of the Duke of York, and though a Protestant, one of James's strongest supporters. He was often a guest in Pall Mall, particularly enjoying the wine Nell provided in generous quantities for her visitors. In June 1678, he was in the Hague on a diplomatic mission, and Nell wrote to him – a chatty, informal letter full of gossip:[20]

Pray, dear Mr Hyde, forgive me for not writing to you before now, for the reason is I have been sick three month, and since I recovered I have had nothing to entertain you withal, nor have nothing now worth writing but that I can hold no longer to let you know I have never been in any company without drinking your health, for I love you with all my soul.

The Pall Mall is now to me a dismal place, since I have utterly lost Sir Carr Scrope, never to be recovered again – for he told me he could not love always at this rate, and so began to be a little uncivil, which I could not suffer from an ugly *beau garçon*.

Mrs Knight's mother is dead, and she has put up a scutcheon no bigger than my Lady Green's scutcheon. My Lord Rochester is gone in the country. Mr Savile has got a misfortune, but is upon recovery and is to marry an heiress, who I think won't have an ill time out if he hold up his thumb. My Lord of Dorset appears worse in three months, for he drinks ale with Shadwell and

Mr Harris at the Duke's home all day long. My Lord Beauclerk is going into France.

We are going to sup with the King at Whitehall and my Lady Harvey. The King remembers his service to you. Now, let's talk of State affairs, for we never carried things so cunningly as now, for we don't know whether we shall have peace or war, but I am for war, and for no other reason but that you may come home. I have a thousand merry conceits, but I can't make her write me, and therefore you must take the will for the deed. Goodbye. Your most loving, obedient, faithful and humble servant, E.G.

The letter is easily decoded: the allusion to 'peace or war' referred to Hyde's reason for being in the Hague – Charles's efforts to bring to an end the conflict between France and Holland. The King had friends and relatives fighting on both sides, and saw the war as an unnecessary drain on the finances of France, in which he had a very considerable personal interest. As to the other references in the letter, Sir Carr Scrope was an uncivil if witty poet, unpopular with almost everyone (and especially with the Duke of York, to whose mistress he had been particularly unpleasant). Mrs Knight was a well-known singer and allegedly for a time the King's mistress. Shadwell (Thomas Shadwell, the Poet Laureate) and Joseph Harris (the actor) were Dryden's drinking companions. Lord Beauclerk, who was only eight years old, indeed went to Paris – but almost immediately died. Lady Green was one of Nell's friends, and a companion in theatre-going. (As Catherine Pegge, she had been the King's mistress during his exile, and had had two children by him – one the popular 'Don Carlos', who became Earl of Plymouth, and the other a girl who became a nun.) Lady Harvey, we know about; Henry Saville failed to capture his heiress, and was sent to the Embassy in Paris.

Later in the summer, Nell – like everyone else about the Court – was swept up in the ramifications of what became known as 'the Popish Plot'. This was fabricated by the notorious Titus Oates, an ugly renegade Anglican priest who alleged that Roman Catholics were plotting to assassinate the King and place his Catholic brother on the throne. Anyone who was anyone knew that the King was in any case determined that the Duke of York should succeed him, and it must seem extremely unlikely that a plotter would have taken the enormous risk of committing treason merely to hurry the process on for a few years. But there is no accounting for the actions of fanatics.

Though the plot was the product of the religious frenzy of a relatively small number of people, it led to mass hysteria on a grand scale. The King's continual efforts to encourage religious freedom, the alliance with Catholic France, the Duke of York's open conversion to Catholicism had all raised the hackles of the fiercer Anglicans, who now saw plots and secret treaties on every side. Danby, the King's Chief Minister, was a sturdy Anglican who nevertheless did his best to dispel suspicion; he argued for an end to the pro-French foreign policy favoured by the King (chiefly for financial reasons) and encouraged – even perhaps contrived – the marriage of the Duke of York's eldest daughter to William of Orange. But Danby was regarded with suspicion by the very folk – the country gentlemen and landowners – he was most anxious to please. They suspected his support for absolute monarchy, and suspected even more his attempts to build a standing army (which they rightly saw as a force that could be employed to enforce the royal will). This made his attempts to dampen down religious hysteria extremely difficult, especially when that hysteria was fanned to a blaze by Titus Oates.

Oates himself seems to have been chiefly motivated by a keen sense of his own importance. He was the son of a Baptist preacher, and the first twenty-nine years of his life were at once obscure and unsuccessful. Ordained into the Church of England, he was imprisoned for perjury while still a curate, and having escaped to join the navy as a chaplain, he was dismissed from the service for misconduct. He succeeded somehow in becoming chaplain to the Protestant servants of the Catholic Duke of Norfolk, and while in that position met for the first time a number of Catholics. He also met – though presumably not in the Duke's house – the fanatically anti-Jesuit Israel Tongue, who suggested that there was a small fortune to be made by betraying Catholics to the government. Oates set about spying on them, attempting to wriggle into their confidence by himself joining the Roman Catholic Church (in March 1677), and going to European seminaries to study – first to Valladolid and then to Saint-Omer. (He was expelled from both places.)

Back in London, he and Tongue concocted a vivid account of an ambitious plot to assassinate the King, and publicised it through the agency of Sir Edmund Berry Godfrey, a Justice of the Peace who was conveniently murdered just after passing on their conspiracy theory to authority, a fact which no doubt lent it additional weight. The tidal wave of terror that swept through London can scarcely be overestimated; one might compare it to the fear that harried Berlin after the assassination attempt on Hitler in 1944. Oates became, briefly, a hero, but went too far when he accused the Queen of plotting to poison her husband, telling the Privy Council that he had been in a room in Somerset House and heard through an open door Catherine protesting to some unseen plotters that she could no longer tolerate the King's infidelities and would be content if he were out of the way.

Oates broke down under intensive questioning, and revealed complete ignorance of the layout of rooms in Somerset House, and, incidentally, other silly anomalies in the fictions he was spreading: he had for instance described the alleged Spanish Prince Don Juan, a supposed intriguer, as tall and dark, when in fact he was short and red-headed.

Infuriated in particular by Oates's apparent wish to involve the Queen, Charles had him thrown into prison. The House of Commons almost immediately ordered his release, and in November both he and another informer, one Bedloe, testified at the bar of the House of Commons, accusing Catherine of high treason; they repeated their slander the following day in the House of Lords. The Commons was completely taken in, and not only invited the King to administer oaths of supremacy to all the Queen's servants, but to remove her, her family, and all papists from Whitehall. The House of Lords quashed this address, but plotters continued to attack the Queen, and it is possible that they might have succeeded in removing her had it not been for Charles's complete loyalty. He said publicly that he had no intention of abandoning her, and that though some people might believe (because she had not succeeded in bearing him an heir) that he wanted a new wife, he would not see an innocent woman condemned.

A number of Jesuit priests were brought to trial, accused of conspiring with her to poison the King, but were acquitted, and Catherine and the King were drawn even closer together as a result of the various plots. Lady Sunderland suggested that the Queen was now as secure in His Majesty's affection as his mistresses, 'the passion her spouse has for her is so great'. Catherine might not have appreciated the compliment had she heard it, but at a dinner at Chiffinch's apartments she pledged the King's health in wine – the first time she had touched alcohol for many years.

Nell was at Windsor when, in August, the trouble began to boil up. She had prepared her house there in readiness for the Court's arrival on the 14th. That morning the King, while walking in St James's Park, was warned of a probable assassination attempt, but declined to alter his plans, and in the evening supped with his mistress at Windsor. No one ever attempted to implicate her in the plot, though her name was mentioned when, later, a sort of sub-plot developed, aimed at the downfall of Danby, whom she was known to dislike. It was inevitable that she knew many of those who Oates and his co-conspirators named as traitors, and who were arrested – among them Miles Prance, a Catholic goldsmith who had made ornaments for her as well as the Queen, and was denounced by a lodger in his house, one John Wren (who probably saw an easy way out of the debts he owed for his lodging).

Prance, like many of those suddenly denounced and arrested, was understandably terrified at the prospect of torture and possible execution, and made his position worse by losing his head and confessing that he had worked for several of the people accused by Oates. This landed him in irons, suspected of complicity in the murder of Godfrey. He grew more and more terrified, and eventually accused several men – including two priests – of murdering Godfrey, and admitted keeping watch while the murder was done. The King now decided to question him personally, whereupon he recanted; returned to Newgate prison and tortured, he reiterated his original story and dictated a confession, for which he was paid £50. There is little doubt that he was entirely innocent not only of complicity in the murder but of any part in the plot. Hysteria and fear prompted the perjury to which he eventually admitted before vanishing from our sight – not executed but possibly exiled.

There is no proof that Nell spoke to the King about Prance, but despite her usual policy of avoiding raising public matters with him, she may have done so. Presuming him innocent of anything except fear for his own skin, she must have tried to excuse him to his monarch. But she was never interested in politics, and when the dust had settled doubtless enjoyed setting out on her card table one of the packs of cards produced in 1679 and sold at the King's Arms in the Poultry to commemorate the Popish Plot.

Because she entertained the great and good (and sometimes the great and troublesome) there were times when despite her lack of interest her house in Pall Mall was thick with political discussion. She kept her counsel (if indeed she ever had any interest in the subject). But whatever their political opinions or acts, she was always faithful to old friends and acquaintances, and did what she could for them. She never seems to have suffered as a result of this, though from time to time there were rumours that she had got herself into trouble – rumours 'as to her death or absence from her house' as one news-sheet put it, adding that 'we are assured that there is no ground for such report, and Madame Gwyn is now at her house in good health and has not been absent from it'.[21]

Danby's position was finally undermined not only by public hysteria but by the revelation that while the alleged plot had been fulminating, he had been secretly negotiating with the French. Parliament voted to impeach him, and an act was passed demanding that 'all and every person or persons that shall bear any office or shall receive any pay, salary, fee or wages by reason of any patent of grant from his Majesty, or shall have command or place of trust from or under his Majesty take the several oaths of supremacy and allegiance and the said respective officers aforesaid shall also receive the Sacrament of the Lord's Supper according of the usage of the Church of England . . .'[22] This banned any non-Anglicans from entering Parliament. The Duke of York escaped by two votes from being excluded from his seat in the House of Lords, and a Bill was introduced to exclude him from succession to the throne. Charles cannily invited the leading exclusionists – including the Earls of Shaftesbury, Halifax and Essex – to join the government. He offered to plan a Bill that would safeguard the Anglican Church after his Catholic brother succeeded – and, when the Commons passed an Exclusion Bill, dissolved Parliament and called an election.

Further drama was provided when, on 17 November 1679, the Earl of Shaftesbury moved in the House of Lords 'a bill of divorce which by separating the King from Catherine might enable him to marry a protestant consort, and thus to leave the crown to his legitimate issue'. There was so little support that he dropped the idea, and on the evening of the debate Charles, to show his support for his wife, 'went straight to the Queen, and to give a proof of his extraordinary affection for her he seated himself after dinner in her apartment, and slept there a long time, which he had been in the habit of doing only in the Duchess of Portsmouth's chamber'.[23]

Shaftesbury continued to make trouble. In June 1680 he attempted to indict the Duke of York as a Catholic recusant,[24] and accused Louise of being a common prostitute. Louise was terrified: found guilty, she would have to sit in the stocks – and the general dislike of the public would have ensured that that would have been an extremely uncomfortable experience. There were cases of crowds actually killing criminals by enthusiastically pelting them with dead cats, filth and bricks. The judges, however, fortunately discharged the jury before the matter came to trial, but Louise in her fright forsook the Duke of York's cause and declared herself for Monmouth: 'the Duchess of Portsmouth was frighted into a reconciliation,' James wrote in his memoirs,[25] 'and did it so effectively as to become even a patron to her pretended prosecutors, to give them private meetings, particularly the Duke of Monmouth . . .'

In July 1679 *The Domestic Intelligencer* announced that 'Madame Ellen Gwyn's mother, sitting by the water-side at her house by the Neat-houses, near Chelsea, fell accidentally into the water and was drowned'. This, it appears, was a polite way of putting it: the old woman apparently fell into the ditch or small stream that ran along the border between Chelsea and Fulham, while drunk. She had become a notorious, happy dipsomaniac. Nell had always cared for her, in every sense; she housed and fed her in the style to which she had been happy to become accustomed, and on hearing of her death immediately returned to London from Windsor to arrange the funeral, the day after her death, at St Martin-in-the-Fields, where the old woman was laid to rest in a respectable vault. She was an extremely well-known personality, and several good-humoured, if scurrilous, verses commemorated both the death and the funeral.

There was for instance 'An Elegy upon that never to be forgotten Matron Old Maddam Gwinn, Who was unfortunately Drown'd in her own Fishpond, on the 29th of July, 1679':

> . . . Since she's gone, our Tiplers need not fear,
> For whilst she lived true Nantes was monstrous dear.
> Yet brandy-merchants sure have cause to grieve
> Because her fate admits of no reprieve.
> Die in their debts she could not, yet they'll find
> Their trade's decayed, for none is left behind
> That in one day could twenty quarts consume
> And bravely vaunt she durst it twice presume . . .
>
> . . . her mighty hulk
> Six foot in compass was supposed to be –
> Too ponderous for a common destiny.
> No fate when she was sober durst avail
> Her well-built structure, nor could ought prevail.
> Too strong the bases were, whereon she stood,
> That solid mass composed with flesh and blood.
> Had not perfidious legs and feet betrayed
> The element could not have conquest made . . .[26]

Another pamphlet suggested that her loss had 'caused a universal grief among the buxom bona-robas, so that it is generally believed that upon so tragical occasion the palace and the fishpond will be forfeited to her most virtuous daughter Madam Ellen Gwin, as Lady of the Soil

and chief of all the bona-robas that the suburban schools of Venus
have fitted for the Game . . .' and offered an elegy for her tombstone:

> Here lies the victim of a cruel fate
> Whom too much Element did ruinate.
> 'Tis something strange, but yet most wondrous true
> That what we live by should our lives undo.
> She that so oft had powerful waters tried
> At last with silence, in a fish-pond died.
> Fate was unjust, for had he proved but kind
> To make it brandy, he had pleased her mind.[27]

Buckingham congratulated Nell on the costliness of her mother's
funeral – 'no cost, no velvet did the daughter spare' – and recorded
that brandy flamed plentifully at the wake.

In August 1679 the King had been quite seriously ill with fever; the
fact that he was cured by administration of 'the Jesuit's powder' –
quinine – seems to suggest that he may have had malaria. In any
event, the illness concentrated the minds of those anxious about the
succession. The Duke of York, who was abroad, hurried back to
England, and a very keen watch was kept on Monmouth, lest if
Charles died he should attempt to seize the throne. Soon, however,
the King was better and agitating to get off to Newmarket for the
racing. But a few months later he took the precaution of signing a
paper declaring that he 'never gave nor made any contract of
marriage, nor was married to any woman whatsoever, but to my
present wife Queen Catherine now living . . .'

Within a month of recovery he was at Newmarket, with Nell in
attendance. She was never as interested in racing as the King. She
loved riding – but in a comfortable carriage; at least on one occasion
she took an uncomfortable tumble from a horse's back. However, she
showed sufficient enthusiasm for the sport to be an agreeable
companion for Charles at the racetrack, and was happy as always to
indulge her taste for gambling. The people of Newmarket regarded
her as a delightful visitor. The fact that she was now as respectable as
any royal mistress could hope to be is reflected in the welcome given

to her by the Vice-Chancellor of Cambridge University and 'certain scholars' who entertained her with wine and a versified address of welcome when she passed through the city on a roundabout way back to town. It was shortly afterwards that, driving through London streets crowded with merrymakers celebrating the anniversary of the accession of Queen Elizabeth I, she was booed under the impression that she was Louise, leaned out of the window of her carriage, and shouted 'Be still, friends – I am the *Protestant* whore!'

It was in 1679 that the King gave her a house at Windsor. Happy enough with her Pall Mall home, and more a town than a country girl, she was nevertheless pleased with the gift of Burford House (as it was known) inside the grounds of the Castle. She was delighted to invite friends to the new red-brick house where, from the entrance hall,

> On painted ceilings you devoutly stare
> Where sprawl the saints of Verrio and Laguerre[28]

decorating the staircase. The Neapolitan painter Antonio Verrio had come to England in 1672, and worked at Windsor between 1675 and 1684, commissioned by the King to decorate the ceilings of his Withdrawing Room, Presence Chamber and Closet in the north range of the Castle. His banal and gaudy paintings (of scenes from Ovid, in fact, rather than from scripture) were in just the style to please Nell – ostentatious and in the height of fashion.

Burford is one of the few houses described as having been occupied by Nell Gwyn where the evidence for her presence is conclusive – though the place is so much altered that it can no longer realistically be said to resemble the original. In other cases, what we have is mostly rumour and gossip. There is another house in Windsor said to have been hers, and others near and in Newmarket, and in various parts of London from Chelsea to Westminster. Only Queen Elizabeth I can be said to have slept within more houses than Nell Gwyn, and it is best to treat every suggestion with suspicion.

CHAPTER NINE

He was My Friend

All matters of state from her soul she doth hate
And leaves to the politic bitches.

Anon

The last eight years of Nell's life – at least until the King's death – were pleasantly placid. She, and to some extent Louise, had become quietly domesticated, and their relationships with Charles resembled a tried and tested marriage, which had had its difficulties but was now in calm waters.

One event that interested many of Nell's earlier biographers was the foundation in 1682 of the Royal Hospital at Chelsea for aged and wounded soldiers. Tradition for two centuries asserted that it was Nell who gave the King the idea after having been solicited by a disabled old soldier, and that she contributed a great deal to the Hospital's building – not least by tearing her handkerchief into quarters and forming a hollow square with it, illustrating the form the building should take. It is not surprising that the tradition clung, for it would have been very much in Nell's generous nature to have proposed such a thing. Unfortunately there is no shred of evidence that she had anything to do with it, though we can believe, if we wish, that she was enthusiastic about the project and may have encouraged it.

The King was now, in seventeenth-century terms, growing old. In 1680 he was fifty, fifteen years older than the average age at which a man might have been expected, in that century, to die, though of course many working men died earlier because of the effects of poverty, bad and insufficient diet, or disease. The upper classes, as ever, lived longer. Still, fifty was a good age. Nell was no longer young: she was thirty – middle-aged. Louise was a year older, and decidedly plump. Barbara – now out of the way, in France – was an elderly thirty-nine.

Louise had been, virtually since 1674, Charles's *maîtresse en titre*, supplanting Barbara, whose succession of lovers gave Charles more amusement than displeasure. She did not trouble herself unduly to disguise her affairs with Jacob, the rope-dancer (who she actually put on a salary), John Ellis (later Secretary of State), or John Churchill (soon to become a national hero as the Duke of Marlborough), and showed no particular embarrassment when they were discovered. Her third daughter, called after herself, was probably Churchill's; the King certainly believed that to be the case and had some sort of reason to do so, for Buckingham, with his usual sense of mischief, managed to manoeuvre the King into discovering the couple in bed. Churchill is said to have leaped from the bed out of an open window, followed by Charles's shouted remark: 'I forgive you, for you do it for your bread.' A week or so later, with characteristic generosity, he gave Churchill a purse of £5,000 – out of which the handsome young guardsman is said to have refused Barbara as much as half a crown.[1] (Her daughter by him accompanied her to France, and was placed in a nunnery in the Rue Charenton in Paris; known as Sister Benedicta, she bore a child to the Earl of Arran, but nevertheless died as Prioress of the nunnery of St Nicholas at Pontoise.)

As a result of the Test Act, Barbara was deprived of her position as Lady of the Bedchamber to the Queen. (The long-suffering, complaisant Catherine may be forgiven for being pleased to see her go.) But Charles gave her what he could afford, when he could afford it, raised all three of her sons – Charles, Henry and George – to dukedoms, and unusually granted their daughters, Anne and Charlotte Fitzroy, the precedence of duke's daughters. Barbara was ambitious for all of her children, not only in social but also in economic terms. In 1671 she had married Charles, her eldest, to a seven-year-old girl who had brought him a small fortune, but a year later spent some considerable time ignoring the marriage and trying to arrange his betrothal to one of the great heiresses of the time, Elizabeth Percy. The Dowager Duchess of Northumberland, Elizabeth's protector, disapproved, and was too much for the diligent mother. In 1674 and 1677 Barbara saw Anne and Charlotte advantageously married – the former to Lord Dacre, later Earl of

Sussex, and the latter to the Earl of Lichfield. It was no doubt the King who arranged for a grant of well over £1,000, from Secret Service money, to pay for 'wedding clothes, millinery, mercery and lace' for the girls' weddings.

Having worked tirelessly for her children, Barbara decided – somewhat, it seems, to Charles's relief – to retire to France, and in 1677 left London for Paris. Her reception there disappointed her: the French court took very little notice of her. The British Ambassador, Ralph Montagu, did take notice, however, and they had a spirited affair until she moved on to the bed of the Marquis de Châtillon, whereupon Montagu made the mistake of revenging himself by seducing Barbara's eldest daughter, Anne, Lady Sussex. Barbara then wrote privately to Charles, passing on the distinctly unflattering comments his Ambassador had made to her about the King, while in bed. Montagu rushed back to London to offer his apologies, was ostracised by the Court, and replaced as Ambassador by the Earl of Sunderland, who flattered Barbara violently, and as a result enjoyed a happy tenure.

Back at home, Louise got over the fright of the Popish Plot, but took care to ingratiate herself with anyone about the Court who she suspected of being her enemy. No one at Whitehall really liked her, in fact, and she was still hated by the ordinary people of the country. Their dislike was mirrored in Parliament, which in 1679 demanded that she should be sent away from the Court; this frightened her into dismissing all her Catholic servants.

That same year, she too went to France, though only on a visit lasting some five months. She took the waters at Bourbon, visited her estate at Aubigny, and presented herself at court at Versailles, where she seems to have been quite well received. At home once more – England was of course now much more her home than France – she settled into her position as, more or less, a member of the royal family: she even took part in arranging the marriage of Princess Anne and Prince George of Denmark. When not busying herself about the Court, she was decorating and redecorating her apartments at Westminster, at the end of the Stone Gallery. She was living handsomely on an income of £10,000 a quarter from the privy purse –

that is, when the money was actually paid to her. She seems more often to have relied on spasmodic gifts from the King, which in 1681 amounted to £136,668[2] – more than Barbara, and certainly more than Nell, ever received in one year.

The increasingly plump Louise was now treated by the King much as he treated his Queen. He was amiably disposed to both of them, liked their company, but had no erotic interest in either. Louise still tried, from time to time, to talk to him about politics, which he found increasingly irritating. He spent more and more time with Nell, who never troubled him in that way. A squib of the time got it right:

> All matters of state from her soul she does hate
> And leaves to the politic bitches.
> The whore's in the right, for 'tis her delight
> To be scratching just where it itches.[3]

As always, the King continued to be short of money. His mistresses certainly did well out of him, but spasmodically; spending freely, they were never absolutely sure when the next purse would arrive. No doubt the King was no more and no less eager to pay his mistresses than anyone else to whom he was in debt. He was generous when he found it possible, however. In 1681 he offered Nell as much of Sherwood Forest as she could ride round before breakfast. This was a joke; she was no great horsewoman. What she got was most of Bestwood Park, which had belonged originally to Edward III. She had also built up, one way and another, a considerable estate surrounding Burford House, and probably owned property elsewhere.

The single notable tragedy of her life struck in June 1680, when she heard of the death of her nine-year-old younger son James – Lord James Beauclerk – in Paris. He had been born on Christmas Day 1671, and everyone had been delighted: the King and the Duke of York had come to see the baby, and he had been named after the latter. Nell often combined Christmas celebrations with a birthday party for James: when he was five there was a particularly opulent one, the King arriving bearing the patent ennobling the child and his elder brother, and coats of arms for them both. James had seemed a perfectly healthy child until Christmas 1678, when he had been out of sorts. Whatever the trouble was, it seemed not to be serious, and Nell let the child go abroad a year later – to Paris, with Henry Saville. Out of the blue came the news that he had died of 'a bad leg'.

Nell never established the real cause of the child's death. Perhaps no one really knew. For a while, she was convinced that he had been poisoned by Louise, but of course there was absolutely no reason to entertain the suspicion. She went into mourning, blaming herself, as a mother would, for ever letting the child out of her sight.

She was now at an age when she began to hear of the death of old friends. Buckingham died a month after young James. Down and out, deserted by his servants, he caught a cold while out hunting in Yorkshire, and expired in a mean ale house at Helmesley. Sir Peter Lely, who so often painted her, had died in November. Few men had as appreciative an eye for female loveliness as the King, but Lely was certainly one of them. Pope wrote of 'the sleepy eye that spoke the melting soul' in so many of his portraits, and Pepys, another amateur of lovely women, was enhanced when after several attempts he was finally allowed to see Lely's portrait of Barbara. The King called him friend, and often visited his studio, particularly when he was painting Nell or some other beauty, either in 'a nightgown fastened with a single pin' (Pope, again) or without a gown of any kind. He painted on until the last: his body was discovered by the Dowager Duchess of Somerset when she arrived at his house in Covent Garden for a sitting for her portrait.

John Lacy, one of Nell's first lovers, who twenty years and more previously had taught her to dance at his rooms in Drury Lane, died there in September 1681. He had been recognised as one of the finest dancers on the stage until forced by age to retire, when he turned to conventional parts, including Falstaff and Tartuffe. His not very good plays had provided him with a small income in addition to a smaller pension.

There were a few not too serious domestic difficulties during Nell's last decade. For instance, she had rather bad luck with the tutors she engaged for her elder son. In 1674 she employed Sir Fleetwood Sheppard to teach young Charles. Sheppard had been recommended to her by his patron Lord Buckhurst, with whom he had a great deal in common, being (as an epitaph was to describe him) 'a votary of Apollo, Bacchus and Venus'.[4] He spent a great deal of time with Buckhurst and the other Wits – Killigrew, Saville, Rochester – 'talking blasphemy and atheism, drinking, and perhaps in what is worse'.[5] But he was a good teacher, and Charles liked him. Nell liked him too, and trusted him; she made him her steward, and for a time he managed her finances. However, when he got one of her maids with child, she felt she must dismiss him, and in his place engaged the playwright Thomas Otway, then in his late twenties. Nell's friend Aphra Behn may have recommended Otway as a replacement (he had appeared unsuccessfully in a play of hers) – or perhaps it was Rochester. In 1675 Otway's first play was produced at the Dorset Garden Theatre. The following year he had a success at the same theatre with *Don Carlos*, which played for ten nights running – a phenomenon for the time.

It is a little surprising that Nell accepted Otway so readily as a tutor for Charles, despite his success as a dramatist, for he had a considerable reputation as a drunkard, and had got into appreciable trouble because of a passion he conceived for the actress Mrs Barry, who appeared in many of his plays, and who he pursued with such ardour that her accepted lover, Rochester, became extremely irritated. He also gave her so many presents that, bankrupt, he was forced to join the army – from which he retired in ill health, to turn again to the drama, producing several more plays, including, in 1681, his masterpiece, *Venice Preserv'd*, still occasionally seen. Presumably, however, he remained in financial trouble – why else (except of course that Charles was the King's son as well as Nell's) would he accept a position as tutor at a mere £200 a year? However, he did so. But then, in 1681, and despite his continued passion for Mrs Barry, he followed his predecessor's example, got one of Nell's maids pregnant, and was dismissed. Of his successor, nothing is known but his name – Clare – so presumably he was satisfactorily restrained in his philandering.

It was probably in 1681 that one of the anecdotes was first told which has been repeated again and again as an example of Nell's good humour: she is said to have been riding across Bagshot Heath when she was stopped by a highwayman with the somewhat unfelicitous name of Old Mobb. When she had handed over everything of value on her person, he remarked that he hoped she would give him 'something personal' – whereat she cheerfully kissed him, and he gave her back her rings. Mobb is said to have robbed Louise under somewhat similar circumstances, and when she was rather less forthcoming stripped her of her jewels, remarking that since the public contributed to keeping her as the King's whore, she might as well contribute to the upkeep of a highwayman's moll.

Louise was never quite as profligate with her favours outside the King's bedroom as Barbara, but from time to time she enjoyed a little amorous diversity. In January 1682, she gave a dinner in her apartments at Whitehall for Nahed Achmet, the Moroccan Ambassador. Evelyn described it: 'a great banquet of sweetmeats and music, at which the ambassador and retinue behaved themselves with extraordinary moderation and modesty, though placed about a long table, a lady between two Moors – viz., a Moor, then a woman, then a Moor, &c.; and most of these were the King's natural children, viz. The Lady Lichfield, Sussex, Duchess of Portsmouth, Nelly &c., concubines and cattle of that sort, as splendid as jewels and excess of bravery could make them, the Moors neither admiring or seeming to regard anything . . .'[6] Achmet presumably regarded at least one thing, for Louise, who (scandal reported) had always liked black men, was happy to entertain him in private later in the week.

Nell, on the contrary, seems to have been absolutely faithful to the King: in an age notorious for gossip, no one ever suggested that she took any lover besides Charles from the moment he became seriously devoted to her. She does not seem ever to have complained that he was less generous to her than to Louise, even when she was short of money, which from time to time continued to be the case. In September 1682 she dictated a letter to the Duke of Ormonde, who had had much to do with certain estates in Ireland granted to her by the King, which brought in a considerable amount of her income. The Irish farmers had not sent their quarterly contribution, and she badly needed it. 'I hope that you will oblige me now upon this request, that we may be paid our arrears and what is growing due . . .'[7]

A while later, Charles offered her the choice between a handsome pearl necklace valued at over £4,000 which Peg Hughes wanted to sell (it had been given to her by Prince Rupert, on his deathbed, but she would rather have had the cash) or the Garter for her son. She took the pearls.

The King spent the summer of 1683 at Windsor with the Queen, Louise and Nell; none of the ladies was apparently in the least disconcerted by the presence of the others. Charles had narrowly escaped assassination – a plot had been laid to kill him and the Duke of York, so that Monmouth could immediately succeed. The plotters were mostly caught, tortured, hanged, drawn and quartered. Whether or not he knew of the plot, Monmouth disappeared. (A reward of £500 was placed on his head.) Charles had never been on specially good terms with his son, but cannot have been particularly happy to be told that the young man was associated with a plot to kill him.[8]

The summer soothed Charles, however: he went riding with a somewhat reluctant Nell, who was still by no means at ease in the saddle; and he played cards with his wife and Louise when Nell wanted to spend some time at Burford House, now a hospitable home where Pepys and others frequently stayed. It was while she was at Windsor, in August 1683, that she heard of the death of her old colleague Charles Hart. After her retirement from the stage, his career had continued: he played many of the great Shakespearean parts – Othello, Cassio, Brutus and (famously) Hotspur – as well as leading rôles in Beaumont and Fletcher, Ben Jonson and of course Dryden. In his chronicle of the seventeenth-century stage, *Roscius Anglicanus*, Downes said that 'towards the latter end of his acting, if he acted in any one of these but once in a fortnight the house was filled as at a new play'. Hart retired in 1680, and (with Edward Kynaston) received a pension of 5s a day for life. For some years he was a virtual partner in running the Theatre Royal, with Tom Killigrew, who survived him only by weeks – another of Nell's early friends and mentors gone.

Her old friend and colleague Mall Davis had retired some time ago, but still occasionally performed – if in somewhat more rarified entertainments than had been her wont. For instance, in 1683 she and her illegitimate daughter Lady Mary Tudor, then nine years old, took part, at Court, in 'a Masque for the entertainment of the King'. This was one of the earliest English operas, *Venus and Adonis*, by the Master of the Children of the Chapel Royal, and Purcell's teacher, John Blow. So the Court had the pleasure of having Mall, the King's mistress, as Venus, and his bastard child, as Cupid, lecture them on morals:

> Courtiers there is no faith in you,
> You change as often as you can:
> Your women they continue true
> But till they see another man . . .
> At court I find constant and true
> Only an aged lord or two . . .

The King must have been amused, but seems still to have been somewhat gloomy and was now encouraged by Nell in a scheme to build a new royal palace at Winchester – for a while seriously considered as a possible rival to Versailles. Louise was scornful, which did not please Charles; and he was even less pleased when she embarked on a passionate affair with one Philippe de Vendôme, a young nephew of Hortense Mancini (herself now living an obscure but lively life in Chelsea). De Vendôme, who was a cousin of the King's (and the illegitimate grandson of Henry IV of France), was sufficiently handsome to turn Louise's head completely – the reason why he should have wished to do so remains obscure. When Charles heard of the affair, he wrote a protesting letter to Louis XIV, and expelled de Vendôme from England. He stopped short of sending Louise from Court, but she took herself off to France for a while. A broadsheet entitled *A Dialogue between the Duchess of Portsmouth and Madam Gwyn at Parting* celebrated her departure, with Nell protesting her own fidelity to the King:

> Let Fame, that never yet spoke well of woman,
> Give out I was a strolling whore and common;
> Yet have I been to him, since the first hour
> As constant as the needle to the flower

and went on to point out the relative cost to the State of Charles's *maîtress en titre* and his less expensive favourite:

> The people's hate, much less their curse, I fear.
> I do them justice with less sums a year.
> I neither run in court nor city's score,
> I pay my debts, distribute to the poor.

Plans for the new Versailles at Winchester were discussed with Sir Christopher Wren, and Charles ordered that ground should be cleared and building start. There was to be a fine palace, connected to the Cathedral by a tree-lined avenue, on each side of which courtiers were to be invited to build their own houses. The King, Wren and Nell rode out frequently to look over the ground and often went hawking together. Nell, it seems, despite her distaste for riding, had come to enjoy the latter sport – so much so that Charles actually made her Grand Falconer of England when the honour became vacant.

Back in town the winter was a cold one. The river froze over: on 9 January 1684, Evelyn 'went across the Thames on the ice (which was now become so incredibly thick as to bear not only whole streets of booths, in which they roasted meat, and had divers shops of wares, quite across as in a town, but coaches, carts and horses passed over).'[9] By the end of the month, 'coaches plied from Westminster to the Temple, and from several other stairs to and fro, as in the streets; also on sleds, sliding with skates. There was likewise bull-baiting, horse and coach-races, puppet plays and interludes, cooks, tippling [and] lewder places, so that it seemed to be a bacchanalian triumph or carnival on the water . . .'[10]

This was just the kind of thing both Nell and the King enjoyed. He ordered the building of a royal pavilion on the ice, and he and Nell entertained there. He seemed to enjoy her company more and more – and rewarded her for it by creating her son Duke of St Albans when the title fell vacant. With the title came apartments in Whitehall and an annuity of £1,500 a year. At Easter, she must have been pleased by an unusual gesture when he invited the new young Duke to take Holy Communion with him at Whitehall. Evelyn, stuffy as usual, disapproved when 'His Majesty, accompanied with three of his natural sons (viz. The Dukes of Northumberland, Richmond and St Albans, base sons of Portsmouth, Cleveland, Nelly – prostitute creatures) went up to the altar, the three boys entering before the King within the rails at the right hand, and three bishops on the left.'[11] A little later, Evelyn compared the bastards when he met them all at dinner:

> The Duke of Northumberland, another of His Majesty's natural sons, by that strumpet Cleveland . . . seemed to be a young gent of good capacity, well-bred, civil and modest . . . Of all His Majesty's children this seemed the most accomplished, and worth the owning; he is likewise extraordinary handsome and well-shaped. What the Dukes of Richmond and St Albans, base sons of the Duchess of Portsmouth, a French lass, and of Nelly, the comedian and applewoman's daughter, will prove their youth does not discover further than they are both very pretty boys and seem to have more wit than the rest.[12]

What the King, impecunious as usual, did not do was ensure that Nell received a regular income, though much of her capital was spent on entertaining him and his friends. She was forced to mortgage Bestwood Park, pawn some of her jewellery, and trouble the Duke of Ormonde again for money from Ireland. Charles gave her the lease of another house in Windsor – in Priest Street – which enlarged her holdings there, but that was no help in her present troubles. Hard up though she was, she continued to be generous to those less fortunate, getting down from her coach to rescue a poor clergyman who was being arrested by the sheriff's officers, and paying his debt for him. This got her the friendship of the Vicar of her parish, Dr Thomas Tenison, who since 1680 had been Vicar of St Martin-in-the-Fields, and was also a chaplain-in-ordinary to the King. He knew most of the eminent men of the day, and was much admired as a preacher, and though he had published a book attacking the Church of Rome, on a personal level he was charitable and kind to the Catholics in his parish – and charitable indeed to all; he was celebrated for his philanthropy.

Short of money though Nell was, she was as always unable to resist a pretty trinket, and when Lady Williams, a former mistress of the Duke of York, moved from her house in St James's Square, she liked the look of some gold ornaments, and borrowed the money with which to buy them from the Commissioner of Excise. (It was probably never repaid.) A letter survives, written to her sempstress 'Madame Jennings, over against the Tub Tavern in Jermyn Street' asking her to 'speak to my Lady Williams to send me the gold stuff and a note with it, because I must sign it, the next day . . . please tell her ladyship that I will send her a note of what quantity of things I'll have bought, if her ladyship will put herself to the trouble; when they are bought I will sign a note for her to be paid . . . Pray tell my Lady Williams that the King's mistresses are accounted ill paymasters, but she shall have her money the next day after I have the stuff.'[13]

There are a few other domestic details in the letter: Nell reminds Mrs Jennings about a mantle lined with musk-coloured satin, which she was evidently to make for her, but which had been forgotten (perhaps conveniently; did Mrs Jennings know how hard up Nell was?). She was pleased with a crochet of diamonds her son had brought down to Windsor with him – 'the finest thing that ever was seen'. She wanted a Mr Beaver, a jeweller, to come down to Burford House 'that I may bespeak a ring for the Duke of Grafton before he goes to France . . .' (a generous gift for Barbara's son).

Nell was unwell when she wrote the letter: 'I have continued extreme ill ever since you left me, and I am so still. I believe I shall die. My service to the Duchess of Norfolk, and tell her I am as sick as her Grace, but I do not know what I ail . . .' Her friends rallied around. Pepys, who had known her since she first went on the stage, and cherished a print of her naked except for angel's wings, put a naval yacht at her disposal so that she could take a little cruise for her health, and did her 'other small favours connected with the sea'.[14]

She was sufficiently well to go with the King to Newmarket in May for the racing, and then on to Winchester in August to see how the plans for the new Versailles were progressing. There, there was a slight spat with the Church when the King invited his chaplain, Thomas Ken, the prebendary of the Cathedral, to put some rooms in his house at her disposal. A biography of Ken gives the story:[15] 'The official known as the "harbinger" fixed on Ken's prebendal house for [Nell] . . . He met the message with an indignant refusal. "A woman of ill repute ought not to be endured in the house of a clergyman, least of all in that of the King's chaplain." "Not for his kingdom" would he comply with the King's demands. A local tradition relates that he took a practical way of settling the matter, by putting his house into the builder's hands for repair, and having it unroofed.'

The Dean was more cooperative, and had a room built for Nell at the south end of the deanery (though she did not occupy it long, as it was extremely damp and she was not in perfect health). The Reverend Ken's obduracy did him no harm with the King. When the bishopric of Bath and Wells became vacant a little later, Charles listened to a recital of the virtues of various candidates, and then remarked: 'Oddsfish! who should have it if not that little black fellow who would not give poor Nelly a lodging?'

The Winchester palace came to little or nothing: Charles died before it could do so. As it happens, Evelyn was impressed by what work had been done when he visited the city with Pepys in the autumn of 1685: 'placed on the side of a hill where formerly stood the old castle: a stately fabric of three sides and a corridor, all built of brick . . . columns at the break and entrance of freestone – intended for a hunting house when His Majesty came to those parts, and having an incomparable prospect. I believe there had already been £20,000 expended – but now His Majesty did not seem to encourage the finishing of it, at least for a while . . .'[16]

At Christmas 1684 Nell gave her usual party, and the King, as usual, attended. He did not join in the dancing, and was clearly not in the best of health. Uncharacteristically, he had been taking little exercise lately, under the excuse of an ulcer in his left leg which obstinately declined to heal. On Sunday 1 February he went to service in his private chapel, lunched with the Queen, dozed during the afternoon, and in the evening went over to Louise's apartments, where Barbara and Hortense Mancini were also present. Evelyn, disapproving as ever, winced at the amount of gaming that was going on, with at least £2,000 in gold wagered at basset. There was the King, 'in the midst of his three concubines' indulging in 'a scene of profuse gaming and luxurious dallying and profaneness'.[17] There was music, food and wine, and it seems a certain amount of mild love-making.

The King was in good spirits, but did not stay until the early hours of the morning. Instead, he went to his bedroom early with Thomas, Lord Bruce, one of the men attending on him, and sat for an hour or so talking with him about the palace at Winchester – the hall was due to be roofed that week. Then he went to bed. He slept ill, and when he got up discussed with Bruce what he should give Nell for her birthday that day. The courtier noticed that he looked pale and that his speech was thick – he seemed to have some difficulty in enunciating. He took a glass of sherry, and the barber and a surgeon came in to shave the King and dress his leg; but as he sat with the barber's sheet around him, he gave a loud cry and collapsed.

When the Duke of York arrived at his bedside, the King asked for the Queen. Catherine came immediately, and sat by her husband's bedside for two days until, exhausted, she had to get some rest in her own rooms. Louise attempted to see her lover, but was not allowed anywhere near. Hortense Mancini made her way from Chelsea, but was similarly excluded. The King was in no condition to insist on their presence, even supposing he wished it. Apart from his illness, he was being tortured by the doctors with bleeding, blistering with cantharides, enemas, red-hot irons applied to his shaven head and feet and all the other ludicrous treatments of the time: 'all the means that the art of man thought proper for the King's distemper', as Lady Anne Mason, the wife of a courtier, put it in her account of his deathbed.

He is perhaps more likely to have wanted to see Nell than Louise, but we have no evidence that she went to Whitehall, or even when she knew how ill the King was. She probably heard soon enough, however, for the news quickly circulated. The French Ambassador, Paul Barillon d'Amoncourt, called on Louise, ostensibly to offer condolences, but no doubt in a fruitless attempt to find out just what was going on. She told him that the King had told her some time previously that he had secretly gone over to Rome. Barillon immediately went to the Duke of York, and asked what could be done about arranging for a priest to have access to Charles. This would not be easy: Bishop Ken was laying siege at the bedroom door, eager to administer the Anglican sacraments.

James asked his brother in a whisper if he wished for a priest, and Charles whispered back that he did. Father Huddlestone, with whom he had discussed the Catholic faith all those years ago, before his exile, came secretly up the back stairs wrapped in a cloak, heard his confession, and administered the last rites.

Louise may have seen the King after this: there is an anecdote which says that the Duke of York interrupted her as she was trying to pull two diamond rings from the King's fingers. She certainly took the precaution of packing some boxes with valuables and sending them over to the French Embassy for safe keeping, in case things should turn nasty after her lover's death. She was still regarded by many people as little more than a common prostitute. So, of course, was Nell; but she was a Protestant. On Thursday, bedridden for four days, Charles made his famous apology for being 'such an unconscionable time dying'. The Queen came again, but fainted when she saw how her husband was suffering – chiefly, it must be said, from the attentions of the doctors. Carried to her own bed, she sent a message asking his forgiveness for her weakness. 'Alas, poor woman!' the King said, 'She beg my pardon! I beg hers, with all my heart.'

Five of his illegitimate sons – St Albans, Grafton, Northumberland, Southampton and Richmond – came to kneel at his bedside to receive his blessing. At dawn the following morning – Friday 6 February 1685 – he asked his attendants to wind up the clock in his room, and then draw the curtains so that he could see the sunrise for the last time. It is Evelyn who reports that 'he spoke to the Duke to be kind to his concubines the Duchess of Cleveland and especially Portsmouth, and that Nelly might not starve. I did not hear [he added drily] that he said anything of the church or his people . . .'[18] The words, if indeed they were spoken, were very possibly his last. He fell into a coma, and died at noon.

Evelyn was not disposed to mourn Charles graciously, speaking of his 'loss of reputation by a universal neglect of the public for the love of a voluptuous and sensual life, which a vicious court has brought into credit'.[19] The general public was more generous: most had rather enjoyed his reputation as a generous, forthright rake, unwilling to apologise for his weakness for wine, women and song. Nell certainly mourned him honestly. There is every reason to believe that she loved him quite as well as she would have loved any husband, and more wholeheartedly than Barbara, Louise or indeed any of his many other women – Hortense, Mall Davis and the rest. It is said that she stood, cloaked in black, in the Abbey when he was buried – unceremoniously, at night – and that when everyone else had left she stepped forward and placed flowers on his grave. Louise did not attend the funeral, and indeed was forbidden to display any signs of mourning – the new King was not going to regard her as a member of the royal family, the Dowager Whore, so to speak.

Nell decided that she had nothing to lose by approaching James II (who was crowned on 23 April) and enquiring about the possibility of a proper pension. 'Had I suffered for my God as I have done for your brother and you, I should not have needed either of your kindness or justice to me', she wrote. 'I beseech you not to do anything to the settling of my business till I speak with you, and appoint me by Mr Graham where I may speak with you privately. God make you as happy as my soul prays you may be.'[20]

She was not particularly poor: it was estimated that she was worth over £100,000. But her wealth was in property and her income was only £2,000 a year. Only? – It was a small fortune. But she had to keep up property, and she was used to living in some style. James understood her concern, received her, made her a present of £500, and promised that her affairs should be thoroughly looked into. Later in the year, Colonel Graham, who distributed funds from the Secret Service accounts, gave her another £500, and paid over £792 2s 3d 'to the several tradesmen, creditors of Mrs Ellen Gwyn, in satisfaction of their debts for which the said Ellen stood outlawed'.[21] She wrote a rather moving letter of thanks to the King:

Sir, This world is not capable of giving me a greater joy and happiness than your Majesty's favour, not as you are King and so have it in your power to do me good, having never loved your brother and yourself upon that account, but as to your person.

Had he lived, he told me before he died that the world should see by what he did for me that he had both love and value for me . . . He was my friend, and allowed me to tell him all my griefs, and did like a friend advise me and told me who was my friend and who was not . . . All you do for me shall be yours, it being my resolution never to have any interest but yours, and as long as I live to serve you, and when I die to die praying for you.[22]

James knew that what she said about her relationship with Charles was nothing less than the truth. He had known her almost as long as his brother, and clearly had considerably more regard for her than for Barbara or Louise, much less for Hortense or any of Charles's minor mistresses such as Mall Davis. The sentence about what Charles would have done for her perhaps related to her belief that at last the King was about to give her a title – that of Countess of Greenwich. There is some slender evidence that this may be the case: a note in a manuscript book written by one Fredrick van Bossen, quoted by Peter Cunningham in his 1908 biography, says that Nell 'should have been advanced to be Countess of Greenwich, but [was] hindered by the King's death'. Whether or not this was the case, it would in a sense have been a pity; Nell the commoner is a more attractive personality than Nell the Countess, however proud she would have been of the honour.

Shortly afterwards, when Colonel Graham was trying to explain the King's titles as King James VII of Scotland and II of England, she remarked that the late King had been her Charles III – Charles I having been Hart, and Charles II, Buckhurst.

She must surely have been somewhat embarrassed when Monmouth staged his abortive revolution in May 1685. She had always liked the boy – though she had always known that he was rash and unwise. His unwisdom led him this time to the scaffold, where Jack Ketch struck him five times with the axe, then had to sever his butchered head with a knife. The onlookers cheered, and many of those who had once entertained him now violently denied ever having taken his hand – just as London (Pepys ironically remarked) had been completely destitute of republicans when his father had marched into the city to reclaim the throne. There is no record that Nell ever said a bad word about Monmouth. She was not given to denying her friends.

After a period of mourning for Charles, she began to go about again in public – to the playhouse, as ever. She was clearly still attractive, at least to one Sir John Germaine, who was said to be the illegitimate son of William of Orange, and propositioned her. He was put down with the elegant remark that she 'would not lay the dog where the deer had lain'. Later, she gave evidence at a divorce case brought by the Duke of Norfolk, in which Germaine was cited as co-respondent. She recalled an evening at Windsor when they had played cards, and in the morning she had asked the Duchess how she had slept, and indeed how Sir John had slept, for the Duchess's hair was in such disorder as to suggest that it had been a pretty warm night.

From 1 January 1686, James granted her a new pension of £1,500 a year and paid off the mortgage of £3,774 2s 6d she had raised on Bestwood Park. But she seems to have been short of money despite this, for by December of that year she had to sell her pearls. In March 1687 – not long after she heard the news of the death of the Duke of Buckingham – she had a stroke. Sir Charles Littleton wrote to a friend that 'Mrs Nelly has been dying of an apoplexy. She is now come to her sense on one side, for the other is dead of a palsy.'[22] There is no reason to suppose that this was not the cause of her death, though naturally there were rumours that she had died of syphilis, and equally inevitably rumours that the late King had infected her.

Richard Lower, a well-known physician, attended her, and she haltingly entertained him with anecdotes of her life at Court. Dr Tenison, who had become a friend, visited her often, certainly with the condolences of the Church, but also because he had come to like and admire her. She had, according to Evelyn,[23] been seen at Mass the previous year in Dryden's company – but this may have simply been a gesture to King James; there is no evidence that she ever ceased to be 'the Protestant whore', though Papism became extremely fashionable after James's accession.[24] Eventually, probably at the beginning of July, Lower had to tell her that she was dying. She made her will, and on 18 October added a codicil containing several small personal bequests. Another doctor, Christian Harel, who had attended the

King, came to care for her, to make her passing as comfortable as possible. Less desperate to keep her alive than he and his colleagues had been to recover the King, he did not torture her with the blistering and hot irons her royal lover had suffered.

There is some uncertainty whether her seventeen-year-old son was at her bedside during her last illness. It seems probable that he was not. He had been continuously with the King in the last months of his life, but had then enlisted in the Imperial Army. Early in 1688 he was fighting against the Turks, so it is almost certainly the case that he had left England before his mother became seriously ill, and was not with her when, on 14 November 1687, aged thirty-seven, she died.

CHAPTER TEN

The Scoundrel Lass

The scoundrel lass
Rais'd from a dung-hill to a king's embrace . . .

Sir George Etherege, from The Lady of Pleasure

The manner of Nell's funeral on 17 November 1687, at St Martin's-in-the-Fields, and the contents of her will, have much to say about her.

First, it was a remarkably opulent and public funeral for someone of her reputation. It cost £375 – more than a year's income for a gentleman – and the church was crowded, particularly with apprentices and young people. She had always been popular, and while she had somewhat sunk out of sight since the King's death, people remembered her kindly – much more kindly than Charles's other two surviving mistresses. The actor and theatre manager Colley Cibber – who was sixteen when she died – expressed the popular view perfectly: 'She had less to be laid to her charge than any other of those ladies who were in the same state of preferment. She never meddled in matters of any serious moment, or was the tool of working politicians. Never broke into those amorous infidelities which others are accused of; but . . . was as visibly distinguished by her particular personal inclination for the King as her rivals were by their titles and grandeur.'[1]

She may have been, as Etherege put it, a 'scoundrel lass/Rais'd from a dung-hill to a king's embrace',[2] but she was buried like a lady. Her funeral sermon was preached by her friend Mr Tenison, who fewer than ten years later was to be enthroned as Archbishop of Canterbury. He was said to be the finest preacher in England: Evelyn (who almost certainly would have disapproved of his saying anything

177

favourable about Nell) called him 'one of the most profitable preachers in the church of England, being also of a most holy conversation, very learned and ingenious'. He had been at the Duke of Monmouth's side at Tyburn and if, as Jonathan Swift alleged, he was intolerant of levity and whist, he was certainly not intolerant when speaking of Nell. Had he unequivocally condemned her, the fact would undoubtedly have been reported with pleasure by her few enemies. Alas, we cannot know what he said, for no notes seem to have been taken of his sermon – though one oral tradition suggested that he quoted Shakespeare on Falstaff's death: she 'made a good end'.

Tenison chose to preach at Nell's funeral. She had hesitated to ask it, on the grounds that it might impede his career in the Church. And indeed, when in 1691 he was considered for the see of Lincoln, Viscount Villiers (the son-in-law of Charles's infamous pimp, Will Chiffinch) suggested to Queen Mary that such an appointment would be improper, for Tenison had preached 'a notable funeral sermon in praise of Ellen Gwyn'. The Queen, however – James's daughter – pointed out that this was surely 'a sign that the poor unfortunate woman died penitent; for, if I have read a man's heart through his looks, had she not made a truly pious end, the doctor could never have been induced to speak well of her'.[3]

Her will, signed with her initials (it described her, formally, as a spinster of the parish of St Martin's) was witnessed by her secretary, James Booth, and by Lady Hamilton Sandys, Edward Wybourne, Bishop John Warner, and William Scarborough. She left 'all houses, lands, tenements, offices, places, pensions, annuities, and hereditaments whatsoever, in England, Ireland or elsewhere' to 'my dear natural son his Grace the Duke of St Albans', together with 'all manner of my jewels, plate, household stuff, goods, chattels, credits, and other estate whatsoever', and with £100 for each of her executors.[4] The codicil, made three months later, was headed 'The last request of Mrs Ellen Gwinn to his Grace the Duke of St Albans'. In it, she asked to be buried in the chancel of St Martin's, and that a 'decent pulpit-cloth and cushion' should be given to the church on her behalf. In addition, £100 should be given to Dr Tenison 'for taking any poor debtors of the said parish out of prison, and for clothes this winter, and other necessities', and the Vicar should have an additional £50 for the use of Roman Catholic poor in the parish. Her son should also lay out £20 each year to get paupers out of prison at Christmas-time. Her sister Rose should have £200 within a year of Nell's death, her porter, Joe, should have £10, and the nurses who had cared for her deserved £10 each. Her servants should be provided with mourning, and paid whatever wages were due to them. There were bequests to 'my kinsman, Mr Cholmly' (of whom we know nothing; possibly he was a cousin – he received £5), and £50 each to Lady Fairborne and John Warner to buy mourning rings.

There was some little controversy later, when a second codicil was produced, allegedly dictated by her to a chaplain, John Warner. It was unsigned but had been 'read to the deceased and by her approval . . . declared as part of her last Will and Testament'.[5] In this, among other bequests, she left an extra £200 to her sister, and 'a ring of the value of £40 or £40 to buy a ring' to Rose's husband, Guy Forster (her first husband, the highwayman John Cassells, had died in 1675, and she had married again), tokens to her doctors, and a pension of £20 a year for life to an old servant, Bridget Long. The executors at first refused to accept the second codicil, but when it came before the Commissary of the Prerogative Court at Canterbury, it was accepted, and later proved.

The will was altogether a generous one, and was also an interesting testimony to Nell's free-thinking attitude to Catholicism (however proud she was to have been 'the Protestant whore'). The Duke of St Albans was left very well off. Nell might never have been treated as generously as either Barbara or Louise, but although she had spent plenty of money furnishing her houses and on entertaining – and gambling – there was an income of £2,000 settled on her son by Charles's widow in addition to the ready money his mother had left, and her considerable property and effects. Returning to England, the Duke set up at his mother's house in Pall Mall, and was on good terms with his uncle, James II. He never took a keen interest in the politics of the throne, and consequently, like Nell, was disliked by very few. He was placed in command of Princess Anne's 8th Regiment of Horse, which in turn was commanded by a Colonel Langston, who when William of Orange took the throne in 1688 placed it in support of the new king. William III liked the young Duke, who took his seat in the House of Lords in November 1691. He served under William at the campaign of Landen, in Flanders, in 1693, and was made Captain of the Gentleman Pensioners and Lord of the Bedchamber. In 1694 he married an heiress, Lady Diana de Vere, and after serving again with the King in Flanders was given a set of coach horses 'spotted like leopards' in recognition of his courage. King George I made him a knight of the Garter and he died, full of honours, in 1742.

He had eight sons – the third was created Lord Vere of Hanworth; the elder succeeded as second Duke of St Albans. The other six all married and had children – in 1901 it was calculated that there were at least 300 direct descendants of Nell Gwyn.

And what of the other major players in her story? Her two chief rivals, for instance?

It really does seem to have been by accident that Barbara was in London at the time of Charles's death. She had been living in France for some time, but a month or so before the King's fatal illness had come to London on a visit, settled into a house in Arlington Street, Piccadilly, and had begun an affair with an actor called Cardonnell Goodman, a highly disreputable character who only the previous year had been convicted of a conspiracy to poison two of her sons. In March 1686 she had a son of whom he was presumed to be the father ('the town has christened [him] Goodman Cleveland', one gossip wrote).[6]

Goodman – who rejoiced in the nickname 'Scum' – does seem to have been devoted to Barbara: when appearing on stage as Julius Caesar or Alexander the Great, he would scan the audience on his first entrance, and not seeing her would cry 'Is my duchess come?' and decline to proceed until she was in her seat. Nevertheless, he was not husband material, and came to a mysterious and probably bad end: arrested for causing a Jacobin riot in London he was sent to Newgate, and when last heard of was languishing in chains in the Bastille.

When the Earl of Castlemaine died in 1705, Barbara married a soldier, Major-General Robert Feilding, ten years her junior. After seven months, Beau Feilding, as he was called – an eccentric who insisted on having his tea ceremoniously beaten in by a drum – was himself sent to Newgate for threatening and beating his wife. He was then found to be already married, and the marriage to Barbara was annulled. She retired to Walpole House, Chiswick, where she looked after her daughter Barbara's illegitimate son (whose mother remained a nun in Paris) and died in October 1709, her body swollen with dropsy. She lies in Chiswick parish church.

Her second son, Henry Fitzroy, became Duke of Grafton in 1675, was Vice-Admiral of England in 1682 and Lord High Constable at the coronation of James II. He commanded his uncle's army against his half-brother, the Duke of Monmouth, but later took the side of William of Orange, and was fatally injured at the siege of Cork. His son, the 2nd Duke, was kind to Barbara in her last illness; the 3rd Duke became Prime Minister and fathered fourteen legitimate and eighteen illegitimate children.

Barbara's second child, Charles Fitzroy, was at first Lord Limerick (the title of the Earl of Castlemaine's elder son), but when Charles recognised him he became Duke of Southampton, and on his mother's death, Duke of Cleveland. He was not an exciting man, and the title only briefly survived his death, for his eldest son died without issue, and the other two never married. Her third son, George Fitzroy, was made Duke of Northumberland in 1683, and was highly regarded (not least by the critical Evelyn). Her first daughter, Anne, married the Earl of Sussex in 1675 and lived until 1722; her sons died young, and the title passed on through her second daughter, Charlotte Fitzroy, who married the Earl of Litchfield. Her daughter by John Churchill, the Duke of Monmouth, having had an illegitimate child by the Earl of Arran (later the Duke of Hamilton), died in 1737 as Prioress of a nunnery at Pontoise.

Though there were rumours that Louise privately accused James II of having poisoned his brother, she was well treated by the new King, who upon his accession gave her £12,000. However, she was entirely aware of just how disliked she was in England, and in August 1685 made for France, where she had salted away a considerable fortune. Her son, the Duke of Richmond, had been granted French citizenship in order to succeed to her title as Duchess of Auvigny and to her estates there, and she took him with her together with every piece of plate and jewellery she could lay her hands on.

She lived in some style in Paris, gambling heavily, as was her wont, and making herself unpopular by malicious gossip and comment. She returned to England for almost a year in 1686, and again in 1688, when her niece was married to the infamous hanging Judge Jeffreys. A number of disasters then fell swiftly upon her. She fell foul of King William III (a staunch Anglican who mistrusted all Catholics) and her pension was withdrawn. Then in 1691 a fire broke out at Westminster and destroyed her apartments with all their luxurious decorations and furniture. Finally, in 1692 her son left her to live permanently in England.

The last years of her life were impoverished. She lived on her estate at Auvigny as it gradually fell into ruin for lack of repairs, and when Voltaire visited her in 1718 she was still beautiful but almost penniless. Her son Richmond became a Catholic soon after his introduction to the Court of Louis XIV in 1685, joined the army as aide-de-camp to the Duc d'Orléans, and was given his own cavalry regiment. Later, he came to England to support William of Orange, renounced his Catholicism, married, and settled at Goodwood House. King William refused Louise permission to land when she tried to visit her son in 1697. After a somewhat rackety life, Richmond died in 1723; Louise followed him in November of 1734, and was buried in the church of the Barefooted Carmelites in Paris.

We know little of the later life of that admired actress, dancer and singer Mall Davis. Her daughter Lady Mary Tudor was married three times and died in Paris in 1726; two of her grandsons were executed for treason as Jacobites. Hortense Mancini continued to live the high life in Chelsea after Charles's death, declined to notice that she was growing old, and had a number of more or less notorious affairs. She eventually died in 1699, and her body was taken to France, where at long last her husband, who had grown no saner with the years, laid hands upon her and took her to his estate. Her coffin lay unburied for some months while local people came to touch it or lay tributes on it, and brought their children to it to be cured of a variety of illnesses. She was eventually buried in the family vault next to the great Cardinal, her relative. A century later, during the French Revolution, the mob broke open her coffin and burned her bones.

Queen Catherine had been shattered by her husband's death. She had come to terms with his lifestyle many years earlier, and while she may not have liked it, she had learned to tolerate his mistresses and be courteous and even friendly towards them. On his death, she retired into the deepest mourning. Evelyn called on her on 5 March 1685 and found her in her apartments in Whitehall 'on a bed of mourning, the whole chamber ceiling and floor hung with black, tapers lighted, so as nothing could be more lugubrious and solemn'.[7] A brief two months after the funeral, she left the Palace of Whitehall – probably with some relief – and went to live in rooms in Somerset House, occasionally travelling out to spend a few days at a convent she had established at Hammersmith. After a while, she recovered sufficiently to enjoy an occasional game of cards, or to listen to music. When the Duke of Monmouth was awaiting execution in the Tower, he sent her frenzied appeals for her intervention on his behalf; but she closed her ears to them. On 10 June 1688, she was present at the birth of the Prince of Wales, and swore a deposition that he was indeed the son of Queen Mary.

King James plainly found her tiresome, and she seems to have become obsessed with money, engaging in lawsuits against Lord Clarendon, once her chamberlain, and others. These delayed her plans to travel to Portugal, and she was caught in London at the time of the Revolution. King William was kindly disposed to her, but the public agitation against Catholics forced him to appeal to her to adopt a low profile and to leave Somerset House. Then there was trouble with Queen Mary, who took offence when a prayer for the King's success in his war in Ireland was omitted from a service in the Savoy Chapel where the services were arranged by Catherine.

She finally left England in complete privacy in March 1692. She was received with great rejoicing in Lisbon, but resisted the public eye and settled into a quiet life in the Palace of Bemposta, which she had built a little way out of the city. Occasionally the nobility of Portugal would ceremoniously call on her, and in 1704 she agreed to act as regent to her brother Pedro, who was sick. She died suddenly, of colic, on the last day of 1705, leaving an enormous estate.

Of all Charles's women, Nell Gwyn is the one everyone remembers. For every person who has heard of Barbara Palmer (whose reputation was somewhat renewed when she appeared as a character in the once scandalous novel *Forever Amber*), a thousand have heard of 'Mrs Nelly'. There is no memorial to her, in St Martin-in-the-Fields or anywhere else, but houses all over the south-east of England are pointed out as places where she once stayed. And well within living memory, on the Sunday next to Christmas, an orange was placed on a chair near her place in the Savoy Chapel in memory of her.

In an age when scandal and gossip left few reputations untarnished, she escaped condemnation by all except the most puritanical. For a few months near the beginning of her life, it might have been possible to call her a common prostitute. But from the moment when the King first summoned her, there was never any suggestion that she granted her sexual favours to anyone but him; she was as faithful to him as the Queen. She was high spirited, witty, beautiful and sexy, good natured and charitable, a faithful friend, loved money no better than most people and disliked hypocrisy more than was usual in the circles in which she moved. If a monarch is to have a mistress, he might do worse than take her as a model.

Nell Gwyn's Birth-chart

Nell Gwyn's birth-chart was set up by Elias Ashmole, who learned astrology from the greatest astrologer of the age, William Lilly. For those interested in the subject, the chart shows that at the time of her birth the rising sign was 8°26' of Capricorn, and the MC 15° of Scorpio. The Sun was on 00°37' of Aquarius, the Moon on 00°40' of Pisces, Mercury on 8°59' of Aquarius, Venus on 21°56' of Capricorn, Mars on 28°54' of Aquarius, Jupiter on 8°52' of Scorpio, and Saturn retrograde on 23°45' of Gemini. These are the only planets Ashmole would have known. Modern astrologers also consider the positions of Uranus (on 16°51' of Sagittarius), Neptune (on 16°35' of Sagittarius) and Pluto (retrograde on 9°11' of Gemini).

All this would reveal to an astrologer (taking into account the effects of the 'modern' planets, traits which Ashmole would have ascribed to other influences) that Nell Gwyn was indeed extremely ambitious and an eager social climber, and that she possessed the kind of glamour we now ascribe to popular performers – that she made a success of her stage career would be no surprise to an astrologer. She would always have had her eye stubbornly on the main chance, something which may have alienated her from her contemporaries, especially in her early life, though the emphasis on Aquarius signifies a natural kindness and a protective element (ascribed to Capricorn); she would not have forgotten old friends. The placing of Jupiter at the top of the chart is often found in the horoscopes of actors (and politicians), and underlines her dramatic magnetism. She did not lack the wiles to persuade men and women to accede to her wishes, though she would seem to have had a quick temper and a certain taste for a dramatic scene off-stage as well as on. The talent to amuse, both verbally and sexually, are underlined. Both a love of money and the capacity to be extremely generous are shown, and her horoscope underlines the probability that she found her earliest experiences of prostitution distasteful, and was eager to move onwards and upwards.

A comparison between her chart and that of Charles II ('synastry' as astrologers call it) shows a number of strong links of the sort often found between long-term partners, those experiencing deep emotional and/or sexual relationships. The sexual pull between them would be ascribed by astrologers to her Mars being in a sextile relationship to his Venus, an aspect found very commonly in strong relationships, and his Mars being conjunct her Jupiter underlines this. A number of other elements link the two charts – and some suggest the nature of the relationship: the trine between their Saturns indicates the way in which she viewed it – the fact that unlike his other mistresses she knew that there were some areas of his life which she could not and should not attempt to share.

Plays in which Nell Gwyn Appeared, 1665–71

Speculative performances are marked *.

PLAYWRIGHT	TITLE	CHARACTER	DATE[1]
John Dryden	The Indian Emperor	Cydaria	March 1665
James Howard	The English Monsieur	Lady Wealthy	8 December 1666
Beaumont and Fletcher	The Humorous Lieutenant	Celia	20 December 1666
Beaumont and Fletcher	The Chances	Constantia	5 February 1667
Richard Rhodes	Flora's Vagueries	Flora	14 February 1667
John Dryden	Secret Love	Florimel	2 March 1667
Beaumont and Fletcher	The Knight of the Burning Pestle	[Prologue]	? March 1667
James Howard	All Mistaken	Mirida	April 1667
Sir Robert Howard	The Surprisal	Samira	April 26, 1667
Sir Robert Howard	The Committee	?	13 May 1667
Beaumont and Fletcher	A King and No King	Panthea	September 1667
Lord Orrery	The Black Prince	Alicia	19 October 1667
Sir Robert Howard	The Duke of Lerma	Donna Maria	20 February 1668
Robert Howard	The Great Favourite	Maria	1668
Sir William Davenant	The Man's the Master	Lucilla	7 May 1668
Sir Charles Sedley	The Mulberry Garden	?	18 May 1668

1. All dates should be taken as approximate first nights.

PLAYWRIGHT	TITLE	CHARACTER	DATE
Beaumont and Fletcher	Philaster	Bellaria	30 May 1668
John Dryden	An Evening's Love	Donna Jacintha	12 June 1668
John Lacy	The Old Troop	Doll Troop	31 July 1668
Richard Flecknoe	Demoiselles á la Mode	Lysette	14 September 1668
Ben Jonson	Cataline's Conspiracy	[Prologue]	19 December 1668
James Shirley	The Sisters	Pulcheria	? 1668
John Dryden	Tyrannic Love	Valeria	? 1669
John Dyrden	The Conquest of Granada	Almahide	1670/1
John Dryden	*The Assignation	?	? August 1673

The *Dictionary of National Biography* lists the following plays: no evidence has been found that she actually appeared in any of them, but they are listed here for interest: they should be treated gingerly – the idea of Nell Gwyn as Queen Elizabeth is ludicrous, if interesting.

Aphra Behn	The Rover	Angelica Bianca	1677
Anon	The Constant Nymph	?	1677
Samuel Pordage	The Siege of Babylon	Thalestris	1677
Thomas Otway	Friendship in Fashion	Lady Squeamish	1678
Aphra Behn	Sir Patient Fancy	Lady Knowell	1678
Thomas Southerne	The Loyal Brother	Sunamire	1682
John Banks	Unhappy Favourite, or the Earl of Essex	Queen Elizabeth	1682

'A Panegyric upon Nelly'

The following text of 'A Panegyric upon Nelly', dated 1681 in its earliest MS, appeared in a collection of Rochester's poems published in 1756. It is stylistically clear that it was not written by Rochester, and the author remains unknown – but it reflects a striking contemporary view.

Of a great heroine I mean to tell,
And by what just degrees her titles swell
To Mrs Nelly grown, from cinder Nell.
Much did she suffer first on bulk[1] and stage
From the blackguard and bullies of the age;
Much more her growing virtue did sustain,
While dear Charles Hart and Buckhurst sued in vain.
In vain they sued; cursed be the envious tongue
That her undoubted chastity would wrong,
For should we fame believe, we then might say
That thousands lay with her, as well as they.
But, fame, thou liest, for her prophetic mind
Foresaw her greatness. Fate had well designed,
And her ambition chose to be before
A virtuous countess, an imperial whore.
Even in her native dirt her soul was high
And did at crowns and shining monarchs fly;
E'en while she cinders raked, her swelling breast
With thoughts of glorious *whoredom* was possessed;
Still did she dream (nor did her birth withstand)
Of dangling scepters in her dirty hand.
But first the basket her fair arm did suit,
Laden with pippins and Hesperian fruit.
This first step raised, to th'wandering pit she sold

The lovely fruit, smiling with streaks of gold.
Fate now for her did its whole force engage,
And from the pit she's mounted to the stage;
There in full lustre did her glories shine,
And, long eclipsed, spread forth their light divine;
There Hart's and Rowley's[2] soul she did ensnare,
And made a *king* the rival to a player.
The *king* o'ercomes; and to the royal bed
The dunghill-offspring is in triumph led –
Nor let the envious her first rags object
To her, that's now in tawdry gayness decked.
Her merit does from this much greater show,
Mounting so high, that took her rise so low.
Less fam'd that Nelly[3] was whose cuckold rage
In ten years wars did half the world engage.
She's now the darling strumpet of the crowd,
Forgets her state, and talks to them aloud;
Lays by her greatness, and descends to prate
With those 'bove whom she's raised by wond'rous fate;
True to th'Protestant government and laws;
The choice delight of the whole *mobile*,
Scarce Monmouth's self is more belov'd than she.
Was this the cause that did their quarrel move,
That both are rivals to the people's love?
No, 'twas her matchless loyalty alone
That bids prince Perkin[4] pack up and be gone.
Illbred thou art, says prince. Nell does reply,
Was Mrs Barlow[5] better bred than I?
Thus sneak'd away the *nephew* overcome;
By *aunt-in-law*'s severer wit struck dumb.
    Her virtue, loyalty, wit, and noble mind
In the foregoing doggerel you may find.
Now, for her piety, one touch, and then
To Rymer[6] I'll resign my muse and pen.
'Twas thus that raised her charity so high
To visit those that did in durance lie;

From Oxford prisons many did she free –
There died her father, and there gloried she
In giving others life and liberty.
So pious a remembrance still she bore
E'en to the fetters that her father wore.
Nor was her mother's funeral less her care,
No cost, no velvet did the daughter spare;
Fine gilded 'scutchions did the hearse enrich
To celebrate the martyr of the ditch,[7]
Burnt brandy did in flaming brimmers flow,
   Drunk at her funeral; while her well-pleased shade
Rejoiced e'en in the sober fields below
   At all the drunkenness her death had made.

Was ever child with such a mother blessed?
Or even mother such a child possessed?
Nor must her cousin[8] be forgot, preferred
From many years command in the black-guard
To be a ensign; –
Whose tattered colours well do represent
His first estate i'th'ragged regiment.
   Thus we in short have all the virtues seen
Of the incomparable madam Gwyn;
Nor wonder, others are not with her shown;
She who no equal has, must be *alone*.

Brit. Mus. MS Harl 7319, BL C.131.b.5 Pp102/5

Estimated Incomes in 1688

In estimating the modern value of sums of money mentioned in the text, *Charles Davenant's Works,* published in 1771, may be helpful. In a table, he showed the annual family income of various classes of people for the year 1688. They included:

Temporal Lords	£3,200
Spiritual Lords	£1,300
Baronets	£800
Knights	£650
Esquires	£450
Gentlemen	£280
Eminent merchants and traders	£400
Persons in law	£154
Eminent clergymen	£72
Lesser clergymen	£50
Farmers	£42 10s
Shopkeepers and tradesmen	£45
Naval officers	£60
Military officers	£60
Common seamen	£20
Labouring people and out-servants	£15
Common soldiers	£14
Cottagers	£6 10s

'Pindaric'

The following 'Pindaric' or mock eulogy of Lady Castlemaine was published, *c.* 1670, by an anonymous satirist.

> Let ancients boast no more
> Their lewd imperial whore
> Whose everlasting lust
> Survived her body's latest thrust,
> And when that transitory dust
> Had no more vigour left in store
> Was still as fresh and active as before.[1]
>
> Her glory must give place
> To one of modern British race
> Whose every daily act exceeds
> The other's most transcendent deeds.
> She has at length made good
> That there is human flesh and blood
> Even able to outdo
> All that their loosest wishes prompt 'em to.
>
> When she has jaded quite
> Her almost boundless appetite,
> Clayed with the choicest banquets of delight,
> She'll still drudge on in tasteless vice
> As if she sinned for exercise
> Disabling stoutest stallions every hour,
> And when they can perform no more
> She'll rain at 'em and kick 'em out of door . . .
>
> Now tell me all ye powers,
> Who e'er could equal this lewd dame of ours?

Lais herself must yield
And vanquished Julia[2] quit the field.
Nor can that princess one day famed
As wonder of the earth
For Minataurus' glorious birth[3]
With admiration any more be named.
These puny heroines of history
Eclipsed by her shall all forgotten be
Whil'st her great name confronts Eternity.

Brit. Mus. MS Harl. 6913

'Last Instructions to a Painter'

In 1667 Andrew Marvell put into verse the anecdote circulating at the time which suggested that Barbara, Lady Castlemaine, ordered her running footman to take a bath with her.

> She through her lackey's drawers, as he ran,
> Discerned love's cause, and a new flame began.
> Her wonted joys thenceforth and Court she shuns,
> And still within her mind the footman runs:
> His brazen calves, his brawny thighs (the face
> She slights), his feet shaped for a smoother race.
> Poring within her glass she readjusts
> Her looks, and oft-tried beauty now distrusts;
> Fears lest he scorn a woman once assayed,
> And now first wished she e'er had been a maid.
> Great love, how dost thou triumph and how reign,
> That to a groom couldst humble her disdain!
> Stripped to her skin, see how she stooping stands,
> Nor scorns to rub him down with those fair hands,
> And washing (lest the scent her crime disclose)
> His sweaty hooves, tickles him 'twixt the toes.
> But envious fame too soon began to note
> More gold in's fob, more lace upon his coat.
> And he, unwary and of tongue too fleet,
> No longer could conceal his fortune sweet.
> Justly the rogue was whipped in porter's den,
> And Jermyn straight has leave to come again.

ll. 70–102

Bill for Nell Gwyn's Bedstead

John Coques's detailed bill for Nell Gwyn's silver bedstead includes the following details:

Delivered ye King's head weighing 197 ounces
One figure weighing 445 ounces
ye other figure with ye character weighing 428 ounces
ye slaves and ye rest belonging unto it 255 ounces
ye two eagles weighing 169 ounces
one of the crowns weighing 94 ounces
ye second crown weighing 97 ounces
ye third crown weighing 90 ounces
ye fourth crown weighing 82 ounces
one of ye cupids weighing 121 ounces
ye second boy weighing 101 ounces
ye third boy weighing 93 ounces
ye fourth boy weighing 88 ounces
Altogether two thousand two hundred sixty five ounces . . . of
sterling silver at 8s per ounce, comes to £906 0s 10d
Paid for Jacob Hall dancing upon ye rope of wire work £1 10s
Paid to ye cabinet maker for ye great board for ye head of the
bedstead and for the other board that comes under it . . . £3

From H. Noel Williams, *Nell Gwyn, Louise de Kéroüalle and Hortense Mancini* (London, 1915), p. 171.

Notes

1. A QUEEN IN IMAGINATION

1. Quoted in Antonia Fraser, *The Weaker Vessel* (London, 1984), p. 467.
2. Quoted in E.J. Burford, *Wits, Wenches and Wantons*, p. 124.
3. But see pp. 90–1.
4. Some biographers have claimed that the best-known astrologer of the time, William Lilly, cast the chart, but a comparison between it and the calligraphy of the charts in Lilly's client book makes it quite clear that he did not.
5. For an assessment of her astrological chart, see Appendix I.
6. There is no official record of the marriage.
7. William Maitland, *The History of London* (1739), p. 32.
8. *The Life and Times of Anthony Wood,* (1632–95) ed. Andrew Clark (Oxford, 1895), vol. iii, p. 167.
9. John Oldham, 'The Streets of London', from *A Satire in imitation of the Third of Juvenal* (*c.* 1670), ll. 1–9.
10. Oldham, ibid., ll. 22–8.
11. Quoted in W.G. Bell, *The Great Fire of London* (London, 1920), p. 38.
12. John Taylor, *The World Run on Wheels* (1623).
13. *Index to Remembrancia* (London, 1878), p. 421.

14. *Memoirs of the Life of Eleanor Gwinn, a celebrated courtesan in the reign of Charles II and Mistress to that Monarch.* Printed for F. Stamper 'in Pope's-Head-Alley, Cornhill'. MDCCLII [BL 1416.h.41]. Subsequent references in notes allude to *Biog. 1752.*
15. *Biog. 1752,* pp. 4–5.
16. Pepys, *Diary,* 26 October 1667. By 'strong water' Nell probably meant the cheap so-called *aqua vitae* made from fermented grain, or sometimes leftover wine, and sold cheaply in innumerable 'strong-water houses'.
17. 'Madam Nelly's Complaint', attributed (probably wrongly) to Sir George Etherege.

2. HIGH DESIRES

1. The chief source of the story is a footnote scribbled by Lord Dartmouth in his copy of G. Burnet's *History of my own Time* in 1720: G. Burnet, *History of my own Time,* 2 vols, ed. Osmond Airey (Oxford, 1897).
2. Saul, son of Kish (I Samuel ix) was 'a choice young man and a goodly . . . from his shoulders and upward he was higher than any of the people'.

3. From 'An Historical Poem' printed in *The Poems and Letters of Andrew Marvell* (Oxford, 1952), p. 201. Though sometimes attributed to Marvell, the poem's provenance is uncertain.

4. Edward Hyde, first Earl of Clarendon (1609–74), statesman and historian, was one of Charles II's principal advisers. His continual efforts to reform the King were unsuccessful.

5. John Wilmot, 2nd Earl of Rochester (1647–80), a close friend of Charles throughout their lives.

6. Letter to Madame St George, 6 May 1630.

7. Ibid.

8. Sir Samuel Tuke, *A Character of Charles II* (1660).

9. Gilbert Burnet, cited by Williams, *Rival Sultanas*, p. 82.

10. 'A Satire on Charles II', Rochester, *Poems*, p. 74.

11. Thurloe State Papers, BL RB. 31.c.185, p. 645.

12. 'Don Carlo', as he was called, was very like his father, and promised well, but died in 1680 before his promise could be fulfilled. His enormous debts at his death included a massive tailor's bill.

13. Theobald Lord Taafe, later Lord Carlingford, was an Anglo-Irish peer who during Charles's exile was (as Cardinal de Retz put it) 'Great Chamberlain, Valet de Chambre, Clerk of the Kitchen, Cup Bearer and all'.

14. Baronne d'Aulnoy, *Memoirs of the Court of England in 1675*, ed. G.D. Gilbert (London), p. 175.

15. Evelyn, *Diary*, 18 July 1649.

16. Quoted Fraser, *King Charles II*, p. 154.

17. Pepys, *Diary*, 21 October 1666. The King, in response, claimed that Killigrew was 'a notorious liar' and ordered the Duke of York to dismiss him from his service.

18. Abel Boyer, *The History of the Life and Reign of Queen Anne* (London, 1722), p. 48 (Appendix).

19. Bodleian Library, Clarendon MSS, 1659–60, vol. 69, fol. 101.

20. Pepys, *Diary*, 7 November 1666.

21. George Vertue MSS, Brit. Mus. Add MSS 23068–76.

22. Portrait in the collection of the Earl Bathurst.

23. *The Times*, 8 March 1950, p. 14.

24. *Dictionary of National Biography*.

25. Nell, when she had a fine silver bed specially constructed, in which to entertain the King, had a little figure of Jacob carved on it, among the cupids and crowns.

26. Pepys, *Diary*, 13 July 1660.

27. Pepys, *Diary*, 14 October 1660.

28. Pepys, *Diary*, 20 April 1661.

29. Pepys, *Diary*, 31 December 1662.

30. John Anderson, *Memoirs of the House of Hamilton* (Edinburgh, 1825).

31. Pepys, *Diary*, 21 May 1662.

32. Pietro Aretino (1492–1556), the Italian satirical poet whose licentious *sonnetti lussuriosi* and illustrations of them have been keenly admired by amateurs of pornography for the past four centuries.

33. 'A man with an erection needs no excuse'.

34. Pepys, *Diary*, 15 May 1663.
35. W.D. Macray, *Notes which passed at Meetings of the Privy Council between Charles II and the Earl of Clarendon* (Roxburghe Club, 1896), n. 26, p. 69.
36. Evelyn, *Diary*, 30 May 1662.
37. Andrew Marvell.
38. Pepys, *Diary*, 17 February 1667.
39. See pp. 30–1.
40. Burnet, *History of my Own Time*, vol. I, p. 307.
41. *Letters of Philip Stanhope, second Earl of Chesterfield, including some short notes for my remembrance of things and accidents as they happened to me*, Brit. Mus. Add MSS 19, 253, fol. 48.
42. *Dictionary of National Biography* entry under Chiffinch.
43. *Poems on Affairs of State* (London, 1698; 1703 edn, i 97).
44. *Continuation of the Life of Edward, Earl of Clarendon*, 2 vols (London, 1827), para. 359.
45. Lord Cornbury to the Marchioness of Worcester, 10 June 1662, HMC (Report of the Royal Commission on Historical MSS), 12, IX p. 52.
46. *Poems on Affairs of State*, op. cit., p. 164.
47. Anon, *A Lampoon*, Bodl. MS Don B18 and see Appendix V.
48. Philip Ziegler, *King Edward VIII* (London, 1990), p. 236.
49. Pepys, *Diary*, 15 May 1663.
50. See *The Kind Mistress*, Appendix V.
51. Pepys, *Diary*, 14 July 1663.
52. Pepys, *Diary*, 21 April 1666.
53. Pepys, *Diary*, 9 November 1663.
54. Pepys, *Diary*, 26 April 1667.
55. C.H. Hartman, *La Belle Stuart* (London, 1924), p. 113.
56. C.H. Hartmann, *Charles II and Madame* (London, 1934), p. 49.
57. Pepys, *Diary*, 4 July 1663.
58. Penis.
59. A ballad called 'The Hay-Market Hectors', attr. Andrew Marvell.

3. FROM THE PIT TO THE STAGE

1. William Prynne, *Histrio-Mastix, the Players' Scourge* (1635).
2. *The Actors Remonstrance* (1643).
3. Aubrey, *Brief Lives*.
4. *Representative Actors*, ed. W. Clark Russell, p. 9n.
5. Richard and Helen Leacroft, *Theatre and Playhouse*, p. 72.
6. Pepys, *Diary*, 8 May 1663.
7. Evelyn, *Diary*, 5 February 1664.
8. 5p.
9. 7½p.
10. 20p.
11. 12½p.
12. Cibber, *An Apology for the Life of Mr Colley Cibber*.
13. About 34p.
14. The cry is recorded by Thomas Shadwell in his play *The Virtuoso* (1676).
15. 'Half crown my play, sixpence my orange cost': from prologue to *The Feign'd Curtizans* (1679).
16. Quoted in Henriques, *Prostitution and Society*, vol. II, pp. 107–8.
17. The petition was successful: eight of the apprentices were executed for riot.
18. £1.50 and £2.50 respectively.
19. Quoted in Fraser, *The Weaker Vessel*, p. 481.

20. Thomas Shadwell, epilogue to *The Libertine* (1676).
21. *The Session of Ladies.*
22. Rochester, 'A Panegyric upon Nelly', see Appendix III.
23. *Biog. 1752*, p. 6.
24. In a letter to Thomas Browne, the Duke of York's cupbearer.
25. 'A Panegyric to Nelly' (see Appendix III).
26. James Wright, *Historia Histrionica* (London, 1699).
27. Ibid.
28. R. Wewitzer, *Dramatic Remains* (1745).
29. *Biog. 1752*, p. 7.
30. Charles Gilden, *Lives and Characters of the English Dramatic Poets* (London, 1790).
31. *Momus Triumphans, or the Plaigaries of the English Stage Exposed* (London, 1687).
32. Cibber, *An Apology.*
33. *Le Grand Cyrus*, by Madeleine de Scudéry.
34. Dryden, *Secret Love, Works*, vol. IX, pp. 127–8.
35. *Enjoué* – playful, vivacious.
36. Dryden, *Secret Love, Works*, vol. IX, pp. 198–9.
37. Pepys, *Diary*, 2 March 1667.
38. J.H. Wilson, *All the King's Ladies* (Chicago, 1958).
39. Prologue, *The Duke of Lerma.*
40. Dryden, *The Indian Emperor, Works*, vol. IX, p. 107.
41. Pepys, *Diary*, 22 August and 11 November 1667.
42. Pepys, *Diary*, 23 January 1667.
43. Thomas Jordan, 'A Prologue to Introduce the First Woman that Came to Act on the Stage in the Tragedy called the Moor of Venice', *A Royal Arbor of Loyal Poesie* (London, 1664), p. 21.
44. Quoted by Geoffrey Tillotson, *The Times Literary Supplement*, 20 July 1933, p. 494.
45. Jordan, 'A Prologue to Introduce the First Woman . . .'
46. See p. 78.
47. John Downes, *Roscius Anglicanus*, (London, 1708), pp. 23–4.
48. Pepys, *Diary*, 14 January 1668.
49. *Biog. 1752*, p. 11.
50. Pepys, *Diary*, 1 May 1667.

4. NELL'S MERRY PARTS

1. Pepys, *Diary*, 15 October 1663.
2. Lists of the dead.
3. Quoted in A.F. Scott, *Every One a Witness: the Stuart Age* (London, 1974), pp. 259–60.
4. Thomas Dekker, *Work for Armourers* (1609).
5. Pepys, *Diary*, 19 March 1666.
6. Anthony Wood, *Diary.*
7. Pepys, *Diary*, 7 December 1666.
8. See pp. 52–4.
9. Pepys, *Diary*, 25 March 1667.
10. See pp. 61–2.
11. Quoted in C.H. Wilson, *Profit and Power* (London, 1957), p. 19.
12. Aubrey, *Brief Lives.*
13. Rochester, 'Song', *Poems*, p. 20.
14. Not to be confused with the other 'Little Sid', the noble young poet Sidney Godolphin, slain during the Civil War.
15. Pepys, *Diary*, 23 October 1668.
16. Buckhurst, 'On Bonny Black Bess'. 'Black Bess' was a Mrs Barnes, one of Buckhurst's mistresses.

17. Pepys, *Diary*, 13 July 1667.
18. E.W. Brayley, *History of Surrey* (London, 1826).
19. Pepys, *Diary*, 14 July 1667.
20. 'The Advice', *The Poems of Charles Sackville Sixth Earl of Dorset*, ed. Brice Harris.
21. Pepys, *Diary*, 12 July 1667.
22. *Biog. 1752*, pp. 32–4.
23. He was one of her trustees when Burford House at Windsor was settled on her.
24. See p. 10.
25. Pepys, *Diary*, 5 October 1667.

5. LOVE'S THEATRE, THE BED

1. Quoted in Barton, *Tunbridge Wells*.
2. *Memoirs of the Comte de Gramont*, pp. 270–1.
3. Rochester, 'Tunbridge Wells: a satyr', *Poems*, pp. 69–74.
4. By scurvy, Rochester meant syphilis.
5. spleen – melancholy.
6. mum – beer.
7. those – menstruation pains.
8. steel-waters – the Wells' waters had a 'steely' taste.
9. Cuff and Kick are two characters in Thomas Shadwell's play *Epsom Wells*, in which Cuff remarks, 'Others come here to procure conception' and Kick replies, 'Ay, pox! – that's not from the waters, but something else that shall be nameless.'
10. Burnet, *History of My Own Time*, vol. I, p. 480.
11. Pepys, *Diary*, 7 September 1667.
12. Jusserand, *A French Ambassador at the Court of Charles II*, p. 89.

13. Rochester, *Poems*, p. 25.
14. Pepys, *Diary*, 11 January 1668.
15. Pepys, *Diary*, 15 January 1668.
16. Lady Mary Tudor, later married to the Earl of Derwentwater.
17. Reresby, *Memoirs*, p. 40.
18. Spence, *Anecdotes*, p. 63.
19. The modern origin of cabal (originally from the Hebrew Cabala or Kabbala), lies with the initials of the names of Charles's five ministers, Clifford, Arlington, Buckingham. Ashley Cooper, and Lauderdale).
20. Frances Stuart (see pp. 34–6).
21. Andrew Browning, *Thomas Osborne, Earl of Danby* (Glasgow, 1951), vol. I, p. 46.
22. Philalethes, *Remarks Upon Bishop Burnet's Posthumous History* (London, 1724), p. 56.
23. MacGregor-Hastie, *Nell Gwyn*, p. 76.
24. Norman E. Himes, *Medical History of Contraception* (London, 1962).
25. *Biog. 1752*, p. 20.
26. See Appendix IV.
27. Dryden, *Tyrannic Love, or The Royal Martyr*, epilogue.
28. Louis de Rouvroy, Duc de Saint-Simon, *Memoirs*, ed. B. St John (London, 1857), vol. II, p. 37.
29. Evelyn, *Diary*, 4 November 1670.
30. Dispatch of 19 September 1670, quoted in P.W. Sergeant, *My Lady Castlemaine* (London, 1912).
31. Andrew Marvell, *Last Instructions to a Painter* (1667), ll. 79–80. For a longer extract from this poem, which describes Barbara's alleged seduction of her footman, see Appendix VI.

32. Pepys, *Diary*, 7 April 1668.
33. Pepys, *Diary*, 27 August 1667.
34. Pepys, *Diary*, 23 December 1662.
35. Pepys, *Diary*, 31 December 1662.
36. Pepys, *Diary*, 30 July 1667.
37. Pepys, *Diary*, 30 July 1667.
38. Pepys, *Diary*, 28 July 1667.
39. William Harris, *An Historical and Critical Account of the Life of Charles II* (London, 1747), vol. II, p. 398.
40. Anthony a Wood.
41. Dryden, *The Conquest of Granada*, part II, iv, iii, ll. 263–4.
42. See Appendix II for a list of plays in which, without hard evidence, she was said to have appeared after this date.

6. FROM WHORE TO WHORE

1. Evelyn, *Diary*, 1 March 1671.
2. A whore 'of the bulk' would operate behind any hedge; a whore of the 'alcove' required a little more privacy.
3. Rochester, 'A Ramble in St James's Park' in *An Anthology of Erotic Verse*, ed. D. Parker (London, 1980), p. 205.
4. *Lettres sur les Anglois*, ed. C. Gould (Paris, 1933).
5. William Cobbett, *Parliamentary History* (London, 1808), vol. IV.
6. *Poems on Affairs of State* (1679).
7. Colbert de Croissy to Louis XIV, 8 October 1670.
8. De Croissy to Louis XIV, 22 October 1670.
9. Evelyn, *Diary*, 9 October 1670.
10. Evelyn, *Diary*, 4 October 1683.
11. Marie de Rabutin-Chantal de Sévigné (1626–96), known for her correspondence.
12. H. Forneron, *Louise de Keroualle, Duchess of Portsmouth* (London, 1887), p. 177.
13. Evelyn, *Diary*, 4 October 1683.
14. William Matthews (ed.), *Charles' Escape from Worcester* (Berkeley, 1966), p. 100.
15. Fraser, *King Charles II*, p. 256.
16. De Croissy to Louis XIV, 21 September 1671.
17. De Croissy to Louis XIV, 24 July 1673.
18. The scholar and bibliophile Elias Ashmole.
19. penis.
20. Anon, 'The Duchess of Portsmouth's Pictures', *Poems of State Affairs* (1716), vol. I, p. 51.
21. *Correspondence Angleterre*, fol. 201, Archives de la Ministèrre des Affaires Etrangères, Paris.

7. PLEASANT DAYS AND EASY NIGHTS

1. Guaiacum, or 'Holy Wood', made up from the wood of a West Indian tree, and used in several ways to treat syphilis, would perhaps leave a less prominent trace in household accounts than mercury; but the latter was an inevitable charge on the patient's purse.
2. J. Granger, *A Biographical History of England* (1775).
3. See Appendix VII for more items from this bill.
4. 'Mrs Cassells' – Rose Cassells, Nell's sister; John Cassell was perhaps a highwayman.

5. Julep was a sugar syrup in which less agreeable medicines were placed to make them more palatable; glysters were used for a species of seventeenth-century colonic irrigation. Many of the above details are quoted from Cunningham, *The Story of Nell Gwyn*, pp. 126–30.
6. *Third Report of the Historical Manuscripts Commission*, p. 266.
7. *Correspondence of the Family of Hatton, AD 1601–1704.*
8. Gaming Act, 1664.
9. Cibber, *An Apology for the Life of Mr Colley Cibber*, but the story is suspiciously like that told of her first meeting with Charles (see p. 90).
10. Cited in MacGregor-Hastie, *Nell Gwyn*, p. 123.
11. MacGregor-Hastie, *Nell Gwyn*, p. 124.
12. *Memoirs de la Duchesse de Mazarin.*
13. *Letters of Charles II*, ed. A. Bryant (London, 1935), pp. 329–30.
14. Edmund Waller, 'The Triple Combat'.
15. Courtin to Louis XIV, 8 June 1676, quoted in Henri Forneron, *Louise de Kéroüalle* (Paris, 1886), p. 167.
16. Courtin to Louis XIV, 3 August 1676, *Third Report of the Royal Commission on Historical Manuscripts*, II, p. 34.
17. 'Rochester's Farewell to the Court', *Poems on Affairs of State* (1716), vol. I, pp. 151–2.
18. Anon, 'The Duchess of Portsmouth's Pictures', *Poems on State Affairs* (1716), vol. I, p. 51.
19. Anon, 'Portsmouth's Looking-Glass', *Poems on Affairs of State* (1716), vol. I, p. 164.

8. FRIENDS AND ACQUAINTANCES

1. Pepys, *Diary*, 27 November 1667.
2. *Reliquiae Baxterianae* (London, 1696), iii, pp. 21–4.
3. Dryden, *Absalon and Achitophel* (1681); the Duke portrayed Zimri.
4. Fought at Barn Elms on 16 January 1668; the Earl died two months later.
5. *The Poems and Letters of Andrew Marvell*, ed. H.M. Margoliouth (Oxford, 1971), II, p. 355.
6. BL Add. MSS 27872, fol. 18.
7. Presumably, the inclination to speak his mind.
8. BL Add. MSS 27872, fol. 20.
9. Hester W. Chapman, *Great Villiers* (1949), p. 240.
10. Lord Chancellor Boyle to the Duke of Ormonde, Hist. MSS. Comm., Ormonde MSS, vol. IV p. 99.
11. Hist. MSS. Comm., Ormonde MSS, vol. IV.
12. MacGregor-Hastie, *Nell Gwyn*, p. 137.
13. Robert Whitcom, *The Lives and Histories of the Heathen Gods, Goddesses and Demigods* (London, 1678).
14. G.G., contributing to *The Dictionary of National Biography*.
15. Charles.
16. Will Chiffinch.
17. *The Rochester–Saville Letters, 1671–1680*, ed. J.H. Wilson.
18. *The Rochester–Saville Letters, 1671–1680.*
19. Sir Robert Howard to the Duke of Ormonde, Christmas Day 1677.

20. *Camden Miscellany* (Royal Historical Society, 1937), vol. V, p. 25. The letter is particularly ill-spelt and punctuated, and I have adjusted it for easier reading.
21. *Mercurius Domesticus*, 17 December 1679. There had apparently been a rumour that Nell had been murdered by Jesuits.
22. Second Test Act.
23. W.D. Christie's *Life of Shaftesbury* (London, 1871), II, p. 378.
24. Refusing to attend the services of the Church of England.
25. J.S. Clarke, *Life of James II, collected out of memoirs writ of his own hand* (London, 1816).
26. BL Lutt.l.51.
27. BL 74/1889.d.l.594.
28. Alexander Pope: 'Epistle IV to Richard, Earl of Burlington'.

9. HE WAS MY FRIEND

1. Hon. F. Wolseley, *Life of Marlborough* (London, 1897), I, pp. 68–9.
2. *Dictionary of National Biography*.
3. Quoted MacGregor-Hastie, *Nell Gwyn*, p. 167.
4. *Gentleman's Magazine* (1778).
5. *Gentleman's Magazine* (1778).
6. Evelyn, *Diary*, 24 January 1682.
7. Hist. MSS Comm., Ormonde MSS NS VI 436.
8. Monmouth, a few months later, asked Charles's forgiveness and was magnanimously pardoned, though later, to the King's fury, he retracted his confession.
9. Evelyn, *Diary*, 9 January 1684.
10. Evelyn, *Diary*, 24 January 1684.

11. Evelyn, *Diary*, 30 March 1684.
12. Evelyn, *Diary*, 23 October 1684.
13. Quoted in MacGregor-Hastie, p. 175.
14. Arthur Bryant, *Samuel Pepys*, vol. III (London, 1938), p. 190; vol. II (London, 1935), p. 374.
15. E.H. Plumtre, *Life of Thomas Ken, D.D.* (London, 1890), I, pp. 158, 178.
16. Evelyn, *Diary*, 15 September 1685.
17. Evelyn, *Diary*, 4 February 1684.
18. Evelyn, *Diary*, 4 January 1685.
19. Evelyn, *Diary*, 4 January 1685.
20. Evelyn, *Diary*, 4 January 1685.
21. *Secret Service Expenses of Charles II and James II*, Camden Society, p. 109.
22. *Hatton Correspondence*, Camden Society, II, pp. 66–7.
23. Evelyn, *Diary*, 19 January 1686.
24. Evelyn, *Diary*, 17 January 1687.

10. THE SCOUNDREL LASS

1. Cibber, *An Apology for the Life of Mr Colley Cibber*, p. 450.
2. Sir George Etherege, *The Lady of Pleasure, a Satire*.
3. *Memoirs of the Life of Archbishop Tenison* (London, 1716), p. 20.
4. Laurence, Earl of Rochester, Thomas, Earl of Pembroke, Sir Robert Sawyer, the King's Attorney-General, and the Hon. Henry Sidney.
5. 'T.C.D.', 'The Will of Nell Gwyn', *The Genealogists' Magazine*, vol. VII (March, 1935), pp. 8–10.
6. Letter from Peregrine Bertie to the Countess of Richmond quoted in Hamilton,

The Illustrious Lady, p. 193, and, *Rutland Papers* (Camdon Society, London, 1902), ii. 107.

7. Evelyn, *Diary*, 5 March 1685.

APPENDIX III

1. Bulk – a rough trestle upon which itinerant actors performed.
2. The King was known as 'Old Rowley'.
3. Helen of Troy.
4. Perkin Warbeck, another Pretender to the throne.
5. Monmouth's mother.

6. The poet Thomas Rymer (1641–1713).
7. Nell's mother (see pp. 154–5).
8. Perhaps a son of Rose, Nell's sister? Perhaps the 'Mr Cholmly' mentioned in her will?

APPENDIX V

1. Presumably one of the great whores of history: Messalina or Lais.
2. Julia, the Emperor Augustus's immoral daughter.
3. Pasiphae.

Bibliography

The earliest biography is a short one, *Memoirs of the Life of Eleanor Gwinn, a celebrated courtesan in the reign of Charles II and Mistress to that Monarch* (London, F. Stamper 'in Pope's-Head-Alley, Cornhill' 1752 [BL 1416.h.41]). This was republished in 1820 by J. Fairburn, 110 Minories, London, price sixpence, somewhat heavily edited, under the title, *The Life, Amours and Exploits of Nell Gwinn, the fortunate orange girl, who, from the above low Sphere of Life became the Bosom Friend and Mistress of King Charles the Second (of merry memory), and who, for the comfort of old soldiers, was the cause of erecting Chelsea Hospital; with an Account of the many Charities she left and Good Deeds she performed in her Retirement from Public Life and the Stage . . . embellished with a Fine Engraving.*

Andrews, Allen, *The Royal Whore: Barbara Villiers, Countess of Castlemaine*, London, 1971

Anon, 'Hopgarden-caller to the Throne! The Life of Nelly'

Aubrey, John, *Brief Lives*, Oxford, 1897

Barton, Margaret, *Tunbridge Wells*, London, 1937

Bevan, Bryan, *Nell Gwyn*, London, 1969

Brett-James, Norman G., *The Growth of Stuart London*, London and Middlesex, 1935

Burford, E.J., *Bawds and Lodgings: a history of the Bankside brothels c. 100–1675*, London, 1976

——, *Wits, Wenches and Wantons*, London 1984

Chancellor, E. Beresford, *The Annals of Covent Garden*, London, 1930

Chetwood, W.R.A., *General History of the English Stage*, London, 1749

Cibber, Colley, *An Apology for the Life of Mr Colley Cibber, Comedian*, London, 1740

Cunningham, Peter, *The Story of Nell Gwyn*, Edinburgh, 1908

Dasent, Arthur Irwin, *Nell Gwynne*, New York, 1969

Dictionary of National Biography

Dorset, Charles Sackville, Sixth Earl of, *Poems*, ed. Brice Harris, New York, 1979

Duffy, Maureen, *The Passionate Shepherdess: Aphra Behn 1640–89*, London, 1977

Ellis, J., *Correspondence*, 1686–88

Etheredge, G., *Letter Book*, London, 1928

Etherege, Sir George, *The Poems of Sir George Etherege*, ed. James Thorpe, Princeton, 1963

Evelyn, John, *Diary*, ed. Guy de Bédoyère, Gwynedd, 1955

Bibliography

Fraser, Antonia, *King Charles II*, London, 1979
Gramont, Comte de, *Memoirs*, tr. Peter Quennell, London, 1930
Greene, Graham, *Lord Rochester's Monkey*, London, 1974
Hamilton, Anthony, *Memoirs of Comte de Gramont*, tr. Peter Quennell, London, 1930
Hamilton, Elizabeth, *The Illustrious Lady*, London, 1980
Hart, Roger, *English Life in the Seventeenth Century*, London, 1970
Henriques, Fernando, *Prostitution and Society*, 3 vols, London, 1962–8
Home, Gordon, *Epsom*, London, 1901
Howe, Elizabeth, *The First English Actresses*, Cambridge, 1992
Jusserand, J.J., *A French Ambassador at the Court of Charles II*, London, 1892
Leacroft, Richard and Helen, *Theatre and Playhouse*, London, 1894
Love, Harold (ed.), *The Penguin Book of Restoration Verse*, London, 1968
MacGregor-Hastie, Roy, *Nell Gwyn*, London, 1987
Magalotti, Count Lorenzo, *Travels of Cosmo the Third Grand Duke of Tuscany Through England During the Reign of King Charles II 1669*, ed. J. Mawman, London, 1821
Mantzius, Karl, *A History of Theatrical Art*, London, 1909
Marvell, Andrew, *The Satires of Andrew Marvell*, London, 1892
Oldys, W., *Short History of the English Stage* , 1741
Pepys, Samuel, *Diary*, ed. Robert Latham and William Matthews, 10 vols, London, 1983
Picard, Liza, *Restoration London*, London, 1997
Reresby, John, *The Memoirs of Sir John Reresby of Thrybergh*, ed. James J. Cartwright, London, 1875
Roberts, Nickie, *Whores in History*, London, 1992
Rochester, John Wilmot, Earl of, *The Poems of John Wilmot, Earl of Rochester*, ed. Keith Walker, Oxford, 1984
——, 'A Panegyric of Nelly' in the volume quoted above
Russell, W. Clark (ed.), *Representative Actors*, London, undated
Skinner, Otis, *Mad Folk of the Theatre*, Indianapolis, 1928
Spence, Joseph, *Anecdotes*, ed. S.W. Singer, London, 1820
Stone, Lawrence, *The Family, Sex and Marriage in England, 1500–1800*, London, 1977
Tannahill, Reay, *Sex in History*, London, 1980
Thormählen, Marianne, *Rochester: the poems in context*, Cambridge, 1993
Waller, Edmund, *The Works of Edmund Waller Esq., in verse and prose*, London, 1772
Williams, H. Noel, *Rival Sultanas*, London, 1915
Wilson, J.H., *Nell Gwyn, Royal Mistress*, London, 1952
Winn, James Anderson, *John Dryden and his World*, Yale, 1987

Index

Dates of birth and death are given here for those who played a major role in the life of Nell Gwyn

Index

'Protestant whore, the' 157
Prynne, William 39
Purcell, Henry 42

Quin, Ann, *see* Marshall, Ann

Reeves, Anne 101
Rhodes, John 41
Richmond, Duchess of, *see* Stuart, Frances
Richmond, Duke of 35, 120
Roberts, Jane 89–90
Rochester, John Wilmot, Earl of (1647–80)
    13, 14, 36, 71–3, 141, 144–5, 147, 163;
    frisks 145; and marriage 71–2; poetry of
    39, 49, 71, 80; satires of 82–5, 104
Rohan, Chevalier de 128–9
Rose Tavern, the 10
Ross, Madam 11
Rowzee, Dr 80
Rupert, Prince 50, 58, 86
Ruvigny, Comte de 118, 127, 131
Rylance, Mark 59

St Albans, Duke of, *see* Beauclerk, Charles
Sandwich, Lord 20, 33, 100
Saville, Henry (1642–87) 146, 147, 162
Scrope, Sir Carr 148–9
Sedley, Catherine 115
Sedley, Sir Charles (1639?–1701) 73, 74, 76, 115
Sévigné, Marie de Rabutin-Chantal 111–12
Shadwell, Thomas 76, 149
Shepherd, Jack 11
Sheppard, Sir Fleetwood 162–3
Sidney, Colonel Algernon 18
Sidney, Robert 18
Southampton, Earl of, *see* Lennox, Charles
Stuart, Frances (1648–1702) 34–6
Sussex, Earl of 135
Sussex, Anne Countess of 133–4, 135, 160
syphilis 119–20

Taafe, Theobald Lord 17, 18
Tenison, Archbishop Thomas (1636–1715)
    168, 177–8
tennis courts, as theatres 42
theatres: Apothecaries Hall 43; Bridges Street
    43; Cockpit 41, 106; Dorset Garden
    163; Duke's 44, 61, 122, 138; King's
    9,12, 41, 49; Lincoln's Inn 42; Red Bull
    41, 43; Salisbury Court 43.; price of
    admission 44, 46; design of 42–3

Tongue, Israel 150
Tudor, Lady Mary 166, 182
Tunbridge Wells 38, 79, 80–5, 118
Tuke, Sir Samuel, 14

Valck, Gerard 22
Vendôme, Philippe de 166
Vere, Diana de 180
Vere, Sir Henry de 18
Verelst, Simon 22
Verrio, Antonio 157
Villiers, Barbara (1640–1709) 19–21, 47, 65,
    130, 159, 180; appearance 19; becomes a
    Catholic 25; created a Duchess 96; 'the
    curse of the Nation' 32; death 181;
    disliked 97, 182; relations with Nell Gwyn
    112; income 97, 131; becomes King's
    mistress 13; and Nonsuch House 96–7;
    and the queen 31–3; sexual magnetism
    23, 33; hot temper 32; turned away 96,
    99; underwear 25; painted as the Virgin
    21; at Whitehall 24, 105
  lovers: *see* Charles II; Ellis, John; Hall,
    Jacob; Hamilton, James; Jermyn,
    Henry; Marlborough, Duke of;
    Montagu, Ralph; Sandwich, Lord;
    Wycherley, Sir William.
Villiers, Viscount 178

Waller, Edmund 130
Walter, Lucy (1630?–58) 17–19, 143–4
Warner, John 179
Whitehall Palace 105–7
'whores to market' 123
Wicker, Henry 75
Wild, Jonathan 11
Williams, Mrs Christabella 14
Winchester 166, 169–70
Windsor 111, 157, 165
Wood, Anthony à, 3, 6
Worcester, Lady 118
Wren, Sir Christopher 167
Wright, Michael 106
Wycherley, Sir William (*c.* 1640–1716) 33, 73,
    94, 98–9

York, James, Duke of (later King James VII of
    Scotland and II of England, 1633–1701)
    24, 77, 117, 140, 149–50; a Catholic 114,
    154; and Charles II's death 171–2;
    kindness to Nell 173–4, 175

212